EVERYMAN, I will go with thee,

and be thy guide,

In thy most need to go by thy side

Kalevala
THE LAND OF THE HEROES

IN TWO VOLUMES . VOLUME TWO

TRANSLATED BY
W. F. KIRBY

INTRODUCTION BY
J. B. C. GRUNDY M.A., PH.D.

DENT: LONDON
EVERYMAN'S LIBRARY
DUTTON: NEW YORK

NO. 260

SBN: 460 00260 0

A Brief Summary of the Contents of Volume II

vi   A Brief Summary of the Contents

KALEVALA

Argument

Lemminkainen, greatly offended that he was not invited to the wedding, resolves to go to Pohjola, although his mother dissuades him from it, and warns him of the many dangers that he will have to encounter (1–382). He sets forth and succeeds in passing all the dangerous places by his skill in magic (383–776).

Ahti dwelt upon an island,
By the bay near Kauko's headland,
And his fields he tilled industrious,
And the fields he trenched with ploughing,
And his ears were of the finest,
And his hearing of the keenest.

Heard he shouting in the village,
From the lake came sounds of hammering,
On the ice the sound of footsteps,
On the heath a sledge was rattling,   10
Therefore in his mind he fancied,
In his brain the notion entered,
That at Pohjola was wedding,
And a drinking-bout in secret.

Mouth and head awry then twisting,
And his black beard all disordered,
In his rage the blood departed
From the cheeks of him unhappy,
And at once he left his ploughing,
'Mid the field he left the ploughshare,   20
On the spot his horse he mounted,
And he rode directly homeward,
To his dearest mother's dwelling,
To his dear and aged mother.

And he said as he approached her,
And he called, as he was coming,
" O my mother, aged woman,

Bring thou food, and bring it quickly,
That the hungry man may eat it,
And the moody man devour it,   30
While they warm the bathroom for me,
And the bathroom set in order,
That the man may wash and cleanse him,
And adorn him like a hero."

Then did Lemminkainen's mother,
Bring him food, and bring it quickly,
That the hungry man might eat it,
And the moody man devour it,
While they put the bath in order,
And arranged the bathroom for him.   40

Then the lively Lemminkainen
Quickly ate the food she gave him,
Hurried then into the bathroom,
Hastened quickly to the bathroom,
There it was the finch now washed him,
There the bullfinch washed and cleansed him,
Washed his head to flaxen whiteness,
And his throat to shining whiteness.

From the bath the room he entered,
And he spoke the words which follow: 50
"O my mother, aged woman,
Seek the storehouse on the mountain,
Bring me thence my shirt, the fine one
Likewise bring the finest clothing,
That I now may put it on me,
And may fitly clothe me in it."

But his mother asked him quickly,
Asked him thus, the aged woman,
"Whither goes my son, my dearest,
Dost thou go to hunt the lynxes,   60
Or to chase the elk on snowshoes,
Or perchance to shoot a squirrel?"

Answered lively Lemminkainen,
Said the handsome Kaukomieli,
"O my mother who hast borne me,
Not to hunt the lynx I wander,
Nor to chase the elk on snowshoes,

Neither go I squirrel shooting,
But I seek the feast at Pohja,
And the secret drinking-party,   70
Therefore fetch my shirt, the fine one,
Bring me, too, the finest clothing,
That I hasten to the wedding,
And may wander to the banquet.

But his mother would forbid him,
Vainly would his wife dissuade him,
Two, whose like were not created,
And three daughters of Creation,
Sought to hold back Lemminkainen
Back from Pohjola's great banquet.   80

To her son then said the mother,
And her child advised the old one,
"Do not go, my son, my dearest,
O my dearest son, my Kauko,
Go not to the feast at Pohja,
To that mansion's drinking-party,
For indeed they did not ask you,
And 'tis plain they do not want you."

Then the lively Lemminkainen
Answered in the words which follow: 90
"Only bad men go for asking;
Uninvited good men dance there.
There are always invitations,
Always a sufficient summons,
In the sword with blade of sharpness,
And the edge so brightly flashing."

Still did Lemminkainen's mother
Do her utmost to restrain him.
"Go not, son, to sure destruction,
Unto Pohjola's great banquet.   100
Full of terrors is thy journey,
On thy way are mighty wonders,
Thrice indeed doth death await thee;
Thrice the man with death is threatened."

Answered lively Lemminkainen,
Said the handsome Kaukomieli,
"Death is only for the women,

Everywhere they see destruction ;
But a hero need not fear it,
Nor need take extreme precautions.   110
But let this be as it may be,
Tell me that my ears may hear it,
Tell me the first death that waits me,
Tell the first and tell the last one."
    Then said Lemminkainen's mother,
Answered then, the aged woman :
" I will tell the deaths that wait you,
Not as you would have me tell them ;
Of the first death I will tell you,
And this death is first among them.   120
When a little way you've travelled
On the first day of your journey,
You will reach a fiery river,
Flaming right across your pathway,
In the stream a cataract fiery,
In the fall a fiery island,
On the isle a peak all fiery,
On the peak a fiery eagle,
One who whets his beak at night-time,
And his claws in daytime sharpens,   130
For the strangers who are coming,
And the people who approach him."
    Answered lively Lemminkainen,
Said the handsome Kaukomieli,
" This is perhaps a death for women,
But 'tis not a death for heroes.
For I know a plan already,
And a splendid scheme to follow.
I'll create, by songs of magic,
Both a man and horse of alder.   140
They shall walk along beside me,
And shall wander on before me,
While I like a duck am diving,
Like a scoter duck am diving,
'Neath the soaring eagle's talons,
Talons of the mighty eagle.
O my mother, who hast borne me,

Tell me now of death the second."
Then said Lemminkainen's mother,
"Such the second death that waits you: 150
When a little way you've journeyed,
On the second day of travel,
You will reach a trench of fire,
Right across the path extending,
Ever to the east extending,
North-west endlessly extending,
Full of stones to redness heated,
Full of blocks of stone all glowing,
And a hundred there have ventured,
And a thousand there have perished, 160
Hundreds with their swords have perished,
And a thousand steel-clad heroes."
Answered lively Lemminkainen,
Said the handsome Kaukomieli,
"Such a death no man will perish,
Nor is this a death for heroes,
For I know a trick already,
Know a trick, and see a refuge;
And a man of snow I'll sing me,
Make of frozen snow a hero, 170
Push him in the raging fire,
Push him in the glowing torment,
Bathe him in the glowing bathroom,
With a bath-whisk made of copper,
I myself behind him pressing,
Pushing through the fire a pathway,
That my beard unburnt remaineth,
And my locks escape a singeing.
O my mother who hast borne me,
Of the third death tell me truly." 180
Then said Lemminkainen's mother,
"Such the third death that awaits you:
When you've gone a little further,
And another day have travelled,
Unto Pohjola's dread gateway,
Where the pathway is the narrowest,
Then a wolf will rush upon you,

And a bear for his companion,
There in Pohjola's dread gateway,
Where the pathway is the narrowest.   190
Hundreds have been there devoured,
Heroes have by thousands perished ;
Wherefore should they not devour thee,
Kill thee likewise, unprotected ? "

Answered lively Lemminkainen,
Said the handsome Kaukomieli,
" Perhaps a young ewe might be eaten,
Or a lamb be torn to pieces,
Not a man, how weak soever,
Not the sleepiest of the heroes !   200
With a hero's belt I'm girded,
And I wear a hero's armour,
Fixed with buckles of a hero,
So be sure I shall not hasten,
Unto Untamo's dread wolf's jaws,
In the throat of that curst creature.

" 'Gainst the wolf I know a refuge,
'Gainst the bear I know a method ;
For the wolf's mouth sing a muzzle,
For the bear sing iron fetters,   210
Or to very chaff will chop them,
Or to merest dust will sift them ;
Thus I'll clear the path before me,
Reach the ending of my journey."

Then said Lemminkainen's mother,
" Even yet your goal you reach not,
There are still upon your pathway,
On your road tremendous marvels.
Three terrific dangers wait you,
Three more deaths await the hero ;   220
And there even yet await you,
On the spot the worst of marvels.

" When a little way you've travelled,
Up to Pohjola's enclosure,
There a fence is reared of iron,
And a fence of steel erected,
From the ground to heaven ascending,

From the heavens to earth descending.
Spears they are which form the hedgestakes,
And for wattles, creeping serpents,   230
Thus the fence with snakes is wattled,
And among them there are lizards,
And their tails are always waving,
And their thick heads always swelling,
And their round heads always hissing,
Heads turned out, and tails turned inwards.
   "On the ground are other serpents,
On the path are snakes and adders,
And above, their tongues are hissing,
And below, their tails are waving.   240
One of all the most terrific
Lies before the gate across it,
Longer is he than a roof-tree,
Than the roof-props is he thicker,
And above, his tongue is hissing,
And above, his mouth is hissing,
Lifted not against another,
Threatening thee, O luckless hero!"
   Answered lively Lemminkainen,
Said the handsome Kaukomieli: 250
"Such a death is perhaps for children;
But 'tis not a death for heroes,
For I can enchant the fire,
And can quench a glowing furnace,
And can ban away the serpents,
Twist the snakes between my fingers.
Only yesterday it happened
That I ploughed a field of adders;
On the ground the snakes were twisting,
And my hands were all uncovered.   260
With my nails I seized the vipers,
In my hands I took the serpents,
Ten I killed among the vipers,
And the serpents black by hundreds.
Still my nails are stained with snake-blood,
And my hands with slime of serpents.
Therefore will I not permit me,

And by no means will I journey
As a mouthful for the serpents,
To the sharp fangs of the adders.   270
I myself will crush the monsters,
Crush the nasty things to pieces,
And will sing away the vipers,
Drive the serpents from my pathway,
Enter then the yard of Pohja,
And into the house will force me."

    Then said Lemminkainen's mother,
"O my son, forbear to venture,
Into Pohjola's dread castle,
House of Sariola all timbered;   280
For the men with swords are girded,
Heroes all equipped for battle,
Men with drink of hops excited,
Very furious from their drinking.
They will sing thee, most unhappy,
To the swords of all the keenest;
Better men their songs have vanquished,
Mighty ones been overpowered."

    Answered lively Lemminkainen,
Said the handsome Kaukomieli: 290
"Well, but I have dwelt already
There in Pohjola's dread fortress.
Not a Lapp with spells shall chain me,
Forth no son of Turja drive me.
I'll enchant the Lapp by singing,
Drive away the son of Turja,
And in twain will sing his shoulders,
From his chin his speech I'll sever,
Tear his shirt apart by singing,
And I'll break in two his breastbone."   300

    Then said Lemminkainen's mother,
"O alas, my son unhappy,
Dost thou think of former exploits,
Brag'st thou of thy former journey?
True it is thou hast resided
There in Pohjola's dread fortress,
But they sent thee all a-swimming,

Floating overgrown with pond-weed,
O'er the raging cataract driven,
Down the stream in rushing waters.   310
Thou hast known the Falls of Tuoni,
Manala's dread stream hast measured,
There would'st thou to-day be swimming,
But for thine unhappy mother!
  "Listen now to what I tell thee.
When to Pohjola thou comest,
All the slope with stakes is bristling,
And the yard with poles is bristling,
All with heads of men surmounted,
And one stake alone is vacant,   320
And to fill the stake remaining,
Will they cut thy head from off thee."
  Answered lively Lemminkainen,
Said the handsome Kaukomieli:
" Let a weakling ponder o'er it,
Let the worthless find such ending!
After five or six years' warfare,
Seven long summers spent in battle,
Not a hero would concern him,
Nor retire a step before it.   330
Therefore bring me now my mail-shirt,
And my well-tried battle armour;
I my father's sword will fetch me,
And my father's sword-blade look to.
In the cold it long was lying,
In a dark place long was hidden;
There has it been ever weeping,
For a hero who should wield it."
  Thereupon he took his mail-shirt,
Took his well-tried battle armour,   340
And his father's trusty weapon,
Sword his father always wielded,
And against the ground he thrust it,
On the floor the point he rested,
With his hand the sword he bended
Like the fresh crown of the cherry,
Or the juniper when growing.

Said the lively Lemminkainen,
" Hard 'twill be in Pohja's castle,
Rooms of Sariola the misty,   350
Such a sword as this to gaze on,
Such a sword-blade to encounter."
    From the wall his bow he lifted,
From the peg he took a strong bow,
And he spoke the words which follow,
And expressed himself in thiswise :
" I would hold the man deserving,
And regard him as a hero,
Who to bend this bow was able,
And could bend it and could string it,   360
There in Pohjola's great castle,
Rooms of Sariola the misty."
    Then the lively Lemminkainen,
He the handsome Kaukomieli,
Put his shirt of mail upon him,
Clad himself in arms of battle,
And his slave he thus commanded,
And he spoke the words which follow :
" O my servant, bought with money,
Workman, whom I got for money,   370
Harness now my horse of battle,
Harness me my fiery war-horse,
That unto the feast I journey,
Drinking-bout at house of Lempo."
    Then the prudent slave, obedient,
Hastened quickly to the courtyard,
And the foal at once he harnessed,
And prepared the fiery red one,
And he said on his returning,
" I have done what you commanded,   380
And the horse have harnessed for you,
And the best of foals have harnessed."
    Then the lively Lemminkainen,
Thought him ready for his journey,
Right hand urging, left restraining,
And his sinewy fingers smarting,
Now would start, and then reflected,

Started then in reckless fashion.
  Then her son his mother counselled,
Warned her child, the aged woman,   390
At the door, beneath the rafters,
At the place where stand the kettles.
" O my only son, my dearest,
O my child, of all the strongest,
When thou com'st to the carousal,
And thou comest where thou wishest,
Drink thou half a goblet only,
Drink the measure to the middle,
And the other half return thou ;
Give the worst half to a worse one.   400
In the goblet rests a serpent,
And a worm within the measure."
  Yet again her son she cautioned,
To her child again gave warning,
At the last field's furthest limit,
At the last of all the gateways.
" When thou com'st to the carousal,
And thou comest where thou wishest,
Sit upon a half-seat only,
Step thou with a half-step only,   410
And the other half return thou ;
Give the worst half to a worse one,
Thus wilt thou a man be reckoned,
And a most illustrious hero,
And through armies push thy pathway,
And will crush them down beneath thee,
In the press of mighty heroes,
In the throng of men of valour."
  Then departed Lemminkainen,
When the horse in sledge was harnessed.   420
With his ready whip he struck him,
With his beaded whip he smote him,
And the fiery steed sprang forward,
Onward sped the rapid courser.
  When a short way he had journeyed,
For about an hour had travelled,
There he saw a flock of blackfowl,

In the air the grouse flew upward,
And the flock ascended rushing
From before the speeding courser.   430
    On the ice there lay some feathers
Cast by grouse upon the roadway;
These collected Lemminkainen,
And he put them in his pocket,
For he knew not what might happen,
Or might chance upon his journey.
In a house are all things useful,
Can at need be turned to something.
    Then he drove a little further,
On his road a little further,   440
When to neigh began the courser,
Pricked his long ears up in terror.
    Then the lively Lemminkainen,
He the handsome Kaukomieli,
In the sledge at once leaned forward,
Bending down to gaze about him.
There he saw, as said his mother,
As his own old mother warned him,
How there flowed a fiery river,
Right across the horse's pathway,   450
In the stream a cataract fiery,
In the fall a fiery island,
On the isle a peak all fiery,
On the peak a fiery eagle.
In his throat the fire was seething,
And his mouth with flame was glowing,
And his plumage fire was flashing,
And the sparks around were scattering.
    Kauko from afar he noticed,
From afar saw Lemminkainen.   460
    "Whither wilt thou go, O Kauko,
Whither goes the son of Lempi?"
    Answered lively Lemminkainen,
Said the handsome Kaukomieli,
"Unto Pohja's feast I journey,
The carousal held in secret.
Turn thee on one side a little,

From the youth's path do thou turn thee,
Let the traveller make his journey,
Do not hinder Lemminkainen,   470
Therefore move aside a little,
Let him now pursue his journey."

Thereupon the eagle answered,
Hissing from his throat of fire,
" I will let the traveller pass me,
Will not hinder Lemminkainen,
Through my mouth will let him hasten,
Let him thus pursue his journey.
Thither shall thy path direct thee,
Fortunate shall be thy journey,   480
To the banquet thou art seeking,
Where thou all thy life may'st rest thee."

Little troubled Lemminkainen,
And he let it not concern him,
But he felt into his pocket,
And his pouch he opened quickly,
Took the feathers of the blackfowl,
Leisurely he rubbed the feathers,
And between his palms he rubbed them,
'Twixt his fingers ten in number,   490
And a flock of grouse created,
And a flock of capercailzies,
In the eagle's beak he thrust them,
To his greedy throat he gave them,
To the eagle's throat all fiery,
In the fire-bird's beak he thrust them,
Thus he freed himself from danger,
And escaped the first day's danger.

With his whip he struck the courser,
With the beaded whip he struck him,   500
And the horse sped quickly onward,
And the steed sprang lightly forward.

Then he drove a little further,
But a little way had travelled,
When the horse again was shying,
And again the steed was neighing.
From the sledge again he raised him,

And he strove to gaze around him,
And he saw, as said his mother,
As his aged mother warned him, 510
Right in front a trench of fire,
Right across the path extending,
Ever to the east extending,
North-west endlessly extending,
Full of stones to redness heated,
Full of blocks of stone all glowing.
Little troubled Lemminkainen,
But he raised a prayer to Ukko.
"Ukko, thou, of Gods the highest,
Ukko, thou, our Heavenly Father, 520
Send thou now a cloud from north-west,
Send thou from the west a second,
And a third to east establish.
"In the north-east let them gather,
Push their borders all together,
Drive them edge to edge together,
Let the snow fall staff-deep round me,
Deep as is the length of spear-shaft,
On these stones to redness heated,
Blocks of stone all fiery glowing." 530
Ukko, then, of Gods the highest,
He the aged Heavenly Father,
Sent a cloud from out the north-west,
From the west he sent a second,
In the east a cloud let gather,
Let them gather in the north-east;
And he heaped them all together,
And he closed the gaps between them,
Let the snow fall staff-deep downward,
Deep as is the length of spear-shaft, 540
On the stones to redness heated,
Blocks of stone all fiery glowing.
From the snow a pond was fashioned,
And a lake with icy waters.
Then the lively Lemminkainen
Sang a bridge of ice together,
Stretching right across the snow-pond,

From the one bank to the other,
O'er the fiery trench passed safely,
Passed the second day in safety.   550
    With his whip he urged the courser,
Cracked the whip all bead-embroidered,
And began to travel quickly,
As the courser trotted onward.
    Quick he ran a verst, a second,
For a short space well proceeded,
When he suddenly stopped standing,
Would not stir from his position.
    Then the lively Lemminkainen
Started up to gaze around him.   560
In the gate the wolf was standing,
And the bear before the passage,
There in Pohjola's dread gateway,
At the end of a long passage.
Then the lively Lemminkainen,
He the handsome Kaukomieli,
Quickly felt into his pocket,
What his pouch contained exploring,
And he took some ewe's wool from it,
And until 'twas soft he rubbed it,   570
And between his palms he rubbed it,
'Twixt his fingers ten in number.
    On his palms then gently breathing,
Ewes ran bleating forth between them,
Quite a flock of sheep he fashioned,
And a flock of lambs among them,
And the wolf rushed straight upon them,
And the bear rushed after likewise,
While the lively Lemminkainen,
Further drove upon his journey.   580
    Yet a little space he journeyed,
Unto Pohjola's enclosure.
There a fence was raised of iron,
Fenced with steel the whole enclosure,
In the ground a hundred fathoms,
In the sky a thousand fathoms,
Spears they were which formed the hedgestakes,

And for wattles creeping serpents,
Thus the fence with snakes was wattled
And among them there were lizards,   590
And their tails were always waving,
And their thick heads always swelling,
Rows of heads erected always,
Heads turned out and tails turned inwards.
    Then the lively Lemminkainen
Gave himself to his reflections.
"This is what my mother told me,
This is what my mother dreaded;
Here I find a fence tremendous
Reared aloft from earth to heaven,   600
Down below there creeps a viper,
Deeper yet the fence is sunken,
Up aloft a bird is flying,
But the fence is builded higher."
    Natheless was not Lemminkainen
Greatly troubled or uneasy;
From the sheath he drew his knife out,
From the sheath an iron weapon,
And he hewed the fence to pieces,
And in twain he clove the hedgestakes;   610
Thus he breached the fence of iron,
And he drove away the serpents
From the space between five hedgestakes,
Likewise from the space 'twixt seven,
And himself pursued his journey,
On to Pohjola's dark portal.
    In the path a snake was twisting,
Just in front across the doorway,
Even longer than the roof-tree,
Thicker than the hall's great pillars,   620
And the snake had eyes a hundred,
And the snake had tongues a thousand,
And his eyes than sieves were larger,
And his tongues were long as spear-shafts,
And his fangs were like rake-handles;
Seven boats' length his back extended.
Then the lively Lemminkainen

Would not instantly move onward
To the snake with eyes a hundred,
And the snake with tongues a thousand.   630
　　Spoke the lively Lemminkainen,
Said the handsome Kaukomieli:
"Serpent black and subterranean,
Worm whose hue is that of Tuoni,
Thou amidst the grass who lurkest,
At the roots of Lempo's foliage,
Gliding all among the hillocks,
Creeping all among the tree-roots,
Who has brought thee from the stubble,
From the grass-roots has aroused thee,   640
Creeping here on ground all open,
Creeping there upon the pathway?
Who has sent thee from thy nettles,
Who has ordered and provoked thee
That thy head thou liftest threatening,
And thy neck thou stiffly raisest?
Was't thy father or thy mother,
Or the eldest of thy brothers,
Or the youngest of thy sisters,
Or some other near relation?   650
　　"Close thy mouth, thy head conceal thou,
Hide thou quick thy tongue within it,
Coil thyself together tightly,
Roll thyself into a circle,
Give me way, though but a half-way,
Let the traveller make his journey,
Or begone from out the pathway.
Creep, thou vile one, in the bushes,
In the holes among the heathland,
And among the moss conceal thee,   660
Glide away, like ball of worsted,
Like a withered stick of aspen.
Hide thy head among the grass-roots,
Hide thyself among the hillocks,
'Neath the turf thy mouth conceal thou,
Make thy dwelling in a hillock.
If you lift your head from out it,

Ukko surely will destroy it,
With his nails, all steely-pointed,
With a mighty hail of iron."   670
     Thus was Lemminkainen talking,
But the serpent heeded nothing,
And continued always hissing,
Darting out its tongue for ever,
And its mouth was always hissing
At the head of Lemminkainen.
     Then the lively Lemminkainen
Of an ancient spell bethought him,
Which the old crone once had taught him,
Which his mother once had taught him.   680
     Said the lively Lemminkainen,
Spoke the handsome Kaukomieli,
" If you do not heed my singing,
And it is not quite sufficient,
Still you will swell up with anguish
When an ill day comes upon you.
Thou wilt burst in two, O vile one,
O thou toad, in three will burst thou,
If I should seek out your mother,
And should search for your ancestress.   690
Well I know thy birth, vile creature,
Whence thou comest, earthly horror,
For Syöjätär was your mother,
And the sea-fiend was your parent.
     " Syöjätär she spat in water,
In the waves she left the spittle,
By the wind 'twas rocked thereafter,
Tossed upon the water-current,
Thus for six years it was shaken,
Thus for seven whole summers drifted,   700
On the ocean's shining surface,
And upon the swelling billows.
Thus for long the water stretched it,
By the sun 'twas warmed and softened,
To the land the billows drove it,
On the beach a wave upcast it.
     " Walked three Daughters of Creation

On the beach of stormy ocean,
On the beach, the waves that bounded,
On the beach they saw the spittle, 710
And they spoke the words which follow:
'What might perhaps of this be fashioned,
If a life by the Creator,
And if eyes were granted to it?'
    "This was heard by the Creator,
And he spoke the words which follow:
'Evil only comes from evil,
And a toad from toad's foul vomit,
If I gave a life unto it,
And if eyes were granted to it.' 720
    "But the words were heard by Hiisi,
One for mischief always ready,
And he set about creating;
Hiisi gave a life unto it,
Of the slime of toad disgusting,
From Syöjätär's filthy spittle,
Formed from this a twisting serpent,
To a black snake he transformed it.
    "Whence the life he gave unto it?
Life he brought from Hiisi's coal-heap. 730
Whence was then its heart created?
Out of Syöjätär's own heartstrings.
Whence the brains for this foul creature?
From a mighty torrent's foaming.
Whence its sense obtained the monster?
From a furious cataract's foaming.
Whence a head, this foul enchantment?
From the bean, a bean all rotten.
Whence were then its eyes created?
From a seed of flax of Lempo. 740
Whence were the toad's ears created?
From the leaves of Lempo's birch-tree.
Whence was then its mouth constructed?
Syöjätär's own mouth supplied it.
Whence the tongue in mouth so evil?
From the spear of Keitolainen.
Teeth for such an evil creature?

From the beard of Tuoni's barley.
Whence its filthy gums created?
From the gums of Kalma's maiden.   750
Whence was then its back constructed?
Of the coals of fire of Hiisi.
Whence its wriggling tail constructed?
From the plaits of Pahalainen.
Whence its entrails were constructed?
These were drawn from Death's own girdle.
  "This thy origin, O serpent,
This thy honour, as reported ;
Black snake from the world infernal,
Serpent of the hue of Tuoni,   760
Hue of earth, and hue of heather,
All the colours of the rainbow.
Go from out the wanderer's pathway,
From before the travelling hero,
Yield the pathway to the traveller,
Make a way for Lemminkainen
To the feast at Pohja holden,
Where they hold the great carousal."
  Then the snake obeyed his orders,
And the hundred-eyed drew backward,   770
And the great snake twisted sideways,
Turning in a new direction,
Giving thus the traveller pathway,
Making way for Lemminkainen
To the feast at Pohja holden,
And the secret-held carousal.

RUNO XXVII.—THE DUEL AT POHJOLA

Argument

Lemminkainen comes to Pohjola and behaves with the greatest insolence (1–204). The Lord of Pohjola grows angry, and as he can do nothing against Lemminkainen by magic, he challenges him to a duel (205–282). In the course of the duel Lemminkainen strikes off the head of the Lord of Pohjola, and to avenge this, the Mistress of Pohjola raises an army against him (283–420).

Now that I have brought my Kauko,
Carried Ahto Saarelainen,
Often past Death's jaw expanded,
Past the very tongue of Kalma,
To the banquet held at Pohja,
And to the concealed carousal,
Now must I relate in detail,
And my tongue relate in fulness,
How the lively Lemminkainen,
He the handsome Kaukomieli,   10
To the homestead came of Pohja,
Halls of Sariola the misty,
Uninvited to the banquet,
To the drinking-bout unbidden.

   Thus the lively Lemminkainen,
Ruddy youth, and arrant scoundrel,
In the room at once came forward,
Walking to the very middle;
'Neath him swayed the floor of linden,
And the room of firwood rattled.   20

   Spoke the lively Lemminkainen,
And he said the words which follow :
" Greetings to ye on my coming,
Greetings also to the greeter !
Hearken, Pohjola's great Master,
Have you here within this dwelling,
Barley for the horse's fodder,
Beer to offer to the hero ? "

There sat Pohjola's great Master,
At the end of the long table,   30
And from thence he made his answer,
In the very words which follow :
" Perhaps there is within this dwelling,
Standing room for your fine courser,
Nor would I indeed forbid you
In the room a quiet corner,
Or to stand within the doorway,
In the doorway, 'neath the rafters,
In the space between two kettles,
There where three large hoes are standing."   40
    Then the lively Lemminkainen
Tore his black beard in his anger,
('Twas the colour of a kettle),
And he spoke the words which follow :
" Lempo might perchance be willing,
Thus to stand within the doorway,
Where he might with soot be dirtied,
While the soot falls all around him !
But at no time did my father,
Never did my aged father   50
Ever stand in such a station,
In the doorway, 'neath the rafters !
There was always room sufficient
For his horse within the stable,
And a clean room for the hero,
And a place to put his gloves in,
Pegs whereon to hang his mittens,
Walls where swords may rest in order.
Why should I not also find it,
As my father always found it ? "   60
    After this he strode on further,
To the end of the long table,
At the bench-end then he sat him,
At the end of bench of firwood,
And the bench it cracked beneath him,
And the bench of firwood tottered.
    Said the lively Lemminkainen,
" Seems to me that I'm unwelcome,

As no ale is offered to me,
To the guest who just has entered."   70
  Ilpotar, the noble Mistress,
Answered in the words which follow:
"O thou boy, O Lemminkainen,
Not as guest thou com'st among us,
But upon my head to trample,
And to make it bow before you,
For our ale is still in barley,
Still in malt the drink delicious,
And the wheatbread still unbaken,
And unboiled the meat remaineth.   80
Yesternight you should have entered,
Or perchance have come to-morrow."
  Then the lively Lemminkainen,
Twisted mouth and turned his head round,
Tore his black beard in his anger,
And he spoke the words which follow:
" Eaten is the feast already,
Finished feast, and drunk the bride-ale,
And the ale has been divided,
To the men the mead been given,   90
And the cans away been carried,
And the pint-pots laid in storage.
  " Pohjola's illustrious Mistress,
Long-toothed Mistress of Pimentola,
Thou hast held the wedding badly,
And in doggish fashion held it,
Baked the bread in loaves enormous,
Thou hast brewed the beer of barley,
Six times sent thy invitations,
Nine times hast thou sent a summons,   100
Thou hast asked the poor, the spectres,
Asked the scum, and asked the wastrels,
Asked the leanest of the loafers,
Labourers with one garment only ;
All folks else thou hast invited,
Me rejected uninvited.
  "Wherefore should I thus be treated,
When I sent myself the barley ?

Others brought it by the spoonful
Others poured it out by dishfuls,   110
But I poured it out in bushels,
By the half-ton out I poured it,
Of my own, the best of barley,
Corn which I had sown aforetime.

"'Tis not now that Lemminkainen,
Is a guest of great distinction,
For no ale is offered to me,
Nor the pot set on the fire.
In the pot is nothing cooking,
Not a pound of pork you give me,   120
Neither food nor drink you give me,
Now my weary journey's ended."

Ilpotar, the noble Mistress,
Uttered then the words which follow:
"O my little waiting-maiden,
O my ever-ready servant,
Put into the pot some dinner,
Bring some ale to give the stranger."

Then the girl, the child so wretched,
Washed the worst of all the dishes,   130
And the spoons she then was wiping,
And the ladles she was scouring,
Then into the pot put dinner,
Bones of meat, and heads of fishes,
Very ancient stalks of turnips,
Crusts of bread of stony hardness,
And a pint of ale she brought him,
And a can of filthy victuals,
Gave it lively Lemminkainen
That he should drink out the refuse,   140
And she spoke the words which follow:
"If you are indeed a hero,
Can you drink the ale I bring you,
Nor upset the can that holds it?"

Lemminkainen, youth so lively,
Looked at once into the pint-pot,
And below a worm was creeping,
In the midst there crept a serpent,

On the edge were serpents creeping,
Lizards also there were gliding.   150
   Said the lively Lemminkainen,
Loudly grumbled Kaukomieli,
"Off to Tuonela the bearer,
Quick to Manala the handmaid,
Ere the moon again has risen,
Or this very day is ended !"
   Afterwards these words he added,
"O thou beer, thou drink so nasty,
In an evil hour concocted,
Evil only lurks within thee !   160
Notwithstanding I will drink it,
On the ground will cast the refuse,
With my nameless finger lift it,
With my left thumb will I lift it."
   Then he felt into his pocket,
And within his pouch was searching,
Took an angle from his pocket,
Iron hooks from out his satchel,
Dropped it down into the pint-pot,
In the ale began to angle,   170
Hooked the snakes upon his fish-hooks,
On his hooks the evil vipers,
Up he drew of toads a hundred,
And of dusky snakes a thousand.
Down upon the ground he threw them,
Threw them all upon the planking,
Thereupon a sharp knife taking,
From the sheath he quickly drew it,
Cut the heads from off the serpents,
Broke the necks of all the serpents.   180
Then he drank the ale with gusto,
Drank the black mead with enjoyment,
And he spoke the words which follow :
"As a guest I am not honoured,
Since no ale was brought unto me
Which was better worth my drinking,
Offered me by hands more careful,
In a larger vessel brought me ;

Since no sheep was slaughtered for me,
No gigantic steer was slaughtered,   190
In the hall no ox they brought me,
From the house of hoofèd cattle."
 Then did Pohjola's great Master,
Answer in the words which follow:
"Wherefore have you then come hither,
Who invited you among us?"
 Answered lively Lemminkainen,
Said the handsome Kaukomieli:
"Good is perhaps the guest invited,
Better still if uninvited.   200
Hearken then, thou son of Pohja,
Pohjola's illustrious Master,
Give me ale for cash directly,
Reach me here some drink for money."
 Then did Pohjola's great Master,
Angry grow and greatly furious,
Very furious and indignant,
Sang a pond upon the flooring,
In the front of Lemminkainen,
And he said the words which follow: 210
"Here's a river you may drink of,
Here's a pond that you may splash in."
 Little troubled Lemminkainen,
And he spoke the words which follow:
"I'm no calf by women driven,
Nor a bull with tail behind me,
That I drink of river-water,
Or from filthy ponds the water."
 Then himself began to conjure,
And himself commenced his singing,   220
Sang upon the floor a bullock,
Mighty ox with horns all golden,
And he soon drank up the puddle,
Drank the river up with pleasure.
 But the mighty son of Pohja,
By his spells a wolf created,
And upon the floor he sang him,
To devour the fleshy bullock.

Lemminkainen, youth so lively,
Sang a white hare to his presence, 230
And upon the floor 'twas leaping,
Near the wolf-jaws widely opened.
But the mighty son of Pohja,
Sang a dog with pointed muzzle;
And the dog the hare devoured,
Rent the Squint-eye into fragments.
Lemminkainen, youth so lively,
On the rafters sang a squirrel,
And it frolicked on the rafters,
And the dog was barking at it. 240
But the mighty son of Pohja,
Sang a golden-breasted marten,
And the marten seized the squirrel,
On the rafter's end while sitting.
Lemminkainen, youth so lively,
Sang a fox of ruddy colour,
And it killed the gold-breast marten,
And destroyed the handsome-haired one.
But the mighty son of Pohja
By his spells a hen created, 250
And upon the ground 'twas walking,
Just before the fox's muzzle.
Lemminkainen, youth so lively,
Thereupon a hawk created,
Quickly with its claws it seized it,
And it tore the hen to pieces.
Then said Pohjola's great Master,
In the very words which follow:
"Better will not be the banquet,
Nor the guest-provision lessened. 260
House for work, the road for strangers,
Unrefreshed from the carousal!
Quit this place, O scamp of Hiisi,
Haste away from all folks' knowledge,
To thy home, O toad the basest,
Forth, O scoundrel, to thy country!"
Answered lively Lemminkainen,
Said the handsome Kaukomieli,

"None would let himself be banished,
Not a man, how bad soever,   270
From this place be ever driven,
Forced to fly from such a station."
    Then did Pohjola's great Master,
Snatch his sword from wall where hanging,
Grasped in haste the sharpened weapon,
And he spoke the words which follow:
"O thou Ahti Saarelainen,
Or thou handsome Kaukomieli,
Let us match our swords together,
Match the glitter of the sword-blades,   280
Whether my sword is the better,
Or is Ahti Saarelainen's."
    Said the lively Lemminkainen,
"Little of my sword is left me,
For on bones it has been shattered,
And on skulls completely broken!
But let this be as it may be,
If no better feast is ready,
Let us struggle, and determine
Which of our two swords is favoured.   290
Ne'er in former times my father
In a duel has been worsted,
Why should then his son be different,
Or his child be like a baby?"
    Sword he took, and bared his sword-blade,
And he drew his sharp-edged weapon,
Drew it from the leather scabbard,
Hanging at his belt of lambskin.
Then they measured and inspected
Which of their two swords was longer,   300
And a very little longer,
Was the sword of Pohja's Master,
As upon the nail the blackness,
Or a half-joint of a finger.
    Spoke then Ahti Saarelainen,
Said the handsome Kaukomieli,
"As your sword is rather longer,
Let the first attack be yours."

Then did Pohjola's great Master,
Aim a blow, and tried to strike him,   310
Aimed his sword, but never struck it,
On the head of Lemminkainen.
Once indeed he struck the rafters,
And the beams resounded loudly,
And across the beam was shattered,
And the arch in twain was broken.

Then spoke Ahti Saarelainen,
Said the handsome Kaukomieli:
" Well, what mischief did the rafters,
And what harm the beam effected,   320
That you thus attack the rafters,
And have made the arch to rattle?

" Hear me, son of Pohja's country,
Pohjola's illustrious Master,
Awkward 'tis in room to combat,
Trouble would it give the women,
If the clean room should be damaged,
And with blood defiled the flooring.
Let us go into the courtyard,
In the field outside to battle,   330
On the grass outside to combat.
In the yard the blood looks better,
In the yard it looks more lovely,
On the snow it looks much better."

Out into the yard they wandered,
And they found therein a cowhide,
And they spread it in the courtyard,
And they took their stand upon it.

Then said Ahti Saarelainen,
" Hearken, O thou son of Pohja!   340
As your sword is rather longer,
And your sword is more terrific,
Perhaps indeed you need to use it,
Just before your own departure,
Or before your neck is broken.
Strike away, O son of Pohja."

Fenced away the son of Pohja,
Struck a blow, and struck a second,

And he struck a third blow after,
But he could not strike him fairly,
Could not scratch the flesh upon him,　　350
From his skin a single bristle.
　　Then spoke Ahti Saarelainen,
Said the handsome Kaukomieli,
"Give me leave to try a little,
For at last my time is coming."
　　Natheless Pohjola's great Master,
Did not pay the least attention,
Striking on, without reflection,
Ever striking, never hitting.　　360
From his sword-blade flashed red fire,
And its edge was always gleaming
In the hands of Lemminkainen,
And the sheen extended further,
As against the neck he turned it,
Of the mighty son of Pohja.
　　Said the handsome Lemminkainen,
"Hearken, Pohjola's great Master,
True it is, thy neck so wretched,
Is as red as dawn of morning."　　370
　　Thereupon the son of Pohja,
He, the mighty lord of Pohja,
Bent his eyes that he might witness
How his own neck had been reddened.
Then the lively Lemminkainen,
Hurriedly a stroke delivered,
With his sword he struck the hero,
Quickly with the sword he struck him.
　　Full and fair he struck the hero,
Struck his head from off his shoulders,　　380
And the skull from neck he severed,
As from off the stalk a turnip,
Or an ear of corn is severed,
From a fish a fin divided.
In the yard the head went rolling,
And the skull in the enclosure,
As when it is struck by arrow
Falls the capercail from tree-top.

In the ground stood stakes a hundred,
In the yard there stood a thousand,   390
On the stakes were heads a hundred,
Only one stake still was headless.
Then the lively Lemminkainen
Took the head of the poor fellow;
From the ground the skull he lifted,
And upon the stake he set it.
    Then did Ahti Saarelainen,
He the handsome Kaukomieli,
Once again the house re-enter,
And he spoke the words which follow: 400
" Wicked maid, now bring me water,
That I wash my hands and cleanse them,
From the blood of wicked Master,
From the gore of man of evil."
    Furious was the Crone of Pohja,
Wild with wrath and indignation,
And at once she sang up swordsmen,
Heroes well equipped for battle.
Up she sang a hundred swordsmen,
Sang a thousand weapon-bearers,   410
Lemminkainen's head to capture,
From the neck of Kaukomieli.
    Now the time seemed really coming,
Fitting time for his departure,
Terror came at length upon him,
And too hard the task before him;
From the house the youthful Ahti
Lemminkainen quick departed,
From the feast prepared at Pohja,
From the unannounced carousal.   420

Runo XXVIII.—Lemminkainen and his Mother

Argument

Lemminkainen escapes with all speed from Pohjola, comes home
and asks his mother where he can hide himself from the people of
Pohjola, who will soon attack him in his home, a hundred to one
(1–164). His mother reproaches him for his expedition to Pohjola,
suggests various places of concealment, and at length advises him to go
far across the lakes to a distant island, where his father once lived in
peace during a year of great war (165–294).

THEN did Ahti Saarelainen,
He the lively Lemminkainen,
Haste to reach a place for hiding,
Hasten quickly to remove him
From the gloomy land of Pohja,
From the gloomy house of Sara.

    From the room he rushed like snowfall,
To the yard like snake he hurried,
That he might escape the evil,
From the crime he had committed.   10

    When he came into the courtyard,
Then he gazed around and pondered,
Seeking for the horse he left there,
But he nowhere saw him standing
In the field a stone was standing,
On the waste a clump of willows.

    Who will come to give him counsel,
Who will now advise and help him,
That his head come not in danger,
And his hair remain uninjured,   20
Nor his handsome hair be draggled
In the courtyard foul of Pohja?
In the village heard he shouting,
Uproar too from other homesteads,
Lights were shining in the village,
Eyes were at the open windows.

Then must lively Lemminkainen,
Then must Ahti Saarelainen,
Alter now his shape completely,
And transform without delaying,   30
And must soar aloft as eagle,
Up to heaven to soar attempting;
But the sun his face was scorching,
And the moon shone on his temples.

Then the lively Lemminkainen,
Sent aloft a prayer to Ukko:
"Ukko, Jumala most gracious,
Thou the wisest in the heavens,
Of the thunderclouds the leader,
Of the scattered clouds the ruler!   40
Let it now be gloomy weather,
And a little cloudlet give me,
So that under its protection
I may hasten homeward quickly,
Homeward to my dearest mother,
Unto the revered old woman."

As he flew upon his journey,
As he chanced to look behind him,
There he saw a hawk, a grey one,
And its eyes were fiery-glowing,   50
As it were the son of Pohja,
Like the former lord of Pohja.

And the grey hawk called unto him,
"Ahti, O my dearest brother,
Think you on our former combat,
Head to head in equal contest?"

Then said Ahti Saarelainen,
Said the handsome Kaukomieli,
"O my hawk, my bird so charming,
Turn thyself and hasten homeward,   60
To the place from which you started,
To the gloomy land of Pohja.
Hard it is to catch the eagle,
Clutch the strong-winged bird with talons."

Then he hurried quickly homeward,
Homeward to his dearest mother,

And his face was full of trouble,
And his heart with care o'erladen.
Then his mother came to meet him,
As along the path he hurried, 70
As he past the fence was walking,
And his mother first bespoke him.
"O my son, my son, my youngest,
Thou the strongest of my children!
Why returnest thou so sadly,
Home from Pohjola's dark regions?
Hast thou harmed thyself by drinking
At the drinking-bout of Pohja?
If the goblet made thee suffer,
Here a better one awaits thee, 80
Which thy father won in battle,
Which he fought for in the contest."
Said the lively Lemminkainen,
"O my mother who hast borne me,
If the goblet made me suffer,
I would overcome the masters,
Overcome a hundred heroes,
And would face a thousand heroes."
Then said Lemminkainen's mother,
"Wherefore art thou then in trouble? 90
If the horse has overcome you,
Wherefore let the horse annoy you?
If the horse has overcome you,
You should buy yourself a better,
With your father's lifelong savings,
Which the aged man provided."
Said the lively Lemminkainen,
"O my mother who hast borne me,
If I quarrelled with the courser,
Or the foal had over-reached me, 100
I myself have shamed the masters,
Overcome the horses' drivers,
Foals and drivers I have vanquished,
And the heroes with their coursers."
Then said Lemminkainen's mother,
"Wherefore art thou then in trouble,

Wherefore is thy heart so troubled,
As from Pohjola thou comest?
Have the women laughed about you,
Or the maidens ridiculed you?   110
If the women laughed about you,
Or the maidens ridiculed you,
There are maidens to be jeered at,
Other women to be laughed at."
    Said the lively Lemminkainen,
" O my mother who hast borne me,
If the women laughed about me,
Or the maidens ridiculed me,
I would laugh at all their menfolk,
And would wink at all the maidens,   120
I would shame a hundred women,
And a thousand brides would make them."
    Then said Lemminkainen's mother,
" What has chanced, my son, my darling,
Hast thou perhaps encountered something
As to Pohjola thou wentest?
Have you eaten perhaps too freely,
Eaten much, too much have drunken,
Or at night perchance when resting
Have you seen a dream of evil?"   130
    Then the lively Lemminkainen,
Answered in the words which follow:
" Perhaps old women may remember,
What in sleep they saw in vision!
Though my nightly dreams I think on,
Yet are those of daytime better.
O my mother, aged woman,
Fill my bag with fresh provisions,
With a good supply of flour,
And a lump of salt add likewise,   140
For thy son must travel further,
Journey to another country,
Journey from this house beloved,
Journey from this lovely dwelling,
For the men their swords are whetting,
And the lance-tips they are sharpening."

Then his mother interrupted,
Asking him his cause of trouble.
"Wherefore whet the men their sword-blades,
Wherefore sharpen they the lance-tips ? "   150
    Answered lively Lemminkainen,
Said the handsome Kaukomieli,
"Therefore do they whet their sword-blades,
Therefore they the lance-tips sharpen :
On the head of me unhappy,
On my neck to bring destruction.
From a quarrel rose a duel,
There in Pohjola's enclosure ;
I have slain the son of Pohja,
Slain the very lord of Pohja,   160
Then rose Pohjola to battle,
Close behind me comes the tumult,
Raging all for my destruction,
To surround a single warrior."
    Then his mother gave him answer,
To her child the old crone answered :
"I myself already told you,
And I had already warned you,
And forbidden you most strictly
Not to Pohjola to venture.   170
Had you stayed at home in quiet,
Living in your mother's dwelling,
Safely in your parent's homestead,
In the home of her who bore thee,
Then no war had ever risen,
Nor appeared a cause of contest.
    "Whither now, my son unhappy,
Canst thou flee, unhappy creature,
Go to hide thee from destruction,
Flying from thy wicked action,   180
Lest thy wretched head be captured,
And thy handsome neck be severed,
That thy hair remain uninjured,
Nor thy glossy hair downtrodden ? "
    Said the lively Lemminkainen,
"No such refuge do I know of,

Where a safe retreat awaits me,
Where I from my crime can hide me.
O my mother who hast borne me,
Where do you advise my hiding?"　　190
　　Answered Lemminkainen's mother,
And she spoke the words which follow:
"No, I know not where to hide you,
Where to hide you or to send you.
As a pine upon the mountain,
Juniper in distant places,
There might still misfortune find thee,
Evil fate might rise against thee.
Often is the mountain pine-tree
Cut to pieces into torches,　　200
And the juniper on heathland,
Into posts is often cloven.
　　"As a birch-tree in the valley,
Or an alder in the greenwood,
There might still misfortune find thee,
Evil fate might rise against thee.
Often is the valley birch-tree
Chopped to pieces into faggots,
Often is the alder-thicket
Cut away to make a clearing.　　210
　　"As a berry on the mountain,
Or upon the heath a cranberry,
Or upon the plain a strawberry,
Or in other spots a bilberry,
There might still misfortune find thee,
Evil fate might rise against thee,
For the girls might come to pluck thee,
Tin-adorned ones might uproot thee.
　　"In the lake as pike when hiding,
Powan in slow-flowing river,　　220
There misfortune still might find thee,
And at last destruction reach thee.
If there came a youthful fisher,
He might cast his net in water,
And the young in net might take thee,
And the old with net might capture.

"Didst thou roam as wolf in forest,
Or a bear in rugged country,
There might still misfortune find thee,
Evil fate might rise against thee;   230
If a sooty tramp was passing,
He perchance might spear the growler,
Or the wolves bring to destruction,
And the forest bears might slaughter."
Then the lively Lemminkainen
Answered in the words which follow:
"I myself know evil places,
Worst of all do I esteem them,
There where any death might seize me,
And at last destruction reach me.   240
O my mother who hast reared me,
Mother who thy milk hast given,
Whither would'st thou bid me hide me,
Whither should I now conceal me?
Death's wide jaws are just before me,
At my beard destruction's standing,
Every day for me it waiteth,
Till my ruin is accomplished."
Then said Lemminkainen's mother,
And she spoke the words which follow: 250
"I can tell the best of places,
Tell you one the best of any,
Where to hide yourself completely,
And your crime conceal for ever,
For I know a little country,
Know a very little refuge,
Wasted not, and safe from battle,
And untrodden by the swordsmen.
Swear me now by oaths eternal,
Binding, free from all deception,   260
In the course of sixty summers,
Nevermore to go to battle,
Neither for the love of silver,
Nor perchance if gold was needed."
Then said lively Lemminkainen,
"Now I swear by oaths the strongest,

Never in the first of summers,
Nor in any other summer,
Mix myself in mighty battles,
In the clashing of the sword-blades.   270
Wounds are still upon my shoulders,
In my breast deep wounds still rankle,
From my former battle-pleasures,
In the midst of all the tumult,
In the midst of mighty battles,
Where the heroes all contended."

Then did Lemminkainen's mother
Answer in the words which follow:
"Take the boat your father left you,
And betake yourself to hiding.   280
Traverse nine lakes in succession,
Half the tenth one must thou traverse.
To an island on its surface,
Where the cliffs arise from water.
There in former times your father
Hid, and kept himself in safety,
In the furious fights of summer,
In the hardest years of battle.
There you'll find a pleasant dwelling,
And a charming place to linger.   290
Hide thyself a year, a second,
In the third year come thou homeward,
To your father's well-known homestead,
To the dwelling of your parents."

Runo XXIX.—Lemminkainen's Adventures on the Island

Argument

Lemminkainen sails across the lakes in his boat and comes safely to the island (1–180). There he lives pleasantly among the girls and women till the return of the men from warfare, who conspire against him (181–290). Lemminkainen flies from the island, much to the grief both of the girls and himself (291–402). His boat is wrecked in a violent storm, but he escapes by swimming to land, makes a new boat, and arrives safely on the shores of his own country (403–452). He finds his old house burned, and the whole surroundings laid waste, when he begins to weep and lament, especially for the loss of his mother (453–514). His mother, however, is still alive, having taken refuge in a thick forest where Lemminkainen finds her to his great joy (515–546). She relates how the army of Pohjola came and burned down the house. Lemminkainen promises to build a finer house after he has revenged himself upon the people of Pohjola, and describes his pleasant life in the island of refuge (547–602).

LEMMINKAINEN, youth so lively,
He the handsome Kaukomieli,
Took provisions in his satchel,
In his wallet summer-butter,
Butter for a year to last him,
For another, pork sufficient,
Then he travelled off to hide him,
Started in the greatest hurry,
And he said the words which follow :
" Now I go, and I'm escaping,   10
For the space of three whole summers,
And for five years in succession.
Be the land to snakes abandoned,
Let the lynxes snarl in greenwood,
In the fields the reindeer wander,
In the brakes the geese conceal them.
    " Fare thee well, my dearest mother,
If the people come from Pohja,
From Pimentola the army,
And about my head they ask you,   20

Say that I have fled before them,
And have taken my departure,
And I have laid waste my clearing,
That which I had reaped so lately."

Then he pushed his boat in water,
On the waves he launched his vessel,
From the rollers steel he launched it,
From the haven lined with copper.
On the mast the sails he hoisted,
And he spread the sails of linen,   30
At the stern himself he seated,
And prepared him for his journey,
Sitting by his birchwood rudder,
With the stern-oar deftly steering.

Then he spoke the words which follow,
And in words like these expressed him :
" Wind, inflate the sails above me,
Wind of spring drive on the vessel,
Drive with speed the wooden vessel,
Onward drive the boat of pinewood   40
Forward to the nameless island,
And the nameless promontory."

So the wind the bark drove onward,
O'er the foaming lake 'twas driven,
O'er the bright expanse of water,
Speeding o'er the open water,
Rocking while two moons were changing,
Till a third was near its ending.

At the cape were maidens sitting,
There upon the blue lake's margin   50
They were gazing, and were casting
Glances o'er the azure billows.
One was waiting for her brother,
And another for her father,
But the others all were waiting,
Waiting each one for a lover.

In the distance spied they Kauko,
Sooner still the boat of Kauko,
Like a little cloud in distance,
Just between the sky and water.   60

And the island-maids reflected,
Said the maidens of the island :
"What's this strange thing in the water,
What this wonder on the billows?
If a boat of our relations,
Sailing vessel of our island,
Hasten then, and speed thee homeward,
To the harbour of the island,
That we hear the tidings quickly,
Hear the news from foreign countries,   70
If there's peace among the shore-folks,
Or if war is waged among them."
    Still the wind the sail inflated,
And the billows drove the vessel.
Then the lively Lemminkainen
Guided to the isle the vessel,
To the island's end he drove it,
Where it ends in jutting headland.
    And he said on his arrival,
To the cape as he was coming,   80
" Is there room upon this island,
On the surface of the island,
Where the boat may land upon it,
And to dry land I may bring it?"
    Said the girls upon the island,
And the island-maidens answered :
"There is room upon this island,
On the surface of the island,
Where the boat may land upon it,
And to dry land you may bring it.   90
There are harbours for the vessel,
On the beach sufficient rollers,
To receive a hundred vessels,
Though the boats should come by thousands."
    Then the lively Lemminkainen
On the land drew up his vessel,
On the wooden rollers laid it,
And he spoke the words which follow :
" Is there room upon this island,
On the surface of the island,   100

Where a little man may hide him,
And a weak man may take refuge
From the din of furious battle,
And the clash of steely sword-blades?"
　　Said the girls upon the island,
And the island-maidens answered:
"There is room upon this island,
On the surface of the island,
Where a little man may hide him,
And a weak man may conceal him.　　　　110
Here are very many castles,
Stately castles to reside in,
Though there came a hundred heroes,
And a thousand men of valour."
　　Said the lively Lemminkainen,
And he spoke the words which follow:
"Is there room upon this island,
On the surface of the island,
Where there stands a birch-tree forest,
And a stretch of other country,　　　　120
Where I perhaps may make a clearing,
Work upon my goodly clearing?"
　　Said the girls upon the island,
And the island-maidens answered:
"There is not upon this island,
On the surface of the island,
Not the space your back could rest on,
Land not of a bushel's measure,
Where you perhaps might make a clearing,
Work upon your goodly clearing.　　　　130
All the land is now divided,
And the fields in plots are measured,
And allotted are the fallows,
Grassland managed by the commune."
　　Said the lively Lemminkainen,
Asked the handsome Kaukomieli,
"Is there room upon this island,
On the surface of the island,
Space where I my songs may carol,
Space where I may sing my ballads?　　　　140

Words within my mouth are melting,
And between my gums are sprouting."
    Said the girls upon the island,
And the island-maidens answered:
"There is room upon this island,
On the surface of the island,
Space where you may sing your ballads,
And intone your splendid verses,
While you sport amid the greenwood,
While you dance among the meadows."   150
    Then the lively Lemminkainen
Hastened to commence his singing.
In the court sang mountain-ashtrees,
In the farmyard oaks grew upward.
On the oaks were equal branches,
And on every branch an acorn,
Golden globes within the acorns,
And upon the globes were cuckoos.
When the cuckoos all were calling,
From their mouths was gold distilling,   160
From their beaks was copper flowing,
Likewise silver pouring onward
To the hills all golden-shining,
And among the silver mountains.
    Once again sang Lemminkainen,
Once again he sang and chanted,
Gravel sang to pearls of beauty,
All the stones to gleaming lustre,
All the stones to glowing redness,
And the flowers to golden glory.   170
    Then again sang Lemminkainen;
In the yard a well created,
O'er the well a golden cover,
And on this a golden bucket,
That the lads might drink the water,
And their sisters wash their faces.
Ponds he sang upon the meadows,
In the ponds blue ducks were floating,
Temples golden, heads of silver,
And their claws were all of copper.   180

Then the island maidens wondered,
And the girls were all astounded
At the songs of Lemminkainen,
And the craft of that great hero.
Said the lively Lemminkainen,
Spoke the handsome Kaukomieli,
"I have sung a song most splendid,
But perchance might sing a better,
If beneath a roof I sang it,
At the end of the deal table.   190
If a house you cannot give me,
There to rest upon the planking,
I will hum my tunes in forest,
Toss my songs among the bushes."
Said the maidens of the island,
Answered after full reflection:
"There are houses you may enter,
Handsome halls that you may dwell in,
Safe from cold to sing your verses,
In the open speak your magic."   200
Then the lively Lemminkainen,
Entered in a house directly,
Where he sang a row of pint-pots,
At the end of the long table.
All the pots with ale were brimming,
And the cans with mead the finest,
Filled as full as one could fill them,
Dishes filled to overflowing.
In the pots was beer in plenty,
And the mead in covered tankards,   210
Butter too, in great abundance,
Pork was likewise there in plenty,
For the feast of Lemminkainen,
And for Kaukomieli's pleasure.
Kauko was of finest manners,
Nor to eat was he accustomed,
Only with a knife of silver,
Fitted with a golden handle.
So he sang a knife of silver,
And a golden-hafted knife-blade,   220

And he ate till he was sated,
Drank the ale in full contentment.
    Then the lively Lemminkainen,
Roamed about through every village,
For the island-maidens' pleasure,
To delight the braidless damsels,
And where'er his head was turning,
There he found a mouth for kissing,
Wheresoe'er his hand was outstretched,
There he found a hand to clasp it.   230
    And at night he went to rest him,
Hiding in the darkest corner;
There was not a single village
Where he did not find ten homesteads,
There was not a single homestead
Where he did not find ten daughters,
There was none among the daughters,
None among the mother's children,
By whose side he did not stretch him,
On whose arm he did not rest him.   240
    Thus a thousand brides he found there,
Rested by a hundred widows;
Two in half-a-score remained not,
Three in a completed hundred,
Whom he left untouched as maidens,
Or as widows unmolested.
    Thus the lively Lemminkainen
Lived a life of great enjoyment,
For the course of three whole summers
In the island's pleasant hamlets,   250
To the island-maidens' rapture,
The content of all the widows;
One alone he did not trouble,
'Twas a poor and aged maiden,
At the furthest promontory,
In the tenth among the hamlets.
    As he pondered on his journey,
And resolved to wend him homeward,
Came the poor and aged maiden,
And she spoke the words which follow: 260

"Handsome hero, wretched Kauko,
If you will not think upon me,
Then I wish that as you travel,
May your boat on rocks be stranded."

Rose he not before the cockcrow,
Nor before the hen's child rose he,
From his sporting with the maiden,
Laughing with the wretched woman.

Then upon a day it happened,
And upon a certain evening,   270
He resolved to rise and wander,
Waiting not for morn or cockcrow.

Long before the time he rose up,
Sooner than the time intended,
And he went around to wander,
And to wander through the village,
For his sporting with the damsels,
To amuse the wretched women.

As alone by night he wandered,
Through the villages he sauntered   280
To the isle's extremest headland,
To the tenth among the hamlets,
He beheld not any homestead
Where three rooms he did not notice,
There was not a room among them
Where he did not see three heroes,
And he saw not any hero,
With a sword-blade left unwhetted,
Sharpened thus to bring destruction
On the head of Lemminkainen.   290

Then the lively Lemminkainen
Spoke aloud the words which follow :
"Woe to me, the day is dawning,
And the pleasant sun is rising
O'er a youth, of all most wretched,
O'er the neck of me unhappy !
Lempo may perchance a hero
With his shirt protect and cover,
Perhaps will cover with his mantle,
Cast it round him for protection   300

Though a hundred men attacked him,
And a thousand pressed upon him."
　　Unembraced he left the maidens,
And he left them unmolested,
And he turned him to his vessel,
Luckless to his boat he hurried,
But he found it burned to ashes,
Utterly consumed to ashes.
　　Mischief now he saw approaching,
O'er his head ill days were brooding,　　　310
So began to build a vessel,
And a new boat to construct him.
　　Wood was failing to the craftsman,
Boards with which a boat to fashion,
But he found of wood a little,
Begged some wretched bits of boarding,
Five small splinters of a spindle,
And six fragments of a bobbin.
　　So from these a boat he fashioned,
And a new boat he constructed,　　　320
By his magic art he made it,
With his secret knowledge made it,
Hammered once, one side he fashioned,
Hammered twice, called up the other,
Hammered then a third time only,
And the boat was quite completed.
Then he pushed the boat in water,
On the waves he launched the vessel,
And he spoke the words which follow,
And expressed himself in thiswise:　　　330
"Float like bladder on the water,
On the waves like water-lily.
Eagle, give me now three feathers,
Eagle, three, and two from raven,
For the wretched boat's protection,
For the wretched vessel's bulwarks."
　　Then he stepped upon the planking,
At the stern he took his station,
Head bowed down, in deep depression,
And his cap awry adjusted,　　　340

Since by night he dare not tarry,
Nor by day could linger longer,
For the island-maidens' pleasure,
Sporting with unbraided damsels.
  Spoke the lively Lemminkainen,
Said the handsome Kaukomieli:
" Now the youth must take departure,
And must travel from these dwellings,
Joyless leave behind these damsels,
Dance no longer with the fair ones.   350
Surely when I have departed,
And have left this land behind me,
Never will rejoice these damsels,
Nor unbraided girls be jesting,
In their homes so full of sadness,
In the courtyards now so dreary."
  Wept the island girls already,
Damsels at the cape lamented:
" Wherefore goest thou, Lemminkainen,
And departest, hero-bridegroom ?   360
Dost thou go for maidens' coyness
Or for scarcity of women ? "
  Spoke the lively Lemminkainen,
Said the handsome Kaukomieli,
" 'Tis not for the maidens' coyness,
Nor the scarcity of women.
I have had a hundred women,
And embraced a thousand maidens ;
Thus departeth Lemminkainen,
Quits you thus your hero-bridegroom,   370
Since the great desire has seized me,
Longing for my native country,
Longing for my own land's strawberries,
For the slopes where grow the raspberries,
For the maidens on the headland,
And the poultry of my farmyard."
  Then the lively Lemminkainen
Pushed into the waves the vessel,
Blew the wind, and then it blustered,
Rising waves drove on the vessel   380

O'er the blue lake's shining surface,
And across the open water.
    On the beach there stood the sad ones,
On the shingles the unhappy,
And the island girls were weeping,
And the golden maids lamenting.
Wept for long the island-maidens,
Damsels on the cape lamented,
Long as they could see the masthead,
And the ironwork was gleaming,   390
But they wept not for the masthead,
Nor bewailed the iron fittings,
By the mast they wept the steersman,
He who wrought the iron fittings.
    Lemminkainen too was weeping,
Long he wept, and long was saddened,
Long as he could see the island,
Or the outline of its mountains;
But he wept not for the island,
Nor lamented for the mountains,   400
But he wept the island-damsels,
For the mountain geese lamented.
    Then the lively Lemminkainen
O'er the blue lake took his journey,
And he voyaged one day, a second,
And at length upon the third day
Rose a furious wind against him,
And the whole horizon thundered.
Rose a great wind from the north-west,
And a strong wind from the north-east,   410
Struck one side and then the other,
Thus the vessel overturning.
    Then the lively Lemminkainen
Plunged his hands into the water,
Rowing forward with his fingers,
While his feet he used for steering.
    Thus he swam by night and daytime
And with greatest skill he steered him,
And a little cloud perceived he,
In the west a cloud projecting,   420

Which to solid land was changing,
And became a promontory.
   On the cape he found a homestead,
Where he found the mistress baking,
And her daughters dough were kneading.
"O thou very gracious mistress,
If you but perceived my hunger,
Thought upon my sad condition,
You would hurry to the storehouse,
To the alehouse like a snowstorm,   430
And a can of ale would fetch me,
And a strip of pork would fetch me,
In the pan would broil it for me,
And would pour some butter on it,
That the weary man might eat it,
And the fainting hero drink it.
Nights and days have I been swimming
Out upon the broad lake's billows,
With the wind as my protector,
At the mercy of the lake-waves."   440
   Thereupon the gracious mistress
Hastened to the mountain storehouse,
Sliced some butter in the storehouse,
And a slice of pork provided,
In the pan thereafter broiled it,
That the hungry man might eat it.
Then she fetched of ale a canful,
For the fainting hero's drinking,
And she gave him a new vessel,
And a boat completely finished,   450
Which to other lands should take him,
And convey him to his birthplace.
   Then the lively Lemminkainen
Started on his homeward journey,
Saw the lands and saw the beaches,
Here the islands, there the channels,
Saw the ancient landing-stages,
Saw the former dwelling-places,
And he saw the pine-clad mountains,
All the hills with fir-trees covered,   460

But he found no more his homestead,
And the walls he found not standing ;
Where the house before was standing,
Rustled now a cherry-thicket,
On the mound were pine-trees growing,
Juniper beside the well-spring.
    Spoke the lively Lemminkainen,
Said the handsome Kaukomieli,
" I have roamed among these forests,
O'er the stones, and plunged in river,   470
And have played about the meadows,
And have wandered through the cornfields.
Who has spoiled my well-known homestead,
And destroyed my charming dwelling ?
They have burned the house to ashes,
And the wind's dispersed the ashes."
    Thereupon he fell to weeping,
And he wept one day, a second,
But he wept not for the homestead,
Nor lamented for the storehouse,   480
But he wept the house's treasure,
Dearer to him than the storehouse.
    Then he saw a bird was flying,
And a golden eagle hovering,
And he then began to ask it :
" O my dearest golden eagle,
Can you not perchance inform me,
What has happened to my mother,
To the fair one who has borne me,
To my dear and much-loved mother ? "   490
    Nothing knew the eagle of her,
Nor the stupid bird could tell him,
Only knew that she had perished ;
Said a raven she had fallen,
And had died beneath the sword-blades,
'Neath the battle-axes fallen.
    Answered lively Lemminkainen,
Said the handsome Kaukomieli :
" O my fair one who hast borne me,
O my dear and much-loved mother !   500

Hast thou perished, who hast borne me,
Hast thou gone, O tender mother?
Now thy flesh in earth has rotted,
Fir-trees o'er thy head are growing,
Juniper upon thy ankles,
On thy finger-tips are willows.
   " Thus my wretched doom has found me,
And an ill reward has reached me,
That my sword I dared to measure,
And I dared to raise my weapons   510
There in Pohjola's great castle,
In the fields of Pimentola.
But my own race now has perished,
Perished now is she who bore me."
   Then he looked, and turned on all sides.
And he saw a trace of footsteps,
Where the grass was lightly trampled,
And the heath was slightly broken.
Then he went the way they led him,
And he found a little pathway;   520
To the forest led the pathway,
And he went in that direction.
   Thus he walked a verst, a second,
Hurried through a stretch of country,
And in darkest shades of forest,
In the most concealed recesses,
There he saw a hidden bath-house,
Saw a little cottage hidden,
In a cleft two rocks protected,
In a nook between three fir-trees;   530
There he saw his tender mother,
There beheld the aged woman.
   Then the lively Lemminkainen,
Felt rejoiced beyond all measure,
And he spoke the words which follow,
And in words like these expressed him:
" O my very dearest mother,
O my mother who hast nursed me,
Thou art living still, O mother,
Watchful still, my aged mother!   540

Yet I thought that thou had'st perished,
And wast lost to me for ever,
Perished underneath the sword-blades,
Or beneath the spears had'st fallen,
And I wept my pretty eyes out,
And my handsome cheeks were ruined."
    Then said Lemminkainen's mother,
"True it is that I am living,
But was forced to fly my dwelling,
And to seek a place of hiding   550
In this dark and gloomy forest,
In the most concealed recesses,
When came Pohjola to battle,
Murderous hosts from distant countries,
Seeking but for thee, unhappy,
And our home they laid in ruins,
And they burned the house to ashes,
And they wasted all the holding."
    Said the lively Lemminkainen :
"O my mother who hast borne me,   560
Do not give thyself to sadness,
Be not sad, and be not troubled.
We will now erect fresh buildings,
Better buildings than the others,
And will wage a war with Pohja,
Overthrowing Lempo's people."
    Then did Lemminkainen's mother
Answer in the words which follow :
"Long hast thou, my son, been absent,
Long, my Kauko, hast been living   570
In a distant foreign country,
Always in the doors of strangers,
On a nameless promontory,
And upon an unknown island."
    Answered lively Lemminkainen,
Said the handsome Kaukomieli :
"There to dwell was very pleasant,
Charming was it there to wander.
There the trees are crimson-shining,
Red the trees, and blue the country,   580

And the pine-boughs shine like silver,
And the flowers of heath all golden,
And the mountains are of honey,
And the rocks are made of hens' eggs,
Flows the mead from withered pine-trees,
Milk flows from the barren fir-trees,
Butter flows from corner-fences,
From the posts the ale is flowing.
   " There to dwell was very pleasant,
Lovely was it to reside there ;   590
Afterwards 'twas bad to live there,
And unfit for me to live there.
They were anxious for the maidens,
And suspicious of the women,
Lest the miserable wenches,
And the fat and wicked creatures,
Might by me be badly treated,
Visited too much at night-time.
But I hid me from the maidens,
And the women's daughters guarded   600
Just as hides the wolf from porkers,
Or the hawks from village poultry."

RUNO XXX.—LEMMINKAINEN AND TIERA

Argument

Lemminkainen goes to ask his former comrade-in-arms, Tiera, to
join him in an expedition against Pohjola (1–122). The Mistress of
Pohjola sends the Frost against them, who freezes the boat in the
sea, and almost freezes the heroes themselves in the boat, but that
Lemminkainen restrains it by powerful charms and invocations (123–
316). Lemminkainen and his companion walk across the ice to the
shore, wander about in the waste for a long time in a miserable plight,
and at last make their way home (317–500).

AHTI, youth for ever youthful,
Lemminkainen young and lively,
Very early in the morning,
In the very earliest morning,

Sauntered downward to the boathouse,
To the landing-stage he wandered.
There a wooden boat was weeping,
Boat with iron rowlocks grieving;
" Here am I, for sailing ready,
But, O wretched one, rejected.   10
Ahti rows not forth to battle,
For the space of sixty summers,
Neither for the lust of silver,
Or if need of gold should drive him."
Then the lively Lemminkainen
Struck his glove upon the vessel,
With his coloured glove he struck it,
And he said the words which follow :
" Care thou not, O deck of pinewood,
Nor lament, O timber-sided.   20
Thou once more shalt go to battle,
And shalt mingle in the combat,
Shalt again be filled with warriors,
Ere to-morrow shall be ended."
Then he went to seek his mother,
And he said the words which follow :
" Do not weep for me, O mother,
Nor lament, thou aged woman,
If I once again must wander,
And again must go to battle ;   30
For my mind resolve has taken,
And a plan my brain has seized on,
To destroy the folk of Pohja,
And revenge me on the scoundrels."
To restrain him sought his mother,
And the aged woman warned him :
" Do not go, my son, my dearest,
Thus 'gainst Pohjola to combat !
There perchance might death o'ercome thee,
And destruction fall upon thee."   40
Little troubled Lemminkainen,
But he thought on his departure,
And he started on his journey,
And he spoke the words which follow :

" Can I find another hero,
Find a man, and find a swordsman,
Who will join in Ahti's battle,
And with all his strength will aid me?
"Well is Tiera known unto me,
Well with Kuura I'm acquainted, 50
He will be a second hero,
He's a hero and a swordsman,
He will join in Ahti's battle,
And with all his strength will aid me."
Through the villages he wandered,
Found his way to Tiera's homestead,
And he said on his arrival,
Spoke the object of his coming:
" O my Tiera, faithful comrade,
Of my friends most loved and dearest, 60
Thinkest thou on days departed,
On the life we lived aforetime,
When we wandered forth together,
To the fields of mighty battles?
There was not a single village
Where ten houses were not numbered,
There was none among the houses,
Where ten heroes were not living,
There was none among the heroes,
Not a man, however valiant, 70
None who did not fall before us,
By us twain who was not slaughtered."
At the window worked the father,
And a spear-shaft he was carving;
By the threshold stood the mother,
Busy as she churned the butter;
At the door the ruddy brothers,
And they wrought a sledge's framework;
At the bridge-end stood the sisters,
And the clothes they there were wringing. 80
From the window spoke the father,
And the mother from the threshold,
From the door the ruddy brothers,
From the bridge-end spoke the sisters,

"Tiera cannot go to battle,
Nor may strike with spear in warfare.
Other duties call for Tiera,
He has made a lifelong compact,
For a young wife has he taken
As the mistress of his household,   90
But untouched is she at present,
Uncaressed is still her bosom."

By the stove was Tiera resting,
By the stove-side Kuura rested,
At the stove one foot he booted,
And the other at the stove-bench,
At the gate his belt he tightened,
In the open girt it round him;
Then did Tiera grasp his spear-shaft,
Not the largest of the largest,   100
Nor the smallest of the smallest,
But a spear of mid dimensions.
On the blade a steed was standing,
On the side a foal was trotting,
At the joint a wolf was howling,
At the haft a bear was growling.

Thus his spear did Tiera brandish,
And he brandished it to whirring,
Hurled it then to fathom-deepness
In the stiff clay of the cornfield,   110
In a bare spot of the meadow,
In a flat spot free from hillocks.

Then his spear was placed by Tiera
With the other spears of Ahti,
And he went and made him ready
Swift to join in Ahti's battle.

Then did Ahti Saarelainen
Push his boat into the water,
Like a snake in grass when creeping,
Even like a living serpent,   120
And he sailed away to north-west,
On the lake that borders Pohja.

Then did Pohjola's old Mistress
Call the wicked Frost to aid her,

On the lake that borders Pohja,
On the deep and open water,
And she said the words which follow,
Thus she spoke and thus commanded :
" O my Frost, my boy so little,
O thou foster-child I nurtured !   130
Go thou forth where I shall bid thee,
Where I bid thee, and I send thee.
Freeze the boat of that great scoundrel,
Boat of lively Lemminkainen,
On the lake's extended surface,
On the deep and open water,
Freeze thou too the master in it,
Freeze thou in the boat the rascal,
That he nevermore escape thee,
In the course of all his lifetime,   140
If myself I do not loose him,
If myself I do not free him."

Then the Frost, that wicked fellow,
And a youth the most malicious,
Went upon the lake to freeze it,
And upon the waves he brooded.
Forth he went, as he was ordered,
And upon the land he wandered,
Bit the leaves from off the branches,
Grass from off the flowerless meadows   150
Then he came upon his journey
To the lake that borders Pohja,
To the endless waste of water,
And upon the first night only
Froze the bays and froze the lakelets,
Hurried forward on the seashore,
But the lake was still unfrozen,
And the waves were still unstiffened.
If a small finch swam the water,
On the waves a water-wagtail,   160
Still its claws remained unfrozen,
And its little head unstiffened.

On the second night, however,
He began to work more strongly,

Growing insolent extremely,
And he now grew most terrific,
Then the ice on ice he loaded,
And the great Frost still was freezing,
And with ice he clothed the mountains
Scattered snow to height of spear-shaft,   170
Froze the boat upon the water,
Ahti's vessel on the billows ;
Then he would have frozen Ahti,
And in ice his feet would fasten,
And he seized upon his fingers,
And beneath his toes attacked him.
Angry then was Lemminkainen,
Very angry and indignant,
Pushed the Frost into the fire,
Pushed him in an iron furnace.   180
  With his hands the Frost then seized he,
Grasped him in his fists securely,
And he spoke the words which follow,
And in words like these expressed him :
" Pakkanen, Puhuri's offspring,
Thou, the son of cold of winter,
Do not make my fingers frozen,
Nor my little toes thus stiffen.
Let my ears remain unhandled,
Do not freeze my head upon me.   190
    " There's enough that may be frozen,
Much is left you for your freezing,
Though the skins of men you freeze not,
Nor the forms of mother's children.
Be the plains and marshes frozen,
Freeze the stones to frozen coldness,
Freeze the willows near the water,
Grasp the aspen till it murmurs,
Peel the bark from off the birch-tree,
And the pine-trees break to pieces,   200
But the men you shall not trouble,
Nor the hair of mother's children.
    " If this is not yet sufficient,
Other things remain for freezing.

Thou may'st freeze the stones when heated,
And the slabs of stone when glowing,
Thou may'st freeze the iron mountains,
And the rocks of steely hardness,
And the mighty river Vuoksi,
Or the Imatra terrific,   210
Stop the course of raging whirlpool,
Foaming in its utmost fury.

  " Shall I tell you of your lineage,
And shall I make known your honours ?
Surely do I know thy lineage,
All I know of thine uprearing ;
For the Frost was born 'mid willows,
Nurtured in the sharpest weather,
Near to Pohjola's great homestead,
Near the hall of Pimentola,   220
Sprung from father, ever crime-stained,
And from a most wicked mother.

  " Who was it the Frost who suckled,
Bathed him in the glowing weather ?
Milkless wholly was his mother,
And his mother wholly breastless.

  " Adders 'twas the Frost who suckled,
Adders suckled, serpents fed him,
Suckled with their pointless nipples,
Suckled with their dried-up udders,   230
And the Northwind rocked his cradle,
And to rest the cold air soothed him,
In the wretched willow-thicket,
In the midst of quaking marshes.

  " And the boy was reared up vicious,
Led an evil life destructive,
But as yet no name was given,
To a boy so wholly worthless ;
When at length a name was given,
Frost it was they called the scoundrel.   240

  " Then he wandered by the hedges,
Always dancing in the bushes,
Wading through the swamps in summer
On the broadest of the marshes,

Roaring through the pines in winter,
Crying out among the fir-trees,
Crashing through the woods of birch-trees,
Sweeping through the alder-thickets,
Freezing all the trees and grasses,
Making level all the meadows.　　　　　　　　250
From the trees he bit the foliage,
From the heather bit the blossoms,
Cracked the bark from off the pine-trees,
And the twigs from off the fir-trees.

"Now that thou hast grown to greatness,
And attained thy fullest stature,
Dar'st thou me with cold to threaten,
And to seize my ears attemptest,
To attack my feet beneath me,
And my finger-tips attacking?　　　　　　　　260

"But I shall not let you freeze me.
Not to miserably freeze me,
Fire I'll thrust into my stockings,
In my boots thrust burning firebrands,
In the seams thrust burning embers,
Fire will thrust beneath my shoestrings,
That the Frost may never freeze me,
Nor the sharpest weather harm me.

"Thither will I now condemn thee,
To the furthest bounds of Pohja,　　　　　　　270
To the place from whence thou camest,
To the home from whence thou camest.
Freeze upon the fire the kettles,
And the coals upon the hearthstone,
In the dough the hands of women,
And the boy in young wife's bosom,
In the ewes the milk congeal thou,
And in mares let foals be frozen.

"If to this thou pay'st no heeding,
Then indeed will I condemn thee　　　　　　　280
To the midst of coals of Hiisi,
Even to the hearth of Lempo,
Thrust thee there into the furnace,
Lay thee down upon the anvil,

Unprotected from the hammer,
From the pounding of the hammer,
That the hammer beat thee helpless,
And the hammer beat thee sorely.
   " If this will not overcome thee,
And my spells are insufficient,   290
Still I know another station,
Know a fitting station for thee.
I will lead thy mouth to summer,
And thy tongue to home of summer,
Whence thou never canst release thee,
In the course of all thy lifetime,
If I do not give thee freedom,
And I should myself release thee."
   Then the Frost, the son of Northwind,
Felt that he was near destruction,   300
Whereupon he prayed for mercy,
And he spoke the words which follow:
" Let us understand each other,
Nor the one the other injure,
In the course of all our lifetime,
While the golden moon is shining.
   "Should'st thou hear that I would freeze you,
Or again should misbehave me,
Thrust me then into the furnace,
Sink me in the blazing fire,   310
In the smith's coals do thou sink me,
Under Ilmarinen's anvil,
Or my mouth to summer turn thou,
And my tongue to home of summer,
Never more release to hope for,
In the course of all my lifetime."
   Then the lively Lemminkainen
Left his vessel in the ice-floes,
Left his captured ship of battle,
And proceeded on his journey;   320
Tiera too, the other hero,
Followed in his comrade's footsteps.
   O'er the level ice they wandered,
'Neath their feet the smooth ice crunching

And they walked one day, a second,
And at length upon the third day,
Then they saw a cape of hunger,
And afar a wretched village.
    'Neath the cape there stood a castle,
And they spoke the words which follow :   330
" Is there meat within the castle,
Is there fish within the household,
For the worn and weary heroes,
And the men who faint with hunger ? "
Meat was none within the castle,
Nor was fish within the household.
    Spoke the lively Lemminkainen,
Said the handsome Kaukomieli :
" Fire consume this wretched castle,
Water sweep away such castles ! "   340
    He himself pursued his journey,
Pushing onward through the forest,
On a path with houses nowhere,
On a pathway that he knew not.
    Then the lively Lemminkainen,
He the handsome Kaukomieli,
Shore the wool from stones in passing,
From the rocks the hair he gathered,
And he wove it into stockings,
Into mittens quickly wrought it,   350
In the mighty cold's dominion,
Where the Frost was freezing all things.
    On he went to seek a pathway,
Searching for the right direction.
Through the wood the pathway led him,
Led him in the right direction.
    Spoke the lively Lemminkainen,
Said the handsome Kaukomieli,
" O my dearest brother Tiera,
Now at length we're coming somewhere,   360
Now that days and months we've wandered,
In the open air for ever."
    Then did Tiera make him answer,
And he spoke the words which follow :

"We unhappy sought for vengeance,
Recklessly we sought for vengeance,
Rushing forth to mighty conflict
In the gloomy land of Pohja,
There our lives to bring in danger,
Rushing to our own destruction,   370
In this miserable country,
On a pathway that we knew not.

"Never is it known unto us,
Never known and never guessed at,
What the pathway is that leads us,
Or the road that may conduct us
To our death at edge of forest,
Or on heath to meet destruction,
Here in the abode of ravens,
In the fields by crows frequented.   380

"And the ravens here are flocking,
And the evil birds are croaking,
And the flesh the birds are tearing,
And with blood the crows are sated,
And the ravens' beaks are moistened
In the wounds of us, the wretched,
To the rocks our bones they carry,
And upon the stones they cast them.

"Ah, my hapless mother knows not,
Never she, with pain who bore me,   390
Where her flesh may now be carried,
And her blood may now be flowing,
Whether in the furious battle,
In the equal strife of foemen,
Or upon a lake's broad surface,
On the far-extending billows,
Or on hills with pine-cones loaded,
Wandering 'mid the fallen branches.

"And my mother can know nothing
Of her son, the most unhappy,   400
Only know that he has perished,
Only know that he has fallen ;
And my mother thus will weep me,
Thus lament, the aged woman :

"'Thus my hapless son has perished,
And the wretched one has fallen;
He has sown the seed of Tuoni,
Harrows now in Kalma's country.
Perhaps the son I love so dearly,
Perhaps my son, O me unhappy,   410
Leaves his bows untouched for ever,
Leaves his handsome bows to stiffen.
Now the birds may live securely,
In the leaves the grouse may flutter,
Bears may live their lives of rapine,
In the fields the reindeer roll them.'"

Answered lively Lemminkainen,
Said the handsome Kaukomieli:
"Thus it is, unhappy mother,
Thou unhappy, who hast borne me!   420
Thou a flight of doves hast nurtured,
Quite a flock of swans hast nurtured,
Rose the wind, and all were scattered,
Lempo came, and he dispersed them,
One in one place, one in other,
And a third in yet another.

"I remember times aforetime,
And the better days remember,
How like flowers we gathered round thee,
In one homeland, just like berries.   430
Many gazed upon our figures,
And admired our forms so handsome,
Otherwise than in the present,
In this time so full of evil.
Once the wind was our acquaintance,
And the sun was gazing on us:
Now the clouds are gathering round us,
And the rain has overwhelmed us.
But we let not trouble vex us,
Even in our greatest sorrow,   440
Though the girls were living happy,
And the braidless maids were jesting,
And the women all were laughing,
And the brides were sweet as honey,

Tearless, spite of all vexation,
And unshaken when in trouble.
 " But we are not here enchanted,
Not bewitched, and not enchanted,
Here upon the paths to perish,
Sinking down upon our journey,   450
In our youth to sadly perish,
In our bloom to meet destruction.
 " Let those whom the sorcerers harassed
And bewitched with eyes of evil,
Let them make their journey homeward,
And regain their native country.
Be the sorcerers' selves enchanted,
And with songs bewitched their children;
Let their race for ever perish,
And their race be brought to ruin.   460
 " Ne'er in former times my father,
Never has my aged father
Yielded to a sorcerer's orders,
Or the wiles of Lapland's children.
Thus my father spoke aforetime,
And I now repeat his sayings:
'Guard me, O thou kind Creator,
Guard me, Jumala most gracious,
Aid me with thy hand of mercy,
With thy mighty power protect me,   470
From the plots of men of evil,
And the thoughts of aged women,
And the curses of the bearded,
And the curses of the beardless.
Grant us now thy aid eternal,
Be our ever-faithful guardian,
That no child be taken from us,
And no mother's child shall wander
From the path of the Creator,
Which by Jumala was fashioned.'"   480
 Then the lively Lemminkainen,
He the handsome Kaukomieli,
From his care constructed horses,
Coursers black composed from trouble,

Reins from evil days he fashioned,
Saddles from his secret sorrows,
Then his horse's back he mounted,
On his white-front courser mounted,
And he rode upon his journey,
At his side his faithful Tiera,   490
And along the shores he journeyed,
On the sandy shores proceeded,
Till he reached his tender mother,
Reached the very aged woman.

Now will I abandon Kauko,
Long from out my song will leave him ;
But he showed the way to Tiera,
Sent him on his homeward journey.
Now my song aside will wander,
While I turn to other matters.   500

Runo XXXI.—Untamo and Kullervo

Argument

Untamo wages war against his brother Kalervo, overthrows Kalervo and his army, sparing only a single pregnant woman of the whole clan. She is carried away to Untamo's people, and gives birth to her son Kullervo (1–82). Kullervo resolves in his cradle to take revenge on Untamo, and Untamo attempts several times to put him to death, but without success (83–202). When Kullervo grows up, he spoils all his work, and therefore Untamo sells him as a slave to Ilmarinen (203–374).

'Twas a mother reared her chickens,
Large the flock of swans she nurtured ;
By the hedge she placed the chickens,
Sent the swans into the river,
And an eagle came and scared them,
And a hawk that came dispersed them,
And a flying bird dispersed them.
One he carried to Carelia,
Into Russia bore the second,
In its home he left the third one.   10

Whom the bird to Russia carried
Soon grew up into a merchant;
Whom he carried to Carelia,
Kalervo was called by others,
While the third at home remaining,
Bore the name of Untamoinen,
For his father's lifelong anguish,
And his mother's deep affliction.

Untamoinen laid his netting
Down in Kalervo's fish-waters: 20
Kalervoinen saw the netting,
In his bag he put the fishes.
Untamo of hasty temper
Then became both vexed and angry,
And his fingers turned to battle,
With his open palms he urged it,
Making strife for fishes' entrails,
And for perch-fry made a quarrel.

Thus they fought and thus contended,
Neither overcame the other,   30
And though one might smite the other,
He himself again was smitten.

At another time it happened,
On the next and third day after,
Kalervoinen oats was sowing,
Back of Untamoinen's dwelling.

Sheep of Untamo most reckless
Browsed the oats of Kalervoinen,
Whereupon his dog ferocious
Tore the sheep of Untamoinen.   40

Untamo began to threaten
Kalervo, his very brother;
Kalervo's race vowed to slaughter,
Smite the great, and smite the little,
And to fall on all the people,
And their houses burn to ashes.

Men with swords in belt he mustered,
Weapons for their hands provided,
Little boys with spears in girdle,
Handsome youths who shouldered axes,   50

And he marched to furious battle,
Thus to fight his very brother.
    Kalervoinen's son's fair consort
Then was sitting near the window,
And she looked from out the window,
And she spoke the words which follow:
" Is it smoke I see arising,
Or a gloomy cloud that rises,
On the borders of the cornfields,
Just beyond the new-made pathway?"   60
    But no dark cloud there was rising,
Nor was smoke ascending thickly,
But 'twas Untamo's assemblage
Marching onward to the battle.
    On came Untamo's assemblage,
In their belts their swords were hanging,
Kalervo's folk overwhelming,
And his mighty race they slaughtered,
And they burned his house to ashes,
Like a level field they made it.   70
    Left of Kalervo's folk only
But one girl, and she was pregnant;
Then did Untamo's assemblage
Lead her homeward on their journey,
That she there might sweep the chamber,
And the floor might sweep from litter.
    But a little time passed over,
When a little boy was born her,
From a most unhappy mother,
So by what name should they call him?   80
Kullervo his mother called him,
Untamo, the Battle-hero.
    Then the little boy they swaddled,
And the orphan child they rested
In the cradle made for rocking,
That it might be rocked to lull him.
    So they rocked the child in cradle,
Rocked it till his hair was tossing,
Rocked him for one day, a second,
Rocked him on the third day likewise,   90

When the boy began his kicking,
And he kicked and pushed about him,
Tore his swaddling clothes to pieces,
Freed himself from all his clothing,
Then he broke the lime-wood cradle,
All his rags he tore from off him.

    And it seemed that he would prosper,
And become a man of mettle.
Untamola thought already
That when he was grown to manhood,   100
He would grow both wise and mighty,
And become a famous hero,
As a servant worth a hundred,
Equal to a thousand servants.
Thus he grew for two and three months,
But already in the third month,
When a boy no more than knee-high,
He began to speak in thiswise:
" Presently when I am bigger,
And my body shall be stronger,   110
I'll avenge my father's slaughter,
And my mother's tears atone for."

    This was heard by Untamoinen,
And he spoke the words which follow:
" He will bring my race to ruin,
Kalervo reborn is in him."
Thereupon the heroes pondered
And the old crones all considered
How to bring the boy to ruin,
So that death might come upon him.   120

    Then they put him in a barrel,
In a barrel did they thrust him,
And they pushed it to the water,
Pushed it out upon the billows.

    Then they went to look about them,
After two nights, after three nights,
If the boy had sunk in water,
Or had perished in the barrel.

    In the waves he was not sunken,
Nor had perished in the barrel,   130

He had 'scaped from out the barrel,
And upon the waves was sitting,
In his hand a rod of copper,
At the end a line all silken,
And for lake-fish he was fishing,
As he floated on the water.
There was water in the lakelet,
Which perchance might fill two ladles,
Or if more exactly measured,
Partly was a third filled also.   140
    Untamo again reflected,
" How can we o'ercome the infant,
That destruction come upon him,
And that death may overtake him?"
    Then he bade his servants gather
First a large supply of birch-trees,
Pine-trees with their hundred needles,
Trees from which the pitch was oozing,
For the burning of the infant,
And for Kullervo's destruction.   150
    So they gathered and collected
First a large supply of birch-trees,
Pine-trees with their hundred needles,
Trees from which the pitch was oozing,
And of bark a thousand sledgefuls,
Ash-trees, long a hundred fathoms.
Fire beneath the wood they kindled,
And the pyre began to crackle,
And the boy they cast upon it,
'Mid the glowing fire they cast him.   160
Burned the fire a day, a second,
Burning likewise on the third day,
When they went to look about them.
Knee-deep sat the boy in ashes,
In the embers to his elbows.
In his hand he held the coal-rake,
And was stirring up the fire,
And he raked the coals together.
Not a hair was singed upon him,
Not a lock was even tangled.   170

Then did Untamo grow angry.
"Where then can I place the infant,
That we bring him to destruction,
And that death may overtake him?"
So upon a tree they hanged him,
Strung him up upon an oak-tree.

Two nights and a third passed over,
And upon the dawn thereafter,
Untamo again reflected:
"Time it is to look around us,   180
Whether Kullervo has fallen,
Or is dead upon the gallows."

Then he sent a servant forward,
Back he came, and thus reported:
"Kullervo not yet has perished,
Nor has died upon the gallows.
Pictures on the tree he's carving,
In his hands he holds a graver.
All the tree is filled with pictures,
All the oak-tree filled with carvings;   190
Here are men, and here are sword-blades,
And the spears are leaning by them."

Where should Untamo seek aidance,
'Gainst this boy, the most unhappy?
Whatsoever deaths he planned him,
Or he planned for his destruction,
In the jaws of death he fell not,
Nor could he be brought to ruin.

And at length he grew full weary
Of his efforts to destroy him,   200
So he reared up Kullervoinen
As a slave beneath his orders.

Thereupon said Untamoinen,
And he spoke the words which follow:
"If you live as it is fitting,
Always acting as is proper,
In my house I will retain you,
And the work of servants give you.
I will pay you wages for it,
As I think that you deserve it,   210

For your waist a pretty girdle,
Or upon your ear a buffet."
   So when Kullervo was taller,
And had grown about a span-length,
Then he found some work to give him,
That he should prepare to labour.
'Twas to rock a little infant,
Rock a child with little fingers.
"Watch with every care the infant,
Give it food, and eat some also,   220
Wash his napkins in the river,
Wash his little clothes and cleanse them."
   So he watched one day, a second,
Broke his hands, and gouged his eyes out,
And at length upon the third day,
Let the infant die of sickness,
Cast the napkins in the river,
And he burned the baby's cradle.
   Untamo thereon reflected,
"Such a one is quite unfitted   230
To attend to little children,
Rock the babes with little fingers.
Now I know not where to send him,
Nor what work I ought to give him.
Perhaps he ought to clear the forest?"
So he went to clear the forest.
   Kullervo, Kalervo's offspring,
Answered in the words which follow:
"Now I first a man can deem me,
When my hands the axe are wielding.   240
I am handsomer to gaze on,
Far more noble than aforetime,
Five men's strength I feel within me
And I equal six in valour."
   Then he went into the smithy,
And he spoke the words which follow:
"O thou smith, my dearest brother,
Forge me now a little hatchet,
Such an axe as fits a hero,
Iron tool for skilful workman,   250

For I go to clear the forest,
And to fell the slender birch-trees."
    So the smith forged what he needed,
And an axe he forged him quickly;
Such an axe as fits a hero,
Iron tool for skilful workman.
    Kullervo, Kalervo's offspring,
Set to work the axe to sharpen,
And he ground it in the daytime,
And at evening made a handle.   260
    Then he went into the forest,
High upon the wooded mountains,
There to seek the best of planking,
And to seek the best of timber.
With his axe he smote the tree-trunks,
With the blade of steel he felled them,
At a stroke the best he severed,
And the bad ones at a half-stroke.
    Five large trees at length had fallen,
Eight in all he felled before him,   270
And he spoke the words which follow,
And in words like these expressed him:
" Lempo may the work accomplish,
Hiisi now may shape the timber ! "
    In a stump he struck his axe-blade,
And began to shout full loudly,
And he piped, and then he whistled,
And he said the words which follow:
" Let the wood be felled around me,
Overthrown the slender birch-trees,   280
Far as sounds my voice resounding,
Far as I can send my whistle.
    " Let no sapling here be growing,
Let no blade of grass be standing,
Never while the earth endureth,
Or the golden moon is shining,
Here in Kalervo's son's forest,
Here upon the good man's clearing.
    " If the seed on earth has fallen,
And the young corn should shoot upward,   290

If the sprout should be developed,
And the stalk should form upon it,
May it never come to earing,
Or the sta k-end be developed."

Then the mighty Untamoinen,
Wandered forth to gaze about him,
Learn how Kalervo's son cleared it,
And the new slave made a clearing.
But he found not any clearing,
And the young man had not cleared it.　　　300

Untamo thereon reflected,
" For such labour he's unsuited,
He has spoiled the best of timber,
And has felled the best for planking.
Now I know not where to send him,
Nor what work I ought to give him.
Should I let him make a fencing?"
So he went to make a fencing.

Kullervo, Kalervo's offspring,
Set himself to make a fencing,　　　310
And for this he took whole pine-trees,
And he used them for the fence-stakes,
Took whole fir-trees from the forest,
Wattled them to make the fencing,
Bound the branches fast together
With the largest mountain-ashtrees;
But he made the fence continuous,
And he made no gateway through it,
And he spoke the words which follow,
And in words like these expressed him:　　　320
" He who cannot raise him birdlike,
Nor upon two wings can hover,
Never may he pass across it,
Over Kalervo's son's fencing!"

Then did Untamo determine
Forth to go and gaze around him,
Viewing Kalervo's son's fencing
By the slave of war constructed.

Stood the fence without an opening
Neither gap nor crevice through it,　　　330

On the solid earth it rested,
Up among the clouds it towered.
    Then he spoke the words which follow :
" For such labour he's unsuited.
Here's the fence without an opening,
And without a gateway through it.
Up to heaven the fence is builded,
To the very clouds uprising ;
None can ever pass across it,
Pass within through any opening.   340
Now I know not where to send him,
Nor what work I ought to give him.
There is rye for threshing ready."
So he sent him to the threshing.
    Kullervo, Kalervo's offspring,
Set himself to do the threshing,
And the rye to chaff he pounded,
Into very chaff he threshed it.
Soon thereafter came the master,
Strolling forth to gaze around him,   350
See how Kalervo's son threshed it,
And how Kullervoinen pounded.
All the rye to chaff was pounded,
Into very chaff he'd threshed it.
    Untamoinen then was angry.
" As a labourer he is useless.
Whatsoever work I give him,
All his work he spoils from malice.
Shall I take him into Russia,
Shall I sell him in Carelia,   360
To the smith named Ilmarinen,
That he there may wield the hammer?"
    Kalervo's son took he with him,
And he sold him in Carelia,
To the smith named Ilmarinen,
Skilful wielder of the hammer.
    What then gave the smith in payment?
Great the payment that he made him ;
For he gave two worn-out kettles,
And three halves of hooks he gave him,   370

And five worn-out scythes he gave him,
And six worn-out rakes he gave him,
For a man the most unskilful,
For a slave completely worthless.

RUNO XXXII.—KULLERVO AND THE WIFE OF ILMARINEN

Argument

The wife of Ilmarinen makes Kullervo her herdsman and maliciously bakes him a stone in his lunch (1–32). She then sends him out with the cattle, after using the usual prayers and charms for their protection from bears in the pastures (33–548).

KULLERVO, Kalervo's offspring,
Old man's son, with blue-dyed stockings,
Finest locks of yellow colour,
And with shoes of best of leather,
To the smith's house went directly,
Asked for work that very evening,
Asked the master in the evening,
And the mistress in the morning:
"Give me something now to work at,
Give me work that I may do it,   10
Set me something now to work at,
Give some work to me the wretched!"
  Then the wife of Ilmarinen,
Pondered deeply on the matter,
What the new slave could accomplish,
What the new-bought wretch could work at,
And she took him as her herdsman,
Who should herd her flocks extensive.
  Then the most malicious mistress,
She, the smith's wife, old and jeering,   20
Baked a loaf to give the herdsman,
And a great cake did she bake him,
Oats below and wheat above it,
And between, a stone inserted.

Then she spread the cake with butter,
And upon the crust laid bacon,
Gave it as the slave's allowance,
As provision for the herdsman.
She herself the slave instructed,
And she spoke the words which follow: 30
" Do not eat the food I give you,
Till in wood the herd is driven."

Then did Ilmarinen's housewife
Send the herd away to pasture,
And she spoke the words which follow,
And in words like these expressed her:
" Send the cows among the bushes,
And the milkers in the meadow,
Those with wide horns to the aspens,
Those with curved horns to the birches,   40
That they thus may fatten on them,
And may load themselves with tallow,
There upon the open meadows,
And among the wide-spread borders,
From the lofty birchen forest,
And the lower growing aspens,
From among the golden fir-woods,
From among the silver woodlands.

" Watch them, Jumala most gracious,
Guard them, O thou kind Creator,   50
Guard from harm upon the pathway,
And protect them from all evil,
That they come not into danger,
Nor may fall in any evil.

" As beneath the roof-tree watch them,
Keep them under thy protection,
Watch them also in the open,
When beyond the fold protect them,
That the herd may grow more handsome,
And the mistress' cattle prosper,   60
To the wish of our well-wishers,
'Gainst the wish of our ill-wishers.

" If my herdsman is a bad one,
Or the herd-girls should be timid,

Make the willow then a herdsman,
Let the alder watch the cattle,
Let the mountain-ash protect them,
And the cherry lead them homeward,
That the mistress need not seek them,
Nor need other folks be anxious.   70
" If the willow will not herd them,
Nor the mountain-ash protect them,
Nor the alder watch the cattle,
Nor the cherry lead them homeward,
Send thou then thy better servants,
Send the Daughters of Creation,
That they may protect my cattle,
And the whole herd may look after.
Very many are thy maidens,
Hundreds are beneath thy orders,   80
Dwelling underneath the heavens,
Noble Daughters of Creation.
" Suvetar, the best of women,
Etelätär, Nature's old one,
Hongatar, the noble mistress,
Katajatar, maiden fairest,
Pihlajatar, little damsel,
Tuometar, of Tapio daughter,
Mielikki, the wood's step-daughter,
Tellervo, the maid of Tapio,   90
May ye all protect my cattle,
And protect the best among them,
Through the beauty of the summer,
In the pleasant time of leafage,
While the leaves on trees are moving,
Grass upon the ground is waving.
" Suvetar, the best of women,
Etelätär, Nature's old one,
Spread thou out thy robe of softness,
And do thou spread out thy apron,   100
As a covering for my cattle,
For the hiding of the small ones,
That no ill winds blow upon them,
Nor an evil rain fall on them.

"Do thou guard my flock from evil,
Guard from harm upon the pathways,
And upon the quaking marshes,
Where the surface all is shifting,
Where the marsh is always moving,
And the depths below are shaking,   110
That they come not into danger,
Nor may fall in any evil,
That no hoof in swamp is twisted,
Nor may slip among the marshes,
Save when Jumala perceives it,
'Gainst the will of him, the Holy.

"Fetch the cow-horn from a distance,
Fetch it from the midst of heaven,
Bring the mead-horn down from heaven,
Let the honey-horn be sounded.   120
Blow into the horn then strongly,
And repeat the tunes resounding,
Blow then flowers upon the hummocks,
Blow then fair the heathland's borders,
Make the meadow's borders lovely,
And the forest borders charming,
Borders of the marshes fertile,
Of the springs the borders rolling.

"Then give fodder to my cattle,
Give the cattle food sufficient,   130
Give them food of honey-sweetness,
Give them drink as sweet as honey,
Feed them now with hay all golden,
And the heads of silvery grasses,
From the springs of all the sweetest,
From the streams that flow most swiftly,
From the swiftly-rushing torrents,
From the swiftly-running rivers,
From the hills all golden-shining,
And from out the silvery meadows.   140

"Dig them also wells all golden
Upon both sides of the pastures,
That the herd may drink the water,
And the sweet juice then may trickle

Down into their teeming udders,
Down into their swelling udders,
That the veins may all be moving,
And the milk may flow in rivers,
And the streams of milk be loosened,
And may foam the milky torrents,   150
And the milk-streams may be silent,
And the milk-streams may be swollen,
And the milk be always flowing,
And the stream be always dropping,
Down upon the greenest haycocks,
And no evil fingers guide it;
That no milk may flow to Mana,
Nor upon the ground be wasted.
   "There are many who are wicked,
And who send the milk to Mana,   160
And upon the ground who waste it,
Give the cattle's yield to others.
They are few, but they are skilful
Who can bring the milk from Mana,
Sourest milk from village storage,
And when new from other quarters.
   "Never has indeed my mother
Sought for counsel in the village,
Brought it from another household;
But she fetched her milk from Mana,   170
Sour milk brought from those who stored it,
And fresh milk obtained from others;
Had the milk from distance carried,
Had it fetched from distant regions,
Fetched the milk from realms of Tuoni,
'Neath the earth in Mana's kingdom.
Secretly at night they brought it,
And in murky places hid it,
That the wicked should not hear it,
Nor the worthless ones should know it,   180
Nor bad hay should fall into it,
And it should be saved from spoiling.
   "Thus my mother always told me
In the very words which follow:

' Where has gone the yield of cattle,
Whither has the milk now vanished?
Has it been conveyed to strangers,
Carried to the village storehouse,
In the laps of beggar-wenches,
In the arms of those who envy,　　　　　　190
Or among the trees been carried,
And been lost amid the forest,
And been scattered in the woodlands,
Or been lost upon the heathlands?

" ' But no milk shall go to Mana,
Nor the yield of cows to strangers,
In the laps of beggar-wenches,
In the arms of those who envy,
Nor among the trees be carried,
Nor be lost amid the forest,　　　　　　200
Nor be scattered in the woodlands
Nor be lost upon the heathlands.
In the house the milk is useful,
And at all times it is needed;
In the house there waits the mistress,
In her hand the wooden milk-pail.'

" Suvetar, the best of women,
Etelätär, Nature's old one,
Go and fodder my Syötikki,
Give thou drink to my Juotikki,　　　　　210
Milk confer upon Hermikki,
And fresh fodder give Tuorikki,
Give thou milk unto Mairikki,
Put fresh milk into the cowhouse,
From the heads of brightest herbage,
And the reeds of all the forest,
From the lovely earth up-springing,
From the hillocks rich in honey,
From the sweetest meadow-grasses,
And the berry-bearing regions,　　　　　220
From the goddess of the heather,
And the nymph who tends the grasses,
And the milkmaid of the cloudlets,
And the maid in midst of heaven.

Give the cows their milk-filled udders
Always filled to overflowing,
To be milked by dwarfish women,
That a little girl may milk them.

" Rise, O virgin, from the valley,
From the spring, in gorgeous raiment,   230
From the spring, O maiden, rise thou,
From the ooze arise, O fairest.
From the spring take thou some water,
Sprinkle thou my cattle with it,
That the cattle may be finer,
And the mistress' cattle prosper,
Ere the coming of the mistress,
Ere the herd-girl look upon them,
She, the most unskilful mistress,
And the very timid herd-girl.   240

" Mielikki, the forest's mistress,
Of the herds the bounteous mother,
Send the tallest of thy handmaids,
And the best among thy servants,
That they may protect my cattle,
And my herd be watched and tended
Through the finest of the summer,
In the good Creator's summer,
Under Jumala's protection,
And protected by his favour.   250

" Tellervo, O maid of Tapio,
Little daughter of the forest,
Clad in soft and beauteous garments,
With thy yellow hair so lovely,
Be the guardian of the cattle,
Do thou guard the mistress' cattle
All through Metsola so lovely,
And through Tapiola's bright regions
Do thou guard the herd securely,
Do thou watch the herd unsleeping.   260

" With thy lovely hands protect them,
With thy slender fingers stroke them,
Rub them with the skins of lynxes,
Comb them with the fins of fishes,

Like the hue of the lake creatures,
Like the wool of ewe of meadow.
Come at evening and night's darkness,
When the twilight round is closing,
Then do thou lead home my cattle,
Lead them to their noble mistress,   270
On their backs the water pouring,
Lakes of milk upon their cruppers.
   " When the sun to rest has sunken,
And the bird of eve is singing,
Then I say unto my cattle,
Speak unto my horned creatures.
   " ' Come ye home, ye curve-horned cattle,
Milk-dispensers to the household,
In the house 'tis very pleasant,
Where the floor is nice for resting.   280
On the waste 'tis bad to wander,
Or upon the shore to bellow,
Therefore you should hasten homeward,
And the women fire will kindle,
In the field of honeyed grasses,
On the ground o'ergrown with berries.'
   " Nyyrikki, O son of Tapio,
Blue-coat offspring of the forest !
Take the stumps of tallest pine-trees,
And the lofty crowns of fir-trees,   290
For a bridge in miry places,
Where the ground is bad for walking,
Deep morass, and swampy moorland,
And the treacherous pools of water.
Let the curve-horned cattle wander,
And the split-hoofed cattle gallop,
Unto where the smoke is rising,
Free from harm, and free from danger,
Sinking not into the marshes,
Nor embogged in miry places.   300
   " If the cattle pay no heeding,
Nor will home return at nightfall,
Pihlajatar, little damsel,
Katajatar, fairest maiden,

Quickly cut a branch of birch-tree,
Take a rod from out the bushes,
Likewise take a whip of cherry,
And of juniper to scourge them,
From the back of Tapio's castle,
From among the slopes of alder.   310
Drive the herd towards the household,
At the time for bathroom-heating ;
Homeward drive the household cattle,
Cows from Metsola's great forest.

"Otso, apple of the forest,
With thy honey-paws so curving,
Let us make a peace between us,
Haste to make a peace between us,
So that always and for ever
In the days that we are living,   320
Thou wilt fell no hooféd cattle,
Nor wilt overthrow the milch-kine,
Through the finest of the summer,
In the good Creator's summer.

"When thou hear'st the cow-bells ringing,
Or thou hear'st the cow-horn sounding,
Cast thee down among the hillocks,
Sleep thou there upon the meadow,
Thrust thine ears into the stubble,
Hide thy head among the hillocks,   330
Or conceal thee in the thickets,
To thy mossy lair retreat thou,
Go thou forth to other districts,
Flee away to other hillocks,
That thou mayst not hear the cow-bells,
Nor the talking of the herdsmen.

"O my Otso, O my darling,
Handsome one, with paws of honey,
I forbid thee to approach them,
Or molest the herd of cattle,   340
Neither with thy tongue to touch them,
Nor with ugly mouth to seize them,
With thy teeth to tear to pieces,
Neither with thy claws to scratch them.

"Go thou slouching through the meadow,
Go in secret through the pasture,
Slinking off when bells are ringing,
Shun the talking of the shepherds.
If the herd is on the heathland,
Then into the swamps retreat thou,　　　　350
If the herd is in the marshes,
Then conceal thee in the thickets,
If the herd should climb the mountain,
Quickly then descend the mountain,
If the herd should wander downward,
Wander then along the mountain,
If they wander in the bushes,
To the thicker woods retreat thou,
If the thicker wood they enter,
Wander then into the bushes,　　　　　　360
Wander like the golden cuckoo,
Like the dove of silver colour,
Move aside as moves the powan,
Glide away like fish in water,
As a flock of wool drifts sideways,
Or a roll of flax the lightest,
In thy fur thy claws conceal thou,
In thy gums thy teeth conceal thou,
That the herd thou dost not frighten,
Nor the little calves be injured.　　　　　370

"Let the cattle rest in quiet,
Leave in peace the hooféd cattle,
Let the herd securely wander,
Let them march in perfect order
Through the swamps and through the open,
Through the tangle of the forest,
Never do thou dare to touch them,
Nor to wickedly molest them.

"Keep the former oath thou sworest,
There by Tuonela's deep river,　　　　　380
By the raging fall of water,
At the knees of the Creator.
Thou hast been indeed permitted,
Three times in the course of summer,

To approach the bells when ringing,
And the tinkling of the cow-bells,
But 'tis not permitted to thee,
Nor permission has been given,
To commence a work of evil,
Or a deed of shame accomplish.   390

"Should thy frenzy come upon thee,
And thy teeth be seized with longing,
Cast thy frenzy in the bushes,
On the heath thy evil longing,
Then attack the trees all rotten,
Overthrow the rotten birch-trees,
Turn to trees in water standing,
Growl in berry-bearing districts.

"If the need for food should seize thee,
Or for food the wish thou feelest,   400
Eat the fungi in the forest,
And do thou break down the ant-hills,
And the red roots do thou delve for;
These are Metsola's sweet dainties.
Eat no grass reserved for fodder,
Neither do thou hurt my pasture.

"When in Metsola the honey
Is fermenting and is working,
On the hills of golden colour,
And upon the plains of silver,   410
There is food for those who hunger,
There is drink for all the thirsty,
There is food to eat that fails not,
There is drink that never lessens.

"Let us make a league eternal,
Make an endless peace between us,
That we live in perfect quiet
And in comfort all the summer,
And to us the lands are common,
And our provender delicious.   420

"If thou dost desire a combat,
And wouldst live in hopes of battle,
Let us combat in the winter,
And contend in time of snowfall.

When the marshes thaw in summer,
And the pools are all unfrozen,
Never venture to approach thou,
Where the golden herd is living.
   "When thou comest to this country,
And thou movest in this forest,   430
We at any time will shoot you,
Though the gunners should be absent.
There are very skilful women,
All of them accomplished housewives,
And they will destroy your pathway,
On your journey bring destruction,
Lest you might work any evil,
Or indulge in any mischief,
Ill by Jumala not sanctioned,
And against his blessed orders.   440
   "Ukko, thou, of Gods the highest,
Shouldst thou hear that he is coming,
Then do thou transform my cattle,
Suddenly transform my cattle,
Into stones convert my own ones,
Change my fair ones into tree-trunks,
When the monster roams the district,
And the big one wanders through it.
   "If I were myself a Bruin,
Roamed about a honey-pawed one,   450
Never would I dare to venture
To the feet of aged women.
There are many other regions,
There are many other penfolds,
Where a man may go to wander,
Roaming aimless at his pleasure.
Therefore move thy paws across them,
Do thou move thy paws across them,
In the blue wood's deep recesses,
In the depths of murmuring forest.   460
   "On the heath o'er pine-cones wander,
Tramp thou through the sandy districts,
Go thou where the way is level,
Do thou bound along the lakeshore,

To the furthest bounds of Pohja,
To the distant plains of Lapland.
There indeed mayst thou be happy,
Good it is for thee to dwell there,
Wandering shoeless in the summer,
Wandering sockless in the autumn,   470
Through the wide expanse of marshland,
And across the wide morasses.

"But if thou should not go thither,
If thou canst not find the pathway,
Hasten then to distant regions,
Do thou wander, on thy pathway
Unto Tuonela's great forest,
Or across the heaths of Kalma.
There are marshes to be traversed,
There are heaths that thou mayst traverse,   480
There is Kirjos, there is Karjos,
There are many other cattle,
Fitted with their iron neck-chains,
Ten among them altogether ;
There the lean kine quickly fatten,
And their bones are soon flesh-covered.

"Be propitious, wood and forest,
Be thou gracious, O thou blue wood,
Give thou peace unto the cattle,
And protection to the hoofed ones,   490
Through the whole length of the summer,
Of the Lord the loveliest season.

"Kuippana, thou king of woodland,
Active greybeard of the forest,
Hold thy dogs in careful keeping,
Watch thou well thy dogs and guard them ;
Thrust some fungus in one nostril,
In the other thrust an apple,
That they may not smell the cattle,
And they may not scent their odour.   500
Bind their eyes with silken ribands,
Likewise bind their ears with linen,
That they may not hear them moving,
And they may not see them walking.

"If this is not yet sufficient,
And they do not much regard it,
Then do thou forbid thy children,
Do thou drive away thy offspring.
Lead them forth from out this forest,
From this lakeshore do thou drive them,　　510
From the lands where roam the cattle,
From among the spreading willows,
Do thou hide thy dogs in caverns,
Nor neglect to bind them firmly,
Bind them with the golden fetters,
With the slender silver fetters,
That they may commit no evil,
And be guilty of no outrage.
　　"If this is not yet sufficient,
And they do not much regard it,　　520
Ukko, then, O golden monarch,
Ukko, O thou silver guardian,
Hearken to my words so golden,
Listen to my lovely sayings!
Take a snaffle made of rowan,
Fix it on their stumpy muzzles,
Or if rowan will not hold them,
Cast thou then a copper muzzle,
If too weak is found the copper,
Forge thou then an iron muzzle,　　530
If they break the iron muzzle,
And it should itself be shattered,
Drive thou then a stake all golden,
Through the chin and through the jawbone,
Do thou close their jaws securely,
Fix them that they cannot move them,
That they cannot move their jawbones,
And their teeth can scarcely open,
If the iron is not opened,
If the steel should not be loosened,　　540
If with knife it is not severed,
If with hatchet 'tis not broken."
　　Then did Ilmarinen's housewife,
Of the smith the wife so artful,

Drive from out their stalls the cattle,
Send the cattle forth to pasture,
After them she sent the shepherd,
That the slave should drive the cattle.

RUNO XXXIII.—THE DEATH OF ILMARINEN'S WIFE

Argument

While Kullervo is in the pasture in the afternoon he tries to cut the cake with his knife which he completely spoils, and this goes to his heart the more because the knife was the only remembrance left to him of his family (1-98). To revenge himself on the mistress, he drives the cattle into the marshes to be devoured by beasts of the forest, and gathers together a herd of wolves and bears, which he drives home in the evening (99-184). When the mistress goes to milk them she is torn to pieces by the wild beasts (185-296).

KULLERVO, Kalervo's offspring,
Put his lunch into his wallet,
Drove the cows along the marshes,
While across the heath he wandered,
And he spoke as he was going,
And repeated on his journey,
" Woe to me, a youth unhappy,
And a youth of wretched fortune !
Wheresoe'er I turn my footsteps,
Nought but idleness awaits me ;   10
I must watch the tails of oxen,
And must watch the calves I follow,
Always tramping through the marshes,
Through the worst of level country."
　　Then upon the ground he rested,
On a sunny slope he sat him,
And he then composed these verses,
And expressed himself in singing :
" Sun of Jumala, O shine thou,
Of the Lord, thou wheel, shine warmly,   20
On the warder of the smith's herd,
And upon the wretched shepherd,

Not on Ilmarinen's household,
Least of all upon the mistress,
For the mistress lives luxurious,
And the wheaten-bread she slices,
And the finest cakes devours,
And she spreads them o'er with butter,
Gives the wretched shepherd dry bread,
Dry crusts only for his chewing,   30
Only oaten-cake she gives me,
Even this with chaff she mixes,
Even straw she scatters through it,
Gives for food the bark of fir-tree,
Water in a birch-bark bucket,
Upscooped 'mid the grassy hillocks.
March, O sun, and wheat, O wander,
Sink in Jumala's own season,
Hasten, sun, among the pine-trees,
Wander, wheat, into the bushes,   40
'Mid the junipers, O hasten,
Fly thou to the plains of alder,
Lead thou then the herdsman homeward,
Give him butter from the barrel,
Let him eat the freshest butter,
Over all the cakes extending."
 But the wife of Ilmarinen
While the shepherd was lamenting,
And while Kullervo was singing,
Ate the butter from the barrel,   50
And she ate the freshest butter,
And upon the cakes she spread it,
And hot soup had she made ready,
But for Kullervo cold cabbage,
Whence the dog the fat had eaten,
And the black dog made a meal from,
And the spotted dog been sated,
And the brown dog had sufficient.
 From the branch there sang a birdling,
Sang a small bird from the bushes,   60
"Time 'tis for the servant's supper,
O thou orphan boy, 'tis evening."

Kullervo, Kalervo's offspring,
Looked, and saw the sun was sinking,
And he said the words which follow:
" Now the time has come for eating,
Yes, the time has come for eating,
Time it is to take refreshment."

So to rest he drove the cattle,
On the heath he drove the cattle,   70
And he sat him on a hillock,
And upon a green hill sat him.
From his back he took his wallet,
Took the cake from out the wallet,
And he turned it round and eyed it,
And he spoke the words which follow:
" Many a cake is outside handsome,
And the crust looks smooth from outside,
But within is only fir-bark,
Only chaff beneath the surface."   80

From the sheath he took his knife out,
And to cut the cake attempted.
On the stone the knife struck sharply,
And against the stone was broken.
From the knife the point was broken;
And the knife itself was broken.

Kullervo, Kalervo's offspring,
Looked, and saw the knife was broken,
And at length he burst out weeping,
And he said the words which follow: 90
" Save this knife I'd no companion,
Nought to love except this iron,
'Twas an heirloom from my father,
And the aged man had used it.
Now against a stone 'tis broken,
'Gainst a piece of rock 'tis shattered
In the cake of that vile mistress,
Baked there by that wicked woman.

" How shall I for this reward her,
Woman's prank, and damsel's mockery,   100
And destroy the base old woman,
And that wicked wench, the bakeress ? "

Then a crow cawed from the bushes,
Cawed the crow, and croaked the raven.
"O thou wretched golden buckle,
Kalervo's surviving offspring,
Wherefore art thou so unhappy,
Wherefore is thy heart so troubled?
Take a switch from out the bushes,
And a birch from forest-valley,   110
Drive the foul beasts in the marshes,
Chase the cows to the morasses,
Half to largest wolves deliver,
Half to bears amid the forest.

"Call thou all the wolves together,
All the bears do thou assemble,
Change the wolves to little cattle,
Make the bears the larger cattle,
Lead them then like cattle homeward,
Lead them home like brindled cattle;   120
Thus repay the woman's jesting,
And the wicked woman's insult."

Kullervo, Kalervo's offspring,
Uttered then the words which follow:
"Wait thou, wait thou, whore of Hiisi,
For my father's knife I'm weeping,
Soon wilt thou thyself be weeping,
And be weeping for thy milchkine."

From the bush a switch he gathered,
Juniper as whip for cattle,   130
Drove the cows into the marshes,
And the oxen in the thickets,
Half of these the wolves devoured,
To the bears he gave the others,
And he sang the wolves to cattle,
And he changed the bears to oxen,
Made the first the little cattle,
Made the last the larger cattle.

In the south the sun was sinking,
In the west the sun descended,   140
Bending down towards the pine-trees
At the time of cattle-milking.

Then the dusty wicked herd-boy,
Kullervo, Kalervo's offspring,
Homeward drove the bears before him,
And the wolf-flock to the farmyard,
And the bears he thus commanded,
And the wolves he thus instructed :
" Tear the mistress' thighs asunder,
See that through her calves you bite her,   150
When she comes to look around her,
And she bends her down to milk you."

     Then he made a pipe of cow-bone,
And a whistle made of ox-horn,
From Tuomikki's leg a cow-horn,
And a flute from heel of Kirjo,
Then upon the horn blew loudly,
And upon his pipe made music.
Thrice upon the hill he blew it,
Six times at the pathway's opening.   160

     Then did Ilmarinen's housewife,
Wife of smith, an active woman,
Who for milk had long been waiting,
And expecting summer butter,
Hear the music on the marshes,
And upon the heath the cattle,
And she spoke the words which follow,
And expressed herself in thiswise :
" Praise to Jumala be given,
Sounds the pipe, the herd is coming,   170
Whence obtained the slave the cow-horn,
That he made a horn to blow on ?
Wherefore does he thus come playing,
Blowing tunes upon the cow-horn,
Blowing till he bursts the eardrums,
And he gives me quite a headache ? "

     Kullervo, Kalervo's offspring,
Answered in the words which follow :
" In the swamp the horn was lying,
From the sand I brought the cow-horn,   180
To the lane I brought your cattle,
In the shed the cows are standing ;

Come you forth to smoke the cattle,
And come out to milk the cattle."
 Then did Ilmarinen's housewife
Bid the mother milk the cattle.
" Mother, go and milk the cattle,
Do thou go to tend the cattle,
For I think I cannot finish
Kneading dough as I would have it."   190
 Kullervo, Kalervo's offspring,
Answered in the words which follow :
" Ever do the thrifty housewives,
Ever do the careful housewives
Go the first to milk the cattle,
Set themselves to milk the cattle."
 Then did Ilmarinen's housewife
Hasten forth to smoke the cattle,
And she went to milk the cattle,
And surveyed the herd before her,   200
Gazed upon the horned cattle,
And she spoke the words which follow :
" Beauteous is the herd to gaze on,
Very sleek the horned cattle,
They have all been rubbed with lynx-skin
And the wool of sheep of forest,
Well-filled, too, are all their udders,
And expanded with their fulness."
 So she stooped her down to milk them,
And she sat her down for milking,   210
Pulled a first time and a second,
And attempted it a third time,
And the wolf sprang fiercely at her,
And the bear came fiercely after.
At her mouth the wolf was tearing,
And the bear tore through her tendons,
Halfway through her calves they bit her,
And they broke across her shinbones.
 Kullervo, Kalervo's offspring
Thus repaid the damsel's jesting,   220
Damsel's jesting, woman's mocking,
Thus repaid the wicked woman.

Ilmarinen's wife illustrious
Then herself was brougnt to weeping,
And she spoke the words which follow :
"Ill thou dost, O wicked herdsman,
Driving bears unto the homestead,
To the yard these wolves gigantic."
    Kullervo, Kalervo's offspring
Heard, and thus he made her answer :   230
"Ill I did, a wicked herd-boy,
Not so great as wicked mistress.
In my cake a stone she baked me,
Baked a lump of rock within it,
On the stone my knife struck sharply,
'Gainst the rock my knife was shattered ;
'Twas the knife of mine own father,
Of our race a cherished heirloom."
    Then said Ilmarinen's housewife,
"O thou herd-boy, dearest herd-boy,   240
Wilt thou alter thy intention,
And recall thy words of magic,
And release me from the wolf's jaws,
From the bear's claws now release me ?
Better shirts will I then give you,
And will give you handsome aprons,
Give you wheaten-bread, and butter,
And the sweetest milk for drinking,
For a year no work will give you,
Give you light work in the second.   250
    "If you haste not to release me,
Come not quickly to my rescue,
Death will quickly fall upon me,
And to earth shall I be altered."
    Kullervo, Kalervo's offspring,
Answered in the words which follow :
"If you die, so may you perish,
If you perish, may you perish !
Room there is in earth to hold you,
Room in Kalma's home for lost ones,   260
For the mightiest there to slumber,
For the proudest to repose them."

Then said Ilmarinen's housewife,
"Ukko, thou, of Gods the highest,
Haste to bend thy mighty crossbow,
Of thy bows the best select thou,
Take thou then a bolt of copper,
And adjust it to the crossbow,
Shoot thou then a flaming arrow,
Shoot thou forth the bolt of copper,   270
Shoot it quickly through the arm-pits,
Shoot it that it split the shoulders.
Thus let Kalervo's son perish,
Shoot thou dead this wicked creature,
Shoot him with the steel-tipped arrow,
Shoot him with thy bolt of copper."

 Kullervo, Kalervo's offspring,
Uttered then the words which follow :
"Ukko, thou, of Gods the highest,
Shoot me not as she has prayed thee,   280
Shoot the wife of Ilmarinen,
Do thou kill this wicked woman,
Ere from off this spot she riseth,
Or can move herself from off it."

 Then did Ilmarinen's housewife,
Wife of that most skilful craftsman,
On the spot at once fall dying,
Fell, as falls the soot from kettle,
In the yard before her homestead,
In the narrow yard she perished.   290

 Thus it was the young wife perished,
Thus the fairest housewife perished,
Whom the smith so long had yearned for,
And for six long years was sought for,
As the joy of Ilmarinen,
Pride of him, the smith so famous.

Runo XXXIV.—Kullervo and his Parents

Argument

Kullervo escapes from the homestead of Ilmarinen, and wanders sorrowfully through the forest, where he meets with the Old Woman of the Forest, who informs him that his father, mother, brothers and sisters are still living (1–128). Following her directions he finds them on the borders of Lapland (129–188). His mother tells him that she had long supposed him to be dead, and also that her elder daughter had been lost when gathering berries (189–246).

KULLERVO, Kalervo's offspring,
He, the youth with blue-dyed stockings,
And with yellow hair the finest,
And with shoes of finest leather,
Hurried quickly on his journey
From the home of Ilmarinen,
Ere report could reach the master
Of the death his wife had suffered,
And might harm him in his anger,
And he might at once destroy him.   10

    From the smith he hurried piping,
Joyful left the lands of Ilma,
On the heath his horn blew loudly,
Shouted loudly in the clearing,
And he dashed through plains and marshes,
While the heath re-echoed loudly,
And his horn kept loudly blowing,
And made horrible rejoicing.

    In the smithy did they hear it,
At the forge the smith was standing,   20
To the lane he went to listen,
To the yard to look around him,
Who was playing in the forest,
And upon the heath was piping.

    Then he saw what just had happened,
Saw the truth without deception,

There he saw his wife was resting,
Saw the fair one who had perished,
Where she in the yard had fallen,
On the grass where she had fallen.   30

   Even while the smith was standing,
All his heart was dark with sorrow;
Many nights he spent in weeping,
Many weeks his tears were flowing,
And his soul like tar was darkened,
And his heart than soot no lighter.

   Kullervo still wandered onwards,
Aimlessly he hurried forward,
For a day through thickest forest,
Through the timber-grounds of Hiisi,   40
And at evening, when it darkened,
Down upon the ground he threw him.

   There the orphan boy was sitting,
And the friendless one reflected :
" Wherefore have I been created,
Who has made me, and has doomed me,
Thus 'neath moon and sun to wander
'Neath the open sky for ever ?

   "Others to their homes may journey,
And may travel to their dwellings,   50
But my home is in the forest,
And upon the heath my homestead.
In the wind I find my fire-place,
In the rain I find my bathroom.

   " Never, Jumala most gracious,
Never in the course of ages,
Form a child thus mis-created,
Doomed to be for ever friendless,
Fatherless beneath the heavens,
From the first without a mother,   60
As thou, Jumala, hast made me,
And hast formed me to be wretched,
Formed me like a wandering seagull,
Like a seagull on the lake-cliffs.
Shines the sun upon the swallow,
Brightly shines upon the sparrow,

In the air the birds are joyous,
I myself am never happy,
On my life the sun shines never,
And my life is always joyless.   70
    " Now I know not who has nursed me,
And I know not who has borne me,
For, as water-hens are used to,
Or as ducks among the marshes,
Like the teal on shore she left me,
Or in hollow stone, merganser.
    " I was small, and lost my father,
I was weak, and lost my mother,
Dead is father, dead is mother,
All my mighty race has perished,   80
Shoes of ice to wear they left me,
Filled with snow they left my stockings,
On the ice they left me lying,
Rolling on the platform left me,
Thus I fell into the marshes,
And amid the mud was swallowed.
    " But in all my life I never,
Never in my life I hastened,
Through the swamp to make a platform,
Or a bridge in marshy places ;   90
But I sank not in the marshes,
For I had two hands to help me,
And I had five nimble fingers,
And ten nails to lift me from it."
    Then into his mind it entered
In his brain he fixed the notion
Unto Untamo to journey,
There his father's wrongs avenging,
Father's wrongs, and tears of mother,
And the wrongs himself had suffered.   100
    Then he spoke the words which follow :
" Wait thou, wait thou, Untamoinen,
Watch thou, of my race destroyer !
If I seek thee out in battle,
I will quickly burn thy dwelling,
And thy farms to flame deliver."

Then an old dame came to meet him,
Blue-robed Lady of the Forest,
And she spoke the words which follow,
And in words like these expressed her: 110
" Whither goeth Kullervoinen,
Where will Kalervo's son hasten ? "

Kullervo, Kalervo's offspring,
Answered in the words which follow :
" In my mind the thought has entered,
In my brain has fixed the notion
Hence to other lands to wander,
Unto Untamo's own village,
There my father's death avenging,
Father's wrongs, and tears of mother,   120
There with fire to burn the houses,
And to burn them up completely."

But the old wife made him answer,
And she spoke the words which follow :
" No, your race has not yet perished,
Nor has Kalervo been murdered ;
For your father still is living,
And on earth in health your mother."

" O my dearest of old women,
Tell me, O my dear old woman,   130
Where I yet may find my father,
Where the fair one who has borne me ? "

" Thither is thy father living,
There the fair one who has borne thee,
Far away on Lapland's borders,
On the borders of a fishpond."

" O my dearest of old women,
Tell me, O my dear old woman,
How I best can journey to them,
And the road I may discover ? "   140

" Easy 'tis for thee to journey,
Though to thee unknown the pathway.
Through the forest must thou journey,
By the river thou must travel,
Thou must march one day, a second,
And must march upon the third day,

Then must turn thee to the north-west,
Till you reach a wooded mountain,
Then march on beneath the mountain,
Go the left side of the mountain, 150
Till thou comest to a river,
(On the right side thou wilt find it,)
By the riverside go further,
Till three waterfalls rush foaming,
When thou comest to a headland,
With a narrow tongue projecting,
And a house at point of headland,
And beyond a hut for fishing.
There thy father still is living,
There the fair one who has borne thee, 160
There thou'lt also find thy sisters,
Two among the fairest maidens."

Kullervo, Kalervo's offspring,
Started then upon his journey,
And he marched one day, a second,
Likewise marched upon the third day,
Then he turned him to the north-west,
Till he reached a wooded mountain,
Then he marched halfway below it,
Turning westward from the mountain, 170
Till at length he found the river,
And he marched along the river,
On the west bank of the river,
Past three water-falls he journeyed,
Till at length he reached a headland
With a narrow tongue projecting,
And a house at point of headland,
And beyond, a hut for fishing.

Thereupon the house he entered,
In the room they did not know him. 180
"From what lake has come the stranger,
From what country is the wanderer?"

"Is your son then all forgotten,
Know you not your child, your offspring,
Who by Untamo's marauders,
With them to their home was carried,

Greater not than span of father,
Longer not than mother's spindle?"
   Then his mother interrupted,
And exclaimed the aged woman,   190
"O my son, my son unhappy,
O my golden brooch so wretched,
Hast thou then, with eyes yet living,
Wandered through these countries hither,
When as dead I long had mourned thee,
Long had wept for thy destruction?
   "I had two sons in the past days,
And two daughters of the fairest,
And among them two have vanished,
Two are lost among the elder,   200
First my son in furious battle,
Then my daughter, how I know not.
Though my son has reached the homestead,
Never has returned my daughter."
   Kullervo, Kalervo's offspring,
In his turn began to question.
"How then has your daughter vanished,
What has happened to my sister?"
   Then his mother made him answer,
And she spoke the words which follow: [210
"Thus has disappeared my daughter,
Thus it happened to your sister.
To the wood she went for berries,
Sought for raspberries 'neath the mountain,
There it is the dove has vanished,
There it is the bird has perished,
Thus she died without our knowledge,
How she died we cannot tell you.
   "Who is longing for the maiden?
Save her mother, no one missed her.   220
First her mother went to seek her,
And her mother sought, who missed her,
Forth I went, unhappy mother,
Forth I went to seek my daughter,
Through the wood like bear I hurried,
Speeding through the wastes like otter,

Thus I sought one day, a second,
Sought her also on the third day.
When the third day had passed over,
For a long time yet I wandered,   230
Till I reached a mighty mountain,
And a peak of all the highest,
Calling ever on my daughter,
Ever grieving for the lost one.

   " 'Where is now my dearest daughter?
O my daughter, come thou homeward!'

   " Thus I shouted to my daughter,
Grieving ever for the lost one,
And the mountains made me answer,
And the heaths again re-echoed,   240
'Call no more upon thy daughter,
Call no more, and shout no longer,
Never will she come back living,
Nor return unto her household,
Never to her mother's dwelling,
To her aged father's boathouse.'"

RUNO XXXV.—KULLERVO AND HIS SISTER

Argument

Kullervo attempts to do different kinds of work for his parents, but only succeeds in spoiling everything, so his father sends him to pay the land-dues (1–68). On his way home he meets his sister who was lost gathering berries, whom he drags into his sledge (69–188). Afterwards, when his sister learns who he is, she throws herself into a torrent, but Kullervo hurries home, relates his sister's terrible fate to his mother, and proposes to put an end to his own life (189–344). His mother dissuades him from suicide, and advises him to retire to some retreat where he may be able to recover from his remorse. But Kullervo resolves before all things to avenge himself on Untamo (345–372).

KULLERVO, Kalervo's offspring,
With the very bluest stockings,
After this continued living,
In the shelter of his parents,

But he comprehended nothing,
Nor attained to manly wisdom,
For his rearing had been crooked,
And the child was rocked all wrongly,
By perversest foster-father,
And a foolish foster-mother.   10

Then to work the boy attempted,
Many things he tried his hand at,
And he went the fish to capture,
And to lay the largest drag-net,
And he spoke the words which follow,
Pondered as he grasped the oar:
"Shall I pull with all my efforts,
Row, exerting all my vigour;
Shall I row with common efforts,
Row no stronger than is needful?"   20

And the steersman made him answer,
And he spoke the words which follow:
"Pull away with all your efforts,
Row, exerting all your vigour,
Row the boat in twain you cannot,
Neither break it into fragments."

Kullervo, Kalervo's offspring,
Pulled thereat with all his efforts,
Rowed, exerting all his vigour,
Rowed in twain the wooden rowlocks,   30
Ribs of juniper he shattered,
And he smashed the boat of aspen.

Kalervo came forth to see it,
And he spoke the words which follow:
"No, you understand not rowing,
You have split the wooden rowlocks,
Ribs of juniper have shattered,
Shattered quite the boat of aspen.
Thresh the fish into the drag-net,
Perhaps you'll thresh the water better."   40

Kullervo, Kalervo's offspring,
Then went forth to thresh the water,
And as he the pole was lifting,
Uttered he the words which follow:

"Shall I thresh with all my efforts,
Putting forth my manly efforts ;
Shall I thresh with common efforts,
As the threshing-pole is able?"
    Answered thereupon the net-man,
"Would you call it proper threshing,   50
If with all your strength you threshed not,
Putting forth your manly efforts?"
    Kullervo, Kalervo's offspring,
Threshed away with all his efforts,
Putting forth his manly efforts.
Into soup he churned the water,
Into tow he threshed the drag-net,
Into slime he crushed the fishes.
    Kalervo came forth to see it,
And he spoke the words which follow: 60
"No, you understand not threshing,
Into tow is threshed the drag-net,
And the floats to chaff are beaten,
And the meshes torn to fragments,
Therefore go and pay the taxes,
Therefore go and pay the land-dues.
Best it is for you to travel,
Learning wisdom on the journey."
    Kullervo, Kalervo's offspring,
With the very bluest stockings,   70
And with yellow hair the finest,
And with shoes of finest leather,
Went his way to pay the taxes,
And he went to pay the land-dues.
    When he now had paid the taxes,
And had also paid the land-dues,
In his sledge he quickly bounded,
And upon the sledge he mounted,
And began to journey homeward,
And to travel to his country.   80
    And he drove, and rattled onward,
And he travelled on his journey,
Traversing the heath of Väino,
And his clearing made aforetime.

And by chance a maiden met him,
With her yellow hair all flowing,
There upon the heath of Väino,
On his clearing made aforetime.
 Kullervo, Kalervo's offspring,
Checked the sledge upon the instant,   90
And began a conversation,
And began to talk and wheedle :
"Come into my sledge, O maiden,
Rest upon the furs within it."
 From her snowshoes said the maiden,
And she answered, as she skated,
"In thy sledge may Death now enter,
On thy furs be Sickness seated."
 Kullervo, Kalervo's offspring,
With the very bluest stockings,   100
With his whip then struck his courser,
With his beaded whip he lashed him.
Sprang the horse upon the journey,
Rocked the sledge, the road was traversed,
And he drove and rattled onward,
And he travelled on his journey,
On the lake's extended surface,
And across the open water,
And by chance a maiden met him,
Walking on, with shoes of leather,   110
O'er the lake's extended surface,
And across the open water.
 Kullervo, Kalervo's offspring,
Checked his horse upon the instant,
And his mouth at once he opened,
And began to speak as follows :
"Come into my sledge, O fair one,
Pride of earth, and journey with me."
 But the maiden gave him answer,
And the well-shod maiden answered :   120
"In thy sledge may Tuoni seek thee,
Manalainen journey with thee."
 Kullervo, Kalervo's offspring,
With the very bluest stockings,

With the whip then struck his courser,
With his beaded whip he lashed him.
Sprang the horse upon his journey,
Rocked the sledge, the way was shortened,
And he rattled on his journey,
And he sped upon his pathway,   130
Straight across the heaths of Pohja,
And the borders wide of Lapland.

    And by chance a maiden met him,
Wearing a tin brooch, and singing,
Out upon the heaths of Pohja,
And the borders wide of Lapland.

    Kullervo, Kalervo's offspring,
Checked his horse upon the instant,
And his mouth at once he opened,
And began to speak as follows: 140
"Come into my sledge, O maiden,
Underneath my rug, my dearest,
And you there shall eat my apples,
And shall crack my nuts in comfort."

    But the maiden made him answer,
And the tin-adorned one shouted:
"At your sledge I spit, O villain,
Even at your sledge, O scoundrel!
Underneath your rug is coldness,
And within your sledge is darkness."   150

    Kullervo, Kalervo's offspring,
With the very bluest stockings,
Dragged into his sledge the maiden,
And into the sledge he pulled her,
And upon the furs he laid her,
Underneath the rug he pushed her.

    And the maiden spoke unto him,
Thus outspoke the tin-adorned one:
"From the sledge at once release me,
Leave the child in perfect freedom,   160
That I hear of nothing evil,
Neither foul nor filthy language,
Or upon the ground I'll throw me,
And will break the sledge to splinters,

And will smash your sledge to atoms,
Break the wretched sledge to pieces."
    Kullervo, Kalervo's offspring,
With the very bluest stockings,
Opened then his hide-bound coffer,
Clanging raised the pictured cover,   170
And he showed her all his silver,
Out he spread the choicest fabrics,
Stockings too, all gold-embroidered,
Girdles all adorned with silver.

    Soon the fabrics turned her dizzy,
To a bride the money changed her,
And the silver it destroyed her,
And the shining gold deluded.

    Kullervo, Kalervo's offspring,
With the very bluest stockings,   180
Thereupon the maiden flattered,
And he wheedled and caressed her,
With one hand the horse controlling,
On the maiden's breast the other.

    Then he sported with the maiden,
Wearied out the tin-adorned one,
'Neath the rug all copper-tinselled,
And upon the furs all spotted.

    Then when Jumala brought morning,
On the second day thereafter,   190
Then the damsel spoke unto him,
And she asked, and spoke as follows:
"Tell me now of your relations,
What the brave race that you spring from,
From a mighty race it seems me,
Offspring of a mighty father."

    Kullervo, Kalervo's offspring,
Answered in the words which follow:
"No, my race is not a great one,
Not a great one, not a small one,   200
I am just of middle station,
Kalervo's unhappy offspring,
Stupid boy, and very foolish,
Worthless child, and good for nothing.

Tell me now about your people,
And the brave race that you spring from,
Perhaps from mighty race descended,
Offspring of a mighty father."

And the girl made answer quickly,
And she spoke the words which follow: 210
"No, my race is not a great one,
Not a great one, not a small one,
I am just of middle station,
Kalervo's unhappy daughter,
Stupid girl, and very foolish,
Worthless child, and good for nothing.

"When I was a little infant,
Living with my tender mother,
To the wood I went for berries,
'Neath the mountain sought for raspberries.   220
On the plains I gathered strawberries,
Underneath the mountain, raspberries,
Plucked by day, at night I rested,
Plucked for one day and a second,
And upon the third day likewise,
But the pathway home I found not,
In the woods the pathways led me,
And the footpath to the forest.

"There I stood, and burst out weeping,
Wept for one day and a second,   230
And at length upon the third day,
Then I climbed a mighty mountain,
To the peak of all the highest.
On the peak I called and shouted,
And the woods made answer to me,
While the heaths re-echoed likewise:
'Do not call, O girl so senseless,
Shout not, void of understanding!
There is no one who can hear you,
None at home to hear your shouting.'   240

"Then upon the third and fourth days,
Lastly on the fifth and sixth days,
I to take my life attempted,
Tried to hurl me to destruction,

But by no means did I perish,
Nor could I, the wretched, perish.
  "Would that I, poor wretch, had perished,
Hapless one, had met destruction,
That the second year thereafter,
Or the third among the summers,   250
I had shone forth as a grass-blade,
As a lovely flower existed,
On the ground a beauteous berry,
Even as a scarlet cranberry,
Then I had not heard these horrors,
Would not now have known these terrors."
  Soon as she had finished speaking,
And her speech had once scarce completed,
Quickly from the sledge she darted,
And she rushed into the river,   260
In the furious foaming cataract,
And amid the raging whirlpool,
There she found the death she sought for,
There at length did death o'ertake her,
Found in Tuonela a refuge,
In the waves she found compassion.
  Kullervo, Kalervo's offspring,
From his sledge at once descended,
And began to weep full loudly,
With a piteous lamentation.   270
  "Woe my day, O me unhappy,
Woe to me, and all my household,
For indeed my very sister,
I my mother's child have outraged!
Woe my father, woe my mother,
Woe to you, my aged parents,
To what purpose have you reared me,
Reared me up to be so wretched!
Far more happy were my fortune,
Had I ne'er been born or nurtured,   280
Never in the air been strengthened,
Never in this world had entered.
Wrongly I by death was treated,
Nor disease has acted wisely,

That they did not fall upon me,
And when two nights old destroy me."
   With his knife he loosed the collar,
From the sledge the chains he severed,
On the horse's back he vaulted,
On the whitefront steed he galloped,   290
But a little way he galloped,
But a little course had traversed,
When he reached his father's dwelling,
Reached the grass-plot of his father.
   In the yard he found his mother,
"O my mother who hast borne me,
O that thou, my dearest mother,
E'en as soon as thou hadst borne me,
In the bath-room smoke hadst laid me,
And the bath-house doors had bolted,   300
That amid the smoke I smothered,
And when two nights old had perished,
Smothered me among the blankets,
With the curtain thou hadst choked me,
Thrust the cradle in the fire,
Pushed it in the burning embers.
   "If the village folk had asked thee,
'Why is in the room no cradle?
Wherefore have you locked the bath-house?'
Then might this have been the answer: 310
'In the fire I burned the cradle,
Where on hearth the fire is glowing,
While I made the malt in bath-house,
While the malt was fully sweetened.'"
   Then his mother asked him quickly,
Asked him thus, the aged woman:
"O my son, what happened to thee,
What the dreadful news thou bringest?
Seems from Tuonela thou comest;
As from Manala thou comest."   320
   Kullervo, Kalervo's offspring,
Answered in the words which follow:
"Horrors now must be reported,
And most horrible misfortunes.

I have wronged my very sister,
And my mother's child dishonoured.
   " First I went and paid the taxes,
And I also paid the land-dues,
And by chance there came a maiden,
And I sported with the maiden,   330
And she was my very sister,
And the child of mine own mother.

   " Thereupon to death she cast her,
Plunged herself into destruction,
In the furious foaming cataract,
And amid the raging whirlpool.
But I cannot now determine
Not decide and not imagine
How myself to death should cast me,
I the hapless one, should slay me,   340
In the mouths of wolves all howling,
In the throats of bears all growling,
In the whale's vast belly perish,
Or between the teeth of lake-pike."

   But his mother made him answer:
" Do not go, my son, my dearest,
To the mouths of wolves all howling,
Nor to throats of bears all growling,
Neither to the whale's vast belly,
Neither to the teeth of lake-pike.   350
Large enough the Cape of Suomi,
Wide enough are Savo's borders,
For a man to hide from evil,
And a criminal conceal him.
Hide thee there for five years, six years,
There for nine long years conceal thee,
Till a time of peace has reached thee,
And the years have calmed thine anguish."

   Kullervo, Kalervo's offspring,
Answered in the words which follow: 360
" Nay, I will not go in hiding,
Fly not forth, a wicked outcast,
To the mouth of Death I wander,
To the gate of Kalma's courtyard,

To the place of furious fighting,
To the battle-field of heroes.
Upright still is standing Unto,
And the wicked man unfallen,
Unavenged my father's sufferings,
Unavenged my mother's tear-drops,   370
Counting not my bitter sufferings,
Wrongs that I myself have suffered."

Runo XXXVI.—The Death of Kullervo

Argument

Kullervo prepares for war and leaves home joyfully, for no one but his mother is sorry that he is going to his death (1–154). He comes to Untamola, lays waste the whole district, and burns the homestead (155–250). On returning home he finds his home deserted, and no living thing about the place but an old black dog, with which he goes into the forest to shoot game for food (251–296). While traversing the forest he arrives at the place where he met his sister, and ends his remorse by killing himself with his own sword (297–360).

KULLERVO, Kalervo's offspring,
With the very bluest stockings,
Now prepared himself for battle,
And prepared himself for warfare.
For an hour his sword he sharpened,
Sharpened spear-points for another.
Then his mother spoke unto him,
" Do not go, my son unhappy,
Go not to this mighty battle,
Go not where the swords are clashing !   10
He who goes for nought to battle,
He who wilful seeks the combat,
In the fight shall find his death-wound,
And shall perish in the conflict,
By the sword-blades shall he perish,
Thus shall fall, and thus shall perish.

" If against a goat thou fightest,
And wouldst meet in fight a he-goat,
Then the goat will overcome thee,
In the mud the he-goat cast thee,   20
That like dog thou home returnest,
Like a frog returnest homeward."
    Kullervo, Kalervo's offspring,
Answered in the words which follow:
" In the swamps I shall not sink me,
Nor upon the heath will stumble,
In the dwelling-place of ravens,
In the fields where crows are croaking.
If I perish in the battle,
Sinking on the field of battle,   30
Noble 'tis to fall in battle,
Fine 'mid clash of swords to perish,
Exquisite the battle-fever,
Quickly hence a youth it hurries,
Takes him quickly forth from evil,
There he falls no more to hunger."
    Then his mother spoke and answered,
" If you perish in the battle,
Who shall cater for your father,
And shall tend the old man daily?"   40
    Kullervo, Kalervo's offspring,
Answered in the words that follow:
" Let him perish on the dust-heap,
Leave him in the yard to perish."
    " Who shall cater for your mother,
And shall tend the old dame daily?"
    " Let her die upon a haycock,
In the cowshed let her stifle."
    " Who shall cater for thy brother,
Tend him day by day in future?"   50
    " Let him perish in the forest,
Let him faint upon the meadow."
    " Who shall cater for thy sister,
Tend her day by day in future?"
    " Let her fall in well, and perish,
Let her fall into the wash-tub."

Kullervo, Kalervo's offspring,
Just as he his home was leaving,
Spoke these words unto his father:
"Now farewell, O noble father!   60
Shall you perhaps be weeping sorely,
If you hear that I have perished,
And have vanished from the people,
And have perished in the battle?"

Then his father gave him answer:
"Not for thee shall I be weeping,
If I hear that you have perished,
For another son I'll rear me,
And a better son will rear me,
And a son by far more clever."   70

Kullervo, Kalervo's offspring,
Answered in the words which follow:
"Nor for you shall I be weeping,
If I hear that you have perished.
I will make me such a father,
Mouth of clay, and head of stonework,
Eyes of cranberries from the marshes,
And a beard of withered stubble,
Legs of willow-twigs will make him,
Flesh of rotten trees will make him."   80

Then he spoke unto his brother:
"Now farewell, my dearest brother.
Shall you weep for my destruction,
If you hear that I have perished,
And have vanished from the people,
And have fallen in the battle?"

But his brother gave him answer,
"Not for you shall I be weeping,
If I hear that you have perished.
I will find myself a brother,   90
Better brother far than thou art,
And a brother twice as handsome."

Kullervo, Kalervo's offspring,
Answered in the words which follow:
"Nor for you shall I be weeping,
If I hear that you have perished.

I will make me such a brother,
Head of stone, and mouth of sallow,
Eyes of cranberries I will make him,
Make him hair of withered stubble,   100
Legs of willow-twigs will make him,
Flesh of rotten trees will make him."

Then he spoke unto his sister,
" Now farewell, my dearest sister.
Shall you weep for my destruction,
If you hear that I have perished,
And have vanished from the people,
And have perished in the battle ? "

But his sister gave him answer:
"Not for you shall I be weeping,   110
If I hear that you have perished.
I will find myself a brother,
Better brother far than thou art,
And a brother far more clever."

Kullervo, Kalervo's offspring,
Answered in the words which follow :
" Nor for you shall I be weeping,
If I hear that you have perished.
I will make me such a sister,
Head of stone and mouth of sallow,   120
Eyes of cranberries I will make her,
Make her hair of withered stubble,
Ears of water-lily make her,
And of maple make her body."

Then he said unto his mother,
"O my mother, O my dearest,
Thou the fair one who hast borne me,
Thou the golden one who nursed me,
Shalt thou weep for my destruction,
Shouldst thou hear that I have perished,   130
And have vanished from the people,
And have perished in the battle ? "

Then his mother gave him answer,
And she spoke the words which follow:
"Not thou knowest a mother's feelings,
Nor a mother's heart esteemest.

I shall weep for thy destruction,
If I hear that thou hast perished,
And from out the people vanished,
And have perished in the battle ;   140
Weep until the house is flooded,
Weep until the floor is swimming,
Weep until the paths are hidden,
And with tears the cowsheds weighted,
Weep until the snows are slippery,
Till the ground is bare and slippery,
Lands unfrozen teem with verdure,
And my tears flow through the greenness.

" If I cannot keep on weeping,
And no strength is left for grieving,   150
Weeping in the people's presence,
I will weep in bath-room hidden,
Till the seats with tears are flowing,
And the flooring all is flooded."

Kullervo, Kalervo's offspring,
With the very bluest stockings,
Went with music forth to battle,
Joyfully he sought the conflict,
Playing tunes through plains and marshes,
Shouting over all the heathland,   160
Crashing onwards through the meadows,
Trampling down the fields of stubble.

And a messenger o'ertook him,
In his ear these words he whispered :
" At thy home has died thy father,
And thy aged parent perished.
Now return to gaze upon him,
And arrange for his interment."

Kullervo, Kalervo's offspring,
Made him answer on the instant :   170
" Is he dead, so let him perish.
In the house there is a gelding,
Which unto the grave can drag him,
And can sink him down to Kalma."

Played he, as he passed the marshes,
And he shouted in the clearings,

And a messenger o'ertook him,
In his ear these words he whispered:
" At thy home has died thy brother,
And thy parent's child has perished.   180
Now return to gaze upon him,
And arrange for his interment."

  Kullervo, Kalervo's offspring,
Made him answer on the instant:
" Is he dead, so let him perish.
In the house there is a stallion,
Which unto the grave can drag him,
And can sink him down to Kalma."

  Through the marshes passed he, playing,
Blew his horn amidst the fir-woods,   190
And a messenger o'ertook him,
In his ear these words he whispered:
" At thy home has died thy sister,
And thy parent's child has perished.
Now return to gaze upon her,
And arrange for her interment."

  Kullervo, Kalervo's offspring,
Made him answer on the instant:
" Is she dead, so let her perish.
In the house a mare is waiting,   200
Which unto the grave can drag her,
And can sink her down to Kalma."

  Through the meadows marched he shouting,
In the grassfields he was shouting,
And a messenger o'ertook him,
In his ear these words he whispered:
" Now has died thy tender mother,
And thy darling mother perished.
Now return to gaze upon her,
And arrange for her interment."   210

  Kullervo, Kalervo's offspring,
Answered in the words which follow:
" Woe to me, a youth unhappy,
For my mother now has perished,
Wearied as she made the curtains,
And the counterpane embroidered.

With her long spool she was working,
As she turned around her spindle.
I was not at her departure,
Near her when her soul was parting.   220
Perhaps the cold was great and killed her,
Or perchance was bread too scanty.
"In the house with care, O wash her,
With the Saxon soap, the finest,
Wind her then in silken wrappings,
Wrap her in the finest linen,
Thus unto the grave convey her,
Sink her gently down to Kalma,
Then upraise the songs of mourning,
Let resound the songs of mourning,   230
For not yet can I turn homeward,
Untamo is still unfallen,
Yet unfelled the man of evil,
Undestroyed is yet the villain."
    Forth he went to battle, playing,
Went to Untola rejoicing,
And he said the words which follow:
"Ukko, thou, of Gods the highest,
Give me now a sword befitting,
Give me now a sword most splendid,   240
Which were worth an army to me,
Though a hundred came against me."
    Then the sword he asked was granted,
And a sword of all most splendid,
And he slaughtered all the people,
Untamo's whole tribe he slaughtered,
Burned the houses all to ashes,
And with flame completely burned them,
Leaving nothing but the hearthstones,
Nought but in each yard the rowan.   250
    Kullervo, Kalervo's offspring,
Then to his own home retired,
To his father's former dwelling,
To the home-fields of his parents.
Empty did he find the homestead,
Desolate the open places;

No one forward came to greet him,
No one came his hand to offer.
   To the hearth he stretched his hand out,
On the hearth the coals were frozen,   260
And he knew on his arrival,
That his mother was not living.
   To the stove he stretched his hand out,
At the stove the stones were frozen,
And he knew on his arrival,
That his father was not living.
   On the floor his eyes then casting,
All he noticed in confusion,
And he knew on his arrival,
That his sister was not living.   270
   To the mooring-place he hastened,
But no boats were at their moorings,
And he knew on his arrival,
That his brother was not living.
   Thereupon he broke out weeping,
And he wept one day, a second,
And he spoke the words which follow:
"O my mother, O my dearest,
Hast thou left me nought behind thee,
When thou livedst in this country?   280
   "But thou hearest not, O mother,
Even though my eyes are sobbing,
And my temples are lamenting,
And my head is all complaining."
   In the grave his mother wakened,
And beneath the mould made answer:
"Still there lives the black dog, Musti,
Go with him into the forest,
At thy side let him attend thee,
Take him to the wooded country,   290
Where the forest rises thickest,
Where reside the forest-maidens,
Where the Blue Maids have their dwelling,
And the birds frequent the pine-trees,
There to seek for their assistance,
And to seek to win their favour."

Kullervo, Kalervo's offspring,
At his side the black dog taking,
Tracked his path through trees of forest,
Where the forest rose the thickest.   300
But a short way had he wandered,
But a little way walked onward,
When he reached the stretch of forest,
Recognized the spot before him,
Where he had seduced the maiden,
And his mother's child dishonoured.

There the tender grass was weeping,
And the lovely spot lamenting,
And the young grass was deploring,
And the flowers of heath were grieving,   310
For the ruin of the maiden,
For the mother's child's destruction.
Neither was the young grass sprouting,
Nor the flowers of heath expanding,
Nor the spot had covered over,
Where the evil thing had happened,
Where he had seduced the maiden,
And his mother's child dishonoured.

Kullervo, Kalervo's offspring,
Grasped the sharpened sword he carried,   320
Looked upon the sword and turned it,
And he questioned it and asked it,
And he asked the sword's opinion,
If it was disposed to slay him,
To devour his guilty body,
And his evil blood to swallow.

Understood the sword his meaning,
Understood the hero's question,
And it answered him as follows:
"Wherefore at thy heart's desire   330
Should I not thy flesh devour,
And drink up thy blood so evil?
I who guiltless flesh have eaten,
Drank the blood of those who sinned not?"

Kullervo, Kalervo's offspring,
With the very bluest stockings,

On the ground the haft set firmly,
On the heath the hilt pressed tightly,
Turned the point against his bosom,
And upon the point he threw him,   340
Thus he found the death he sought for,
Cast himself into destruction.

Even so the young man perished,
Thus died Kullervo the hero,
Thus the hero's life was ended,
Perished thus the hapless hero.

Then the aged Väinämöinen,
When he heard that he had perished,
And that Kullervo had fallen,
Spoke his mind in words that follow: 350
" Never, people, in the future,
Rear a child in crooked fashion,
Rocking them in stupid fashion,
Soothing them to sleep like strangers.
Children reared in crooked fashion,
Boys thus rocked in stupid fashion,
Grow not up with understanding,
Nor attain to man's discretion,
Though they live till they are aged,
And in body well-developed."   360

Runo XXXVII.—The Gold and Silver Bride

Argument

Ilmarinen weeps long for his dead wife and then forges himself a
wife of gold and silver with great labour and trouble (1–162). At night
he rests by the golden bride, but finds in the morning that the side which
he has turned towards her is quite cold (163–196). He offers his golden
bride to Väinämöinen, who declines to receive her, and advises him to
forge more useful things, or to send her to other countries where people
wish for gold (197–250).

AFTERWARDS smith Ilmarinen
Mourned his wife throughout the evenings,
And through sleepless nights was weeping,
All the days bewailed her fasting,

And he mourned her all the mornings,
In the morning hours lamented,
Since the time his young wife perished,
Death the fair one had o'ertaken.
In his hand he swung no longer,
Copper handle of his hammer,   10
Nor his hammer's clang resounded,
While a month its course was running.

Said the smith, said Ilmarinen,
"Hapless youth, I know no longer,
How to pass my sad existence,
For at night I sit and sleep not,
Always in the night comes sorrow,
And my strength grows weak from trouble.

"All my evenings now are weary,
Sorrowful are all my mornings,   20
And the nights indeed are dismal,
Worst of all when I am waking.
Grieve I not because 'tis evening,
Sorrow not because 'tis morning,
Trouble not for other seasons;
But I sorrow for my fair one,
And I sorrow for my dear one,
Grieve for her, the dark-browed beauty.

"Sometimes in these times so dismal.
Often in my time of trouble,   30
Often in my dreams at midnight,
Has my hand felt out at nothing,
And my hand seized only trouble,
As it strayed about in strangeness."

Thus the smith awhile lived wifeless,
And without his wife grew older,
Wept for two months and for three months,
But upon the fourth month after,
Gold from out the lake he gathered,
Gathered silver from the billows,   40
And a pile of wood collected,
Nothing short of thirty sledgeloads,
Then he burned the wood to charcoal,
Took the charcoal to the smithy.

Of the gold he took a portion,
And he chose him out some silver,
Even like a ewe of autumn,
Even like a hare of winter,
And the gold to redness heated,
Cast the silver in the furnace,   50
Set his slaves to work the bellows,
And his labourers pressed the bellows.

Toiled the slaves, and worked the bellows,
And the labourers pressed the bellows,
With their ungloved hands they pressed them,
Worked them with their naked shoulders,
While himself, smith Ilmarinen,
Carefully the fire was tending,
As he strove a bride to fashion
Out of gold and out of silver.   60

Badly worked the slaves the bellows,
And the labourers did not press them,
And on this smith Ilmarinen
Went himself to work the bellows.
Once and twice he worked the bellows,
For a third time worked the bellows,
Then looked down into the furnace,
Looking closely to the bellows,
What rose up from out the furnace,
What from out the flames ascended.   70

Then a ewe rose from the furnace,
And it rose from out the bellows.
One hair gold, another copper,
And the third was all of silver;
Others might therein feel pleasure,
Ilmarinen felt no pleasure.

Said the smith, said Ilmarinen,
"Such as you a wolf may wish for,
But I want a golden consort,
One of silver half constructed."   80

Thereupon smith Ilmarinen
Thrust the ewe into the furnace,
Gold unto the mass he added,
And he added silver to it,

Set his slaves to work the bellows,
And his labourers pressed the bellows.
    Toiled the slaves and worked the bellows,
And the labourers pressed the bellows,
With their ungloved hands they pressed them
Worked them with their naked shoulders,   90
While himself, smith Ilmarinen,
Carefully the fire was tending,
As he strove a bride to fashion
Out of gold and out of silver.
    Badly worked the slaves the bellows,
And the labourers did not press them,
And on this smith Ilmarinen
Went himself to work the bellows.
Once and twice he worked the bellows,
For the third time worked the bellows,   100
Then looked down into the furnace,
Looking closely to the bellows,
What rose up from out the furnace,
What from out the flames ascended.
    Then a foal rose from the furnace,
And it rose from out the bellows,
Mane of gold, and head of silver,
And his hoofs were all of copper;
But though others it delighted,
Ilmarinen felt no pleasure.   110
    Said the smith, said Ilmarinen,
" Such as you a wolf may wish for,
But I want a golden consort,
One of silver half constructed."
    Thereupon smith Ilmarinen
Thrust the foal into the furnace,
Gold unto the mass he added,
And he added silver to it,
Set his slaves to work the bellows,
And his labourers pressed the bellows.   120
    Toiled the slaves and worked the bellows,
And the labourers pressed the bellows,
With their ungloved hands they pressed them,
Worked them with their naked shoulders,

While himself, smith Ilmarinen,
Carefully the fire was tending,
As he strove a bride to fashion,
Out of gold and out of silver.

Badly worked the slaves the bellows,
And the labourers did not press them,   130
And on this, smith Ilmarinen
Went himself to work the bellows,
Once and twice he worked the bellows,
For a third time worked the bellows,
Then looked down into the furnace,
Looking closely to the bellows,
What rose up from out the furnace,
What from out the flames ascended.

Then a maid rose from the furnace,
Golden-locked, from out the bellows,   140
Head of silver, hair all golden,
And her figure all was lovely.
Others might have shuddered at her,
Ilmarinen was not frightened.

Thereupon smith Ilmarinen
Set to work to shape the image,
Worked at night without cessation,
And by day he worked unresting.
Feet he fashioned for the maiden,
Fashioned feet ; and hands he made her,   150
But the feet would not support her,
Neither would the arms embrace him.

Ears he fashioned for the maiden,
But the ears served not for hearing,
And a dainty mouth he made her,
Tender mouth and shining eyeballs,
But the mouth served not for speaking,
And the eyes served not for smiling.

Said the smith, said Ilmarinen
"She would be a pretty maiden,   160
If she had the art of speaking,
And had sense, and spoke discreetly."

After this he laid the maiden
On the softest of the blankets,

Smoothed for her the softest pillows,
On the silken bed he laid her.
    After this smith Ilmarinen,
Quickly warmed the steaming bath-room,
Took the soap into the bath-room,
And provided twigs for bath-whisks,   170
And of water took three tubs full,
That the little finch should wash her,
And the little goldfinch cleanse her,
Cleanse her beauty from the ashes.
    When the smith had also bathed him,
Washed him to his satisfaction,
At the maiden's side he stretched him,
On the softest of the blankets,
'Neath the steel-supported hangings,
'Neath the over-arching iron.   180
    After this smith Ilmarinen,
Even on the very first night,
Asked for coverlets in plenty,
And for blankets to protect him,
Also two and three of bearskins,
Five or six of woollen mantles,
All upon one side to lay him,
That towards the golden image.
    And one side had warmth sufficient
Which was covered by the bedclothes;   190
That beside the youthful damsel,
Turned towards the golden image,
All that side was fully frozen,
And with frost was quite contracted,
Like the ice on lake when frozen,
Frozen into stony hardness.
    Said the smith, said Ilmarinen,
"This is not so pleasant for me.
I will take the maid to Väinö,
Pass her on to Väinämöinen,   200
On his knee as wife to seat her,
Dovelike in his arms to nestle."
    So to Väinölä he took her,
And he said upon his coming,

In the very words which follow :
"O thou aged Väinämöinen,
Here I bring a damsel for you,
And a damsel fair to gaze on,
And her mouth gapes not too widely,
And her chin is not too broadened."   210
    Väinämöinen, old and steadfast,
Looked upon the golden image,
Looked upon her head all golden,
And he spoke the words which follow :
" Wherefore have you brought her to me,
Brought to me this golden spectre ? "
    Said the smith, said Ilmarinen,
"With the best intent I brought her,
On your knee as wife to rest her,
Dovelike in your arms to nestle."   220
    Said the aged Väinämöinen,
"O thou smith, my dearest brother,
Thrust the damsel in the furnace,
Forge all sorts of objects from her,
Or convey her hence to Russia,
Take your image to the Saxons,
Since they wed the spoils of battle,
And they woo in fiercest combat ;
But it suits not my position,
Nor to me myself is suited,   230
Thus to woo a bride all golden,
Or distress myself for silver."
    Then dissuaded Väinämöinen,
And forbade the wave-sprung hero,
All the rising generation,
Likewise those upgrown already,
For the sake of gold to bow them,
Or debase themselves for silver,
And he spoke the words which follow,
And in words like these expressed him :   240
"Never, youths, however wretched,
Nor in future, upgrown heroes,
Whether you have large possessions,
Or are poor in your possessions,

In the course of all your lifetime,
While the golden moon is shining,
May you woo a golden woman,
Or distress yourselves for silver,
For the gleam of gold is freezing,
Only frost is breathed by silver."   250

Runo XXXVIII.—Ilmarinen's New Bride from Pohjola

Argument

Ilmarinen goes to Pohjola to woo the younger sister of his first wife,
but as he receives only insulting words in reply, he becomes angry,
seizes the maiden, and starts on his homeward journey (1–124). On
the way the maiden treats Ilmarinen with contempt, and provokes him
till he changes her into a seagull (125–286). When Ilmarinen comes
home, he relates to Väinämöinen how the inhabitants of Pohjola live
free from care since they possessed the Sampo ; and also tells him how
badly his wooing has prospered (287–328).

Thereupon smith Ilmarinen,
He the great primeval craftsman,
Cast away the golden image,
Cast away the silver damsel,
Afterwards his horse he harnessed,
Yoked before the sledge the chestnut,
On the sledge himself he mounted,
And within the sledge he sat him,
And departed on his journey,
And proposed, as he was driving,   10
He to Pohjola would travel,
There to ask another daughter.
    So he drove for one day onward,
Journeyed also on the second,
And at length upon the third day,
Came to Pohjola's broad courtyard.
    Louhi, Pohjola's old Mistress
Came into the yard to meet him,

And began the conversation,
And she turned to him and asked him   20
How her child's health was at present,
If her daughter was contented,
As the daughter-in-law of master,
And the daughter-in-law of mistress.

Thereupon smith Ilmarinen,
Head bowed down, and deeply grieving,
And his cap all sloping sideways,
Answered in the words which follow:
"Do thou not, O mother, ask me,
Do not question me in thiswise   30
How your daughter may be living,
How your dear one now is dwelling!
Death has borne her off already,
Grisly death has seized upon her.
In the ground is now my berry,
On the heath is now my fair one,
And her dark locks 'neath the stubble,
'Neath the grass my silver-fair one.
Give me now your second daughter,
Give me now that youthful maiden,   40
Give her to me, dearest mother,
Give me now your second daughter,
Thus to occupy the dwelling,
And the station of her sister."

Louhi, Pohjola's old Mistress,
Answered in the words which follow:
"Ill have I, unhappy, acted,
And it was a sad misfortune
When to thee my child I promised,
And I gave to thee the other,   50
In her early youth to slumber,
For the rosy-cheeked one perished.
To the mouth of wolf I gave her,
To the jaws of bear when growling.

"No more daughters will I give you,
Nor my daughter will I give you,
That she wash the soot from off you,
And she scratch the soot from off you,

Sooner would I give my daughter,
And would give my tender daughter.   60
To the fiercely-foaming cataract,
To the ever-seething whirlpool,
As a prey to worms of Mana,
To the teeth of pike of Tuoni."

   Thereupon smith Ilmarinen,
Mouth and head both turning sideways,
With his black hair in disorder,
As his head he shook in anger,
Pushed his way into the chamber,
And beneath the roof he entered,   70
And he spoke the words which follow :
"Come thou now with me, O maiden,
In the station of thy sister,
And to occupy her dwelling,
Cakes of honey there to bake me,
And the best of ale to brew me."

   From the floor there sang a baby,
Thus he sang, and thus made answer :
"Quit our castle, guest unwelcome,
From our doors, O stranger, hasten !   80
Thou before hast harmed our castle,
Evil much hast wrought our castle,
When the first time here thou camest,
And within our doors hast entered.

   "Maiden, O my dearest sister,
O rejoice not in this lover,
Neither in his mouth so subtle,
Neither in his feet well-shapen,
For his gums are like a wolf's gums,
Curved his claws like those of foxes,   90
And the claws of bears conceals he,
And his belt-knife blood is drinking,
'Tis with this that heads he severs,
And with this the backs lays open."

   Then the maiden's self made answer,
Thus she spoke to Ilmarinen :
"I myself will not go with you,
Trouble not for such a scoundrel,

For your first wife you have murdered,
And my sister you have slaughtered.   100
You perchance would also slay me,
Murder me, as her you murdered.
Such a maiden is deserving
Of a man of greater standing,
And whose form is far more handsome,
In a finer sledge to take me,
To a larger, finer dwelling,
To a better home than thou hast,
Not unto a smith's black coalhouse,
To a stupid husband's homestead."   110
　　Thereupon smith Ilmarinen,
He the great primeval craftsman,
Mouth and head both turning sideways,
And his black hair in disorder,
Seized without ado the maiden,
In his grasp he seized the maiden,
From the room he rushed like snowstorm,
Dragged her where his sledge was standing,
In the sledge he pushed the maiden,
And within the sledge he cast her,   120
Started quickly on his journey,
And prepared him for his journey,
With one hand the horse he guided,
On the girl's breast laid the other.
　　Wept the maiden and lamented,
And she spoke the words which follow:
"Now I come where grow the cranberries,
To the swamps where grow the arums,
Now the dove approaches ruin,
And the bird is near destruction.   130
　　"Hear me now, smith Ilmarinen,
If you will not now release me,
I will smash your sledge to pieces,
And will break it into fragments,
Break it with my knees asunder,
Break it with my legs to fragments."
　　Thereupon smith Ilmarinen
Answered in the words that follow:

"Know, the sledge by smith was fashioned,
And the boards are bound with iron,   140
And it can withstand the pushing,
And the noble maiden's struggles."
   Then the hapless girl lamented,
And bewailed, the copper-belted,
Struggled till she broke her fingers,
Struggled till her hands were twisted,
And she spoke the words which follow:
"If you will not now release me,
To a lake-fish I'll transform me,
In the deepest waves a powan."   150
   Thereupon smith Ilmarinen
Answered in the words which follow:
"Even so you will not 'scape me,
I myself as pike will follow."
   Then the hapless girl lamented,
And bewailed, the copper-belted,
Struggled till she broke her fingers,
Struggled till her hands were twisted,
And she spoke the words which follow:
"If you will not now release me,   160
To the wood will I betake me,
Hiding in the rocks like ermine."
   Thereupon smith Ilmarinen
Answered in the words which follow:
"Even thus you will not 'scape me,
For as otter I'll pursue you."
   Then the hapless girl lamented,
And bewailed the copper-belted,
Struggled till she broke her fingers,
Struggled till her hands were twisted,   170
And she spoke the words which follow:
"If you will not now release me,
As a lark I'll soar above you,
And behind the clouds will hide me."
   Thereupon smith Ilmarinen,
Answered in the words which follow:
"Even thus you will not 'scape me,
For as eagle I'll pursue you."

But a little way they journeyed,
Short the distance they had traversed,   180
When the horse pricked ears to listen,
And the long-eared steed was shying.
  Then her head the maiden lifted,
In the snow she saw fresh footprints,
And she thereupon inquired,
"What has passed across our pathway?"
  Said the smith, said Ilmarinen,
"'Twas a hare that ran across it."
  Then the hapless girl was sighing,
Much she sobbed, and much was sighing,   190
And she spoke the words which follow:
"Woe to me, unhappy creature!
Better surely had I found it,
And my lot were surely better
If the hare's track I could follow,
In the traces of the Crook-leg,
Than in sledge of such a suitor,
'Neath the rug of one so wrinkled,
For the hairs of hare are finer,
And his mouth-cleft is more handsome."   200
  Thereupon smith Ilmarinen,
Bit his lips, his head turned sideways,
And the sledge drove rattling onward,
And a little way they journeyed,
When the horse pricked ears to listen,
And the long-eared steed was shying.
  Then her head the maiden lifted,
In the snow she saw fresh footprints,
And she thereupon inquired,
"What has passed across our pathway?"   210
  Said the smith, said Ilmarinen,
"'Twas a fox that ran across it."
  Then the hapless girl was sighing,
Much she sobbed, and much was sighing,
And she spoke the words which follow:
"Woe to me, unhappy creature,
Better surely had I found it,
And my lot were surely better,

Were I riding in a fox-sledge,
And in Lapland sledge were fleeing,   220
Than in sledge of such a suitor,
'Neath the rug of one so wrinkled,
For the hairs of fox are finer,
And his mouth-cleft is more handsome.
    Thereupon smith Ilmarinen
Bit his lips, his head turned sideways,
And the sledge drove rattling onward,
And a little way they journeyed,
When the horse pricked ears to listen,
And the long-eared steed was shying.   230
    Then her head the maiden lifted,
In the snow she saw fresh footprints,
And she thereupon inquired,
" What has passed across our pathway ? "
    Said the smith, said Ilmarinen,
" 'Twas a wolf that ran across it."
    Then the hapless girl was sighing,
Much she sobbed, and much was sighing,
And she spoke the words which follow :
" Woe to me, unhappy creature !   240
Better surely had I found it,
And my lot were surely better
If a growling wolf I followed,
Tracked the pathway of the Snouted,
Than in sledge of such a suitor,
'Neath the rug of one so wrinkled,
For the hair of wolf is finer,
And his mouth-cleft is more handsome."
    Thereupon smith Ilmarinen
Bit his lips, his head turned sideways,   250
And the sledge drove rattling onwards,
And at night they reached a village.
    With the journey overwearied,
Slept the smith, and slept profoundly,
And another than her husband
Made the girl laugh as he slept there.
    Thereupon smith Ilmarinen
In the morning when he wakened,

Mouth and head both twisted sideways,
Tossed his black hair in disorder.   260
    After this, smith Ilmarinen
Pondered till he spoke as follows :
"Shall I now commence my singing,
Shall I sing a bride like this one,
To a creature of the forest,
Or a creature of the water ?

    "Not to forest beast I'll sing her,
All the forest would be troubled ;
Neither to a water-creature,
Lest the fishes all should shun her ;   270
Better slay her with my hanger,
With my sword will I despatch her."
    But the sword perceived his object,
Understood the hero's language,
And it spoke the words which follow :
"Not for this was I constructed,
That I should despatch the women,
And the weak I thus should slaughter."
    Thereupon smith Ilmarinen
Presently commenced his singing,   280
And began to speak in anger,
Sung his wife into a seamew,
Thenceforth round the cliffs to clamour,
Scream upon the rocks in water,
Moan around the jutting headlands,
Struggle with the winds against her.
    After this smith Ilmarinen
In his sledge again dashed forward,
And the sledge drove rattling onward,
Head bowed down in great depression,   290
Back he journeyed to his country,
Till he reached the well-known regions.
    Väinämöinen, old and steadfast,
Came upon the road to meet him,
And began to speak as follows :
"Ilmarinen, smith and brother,
Wherefore is your mood so gloomy,
Wherefore is your cap pushed sideways,

As from Pohjola thou comest?
How at Pohjola exist they?"   300
    Said the smith, said Ilmarinen,
"How at Pohjola exist they?
There the Sampo grinds for ever,
And revolves the pictured cover,
And one day it grinds provisions,
Grinds for sale upon the second,
On the third what needs the household.
    "Thus I speak, and tell you truly,
And again repeat it to you,
How at Pohjola exist they,   310
When at Pohjola's the Sampo!
There is ploughing, there is sowing,
There is every kind of increase,
And their welfare is eternal."
    Said the aged Väinämöinen,
"Ilmarinen, smith and brother,
Where hast thou thy wife abandoned,
Where thy youthful bride so famous,
That you here return without her,
Ever driving homeward wifeless?"   320
    Thereupon smith Ilmarinen,
Answered in the words which follow:
"Such a wife she was, I sang her
To the sea-cliffs as a seamew;
Now she screams aloud as seagull,
Shrieks aloud without cessation,
Moans about the rocks in water,
And around the cliffs she clamours."

RUNO XXXIX.—THE EXPEDITION AGAINST POHJOLA

Argument

Väinämöinen persuades Ilmarinen to go with him to Pohjola to bring away the Sampo. Ilmarinen consents, and the heroes start off on their journey in a boat (1–330). Lemminkainen hails them from the shore, and on hearing where they are going, proposes to join them, and is accepted as a third comrade (331–426).

VÄINÄMÖINEN, old and steadfast,
Uttered then the words which follow:
" O thou smith, O Ilmarinen,
Unto Pohjola we'll travel,
And will seize this splendid Sampo,
And behold its pictured cover."
　　Thereupon smith Ilmarinen
Answered in the words which follow:
" No, we cannot seize the Sampo,
Cannot bring the pictured cover,　　　　　10
From the gloomy land of Pohja,
Sariola for ever misty.
There the Sampo has been carried,
And removed the pictured cover
Unto Pohjola's stone mountain,
And within the hill of copper.
There by nine locks is it fastened,
And three roots have sprouted from it,
Firmly fixed, nine fathoms deeply.
In the earth the first is rooted,　　　　　20
By the water's edge the second,
And the third within the home-hill."
　　Said the aged Väinämöinen,
" O thou smith, my dearest brother,
Unto Pohjola we'll travel,
And will carry off the Sampo.
Let us build a ship enormous,
Fit to carry off the Sampo,
And convey the pictured cover,
Forth from Pohjola's stone mountain,　　　30

From within the hill of copper,
And the ninefold locks that hold it."
  Said the smith, said Ilmarinen,
"Safest is by land the journey.
Lempo on the lake is brooding,
Death upon its mighty surface,
And the wind might drive us onward,
And the tempest might o'erturn us;
We might have to row with fingers,
And to use our hands for steering." 40
  Said the aged Väinämöinen,
"Safest is by land the journey,
Safest, but the most fatiguing,
And moreover, full of windings.
Pleasant 'tis in boat on water,
Swaying as the boat glides onward,
Gliding o'er the sparkling water,
Driving o'er its shining surface,
While the wind the boat is rocking,
And the waves drive on the vessel, 50
While the west-wind rocks it gently,
And the south-wind drives it onward,
But let this be as it may be,
If you do not like the lake-voyage,
We by land can journey thither,
And along the shore can journey.
  "First a new sword do you forge me,
Make me now a keen-edged weapon,
So that I with beasts can struggle,
Chase away the folks of Pohja. 60
Forth I go to seize the Sampo,
From the cold and dismal village,
From the gloomy land of Pohja,
Sariola for ever misty."
  Thereupon smith Ilmarinen
He the great primeval craftsman,
Cast some iron in the fire,
Steel upon the glowing charcoal,
And of gold he took a handful,
And of silver took a handful, 70

Set the slaves to work the bellows,
And he made the labourers press them.
　Worked the slaves the bellows strongly,
Well the labourers pressed the bellows,
Till like soup spread out the iron,
And like dough the steel was yielding,
And the silver shone like water,
And the gold swelled up like billows.
　Thereupon smith Ilmarinen,　　　　　　　80
He the great primeval craftsman,
Stooped to look into the furnace,
At the edges of the bellows,
And he saw a sword was forming,
With a hilt of gold constructed.
　From the fire he took the weapon,
Took the work so finely fashioned,
From the furnace to the anvil,
To the hammer and the mallet,
Forged the sword as he would wish it,
And a blade the best of any,　　　　　　　90
And with finest gold inlaid it,
And with silver he adorned it.
　Väinämöinen, old and steadfast,
Entered then to view the weapon,
And he found a keen-edged sword-blade.
Straightway in his hand he raised it,
And he turned it and surveyed it,
And he spoke the words which follow:
"Does this sword befit a hero,
Is the sword to bearer suited?"　　　　　　100
　And the sword the hero suited,
Well did it befit the bearer.
On its point the moon was shining,
On its side the sun was shining,
On the haft the stars were gleaming,
At the tip a horse was neighing,
On the knob a cat was mewing,
On the sheath a dog was barking.
　After this the sword he brandished,
And he cleft an iron mountain,　　　　　　110

And he spoke the words which follow:
"Thus, with such a blade as this is,
Can I cleave the mountains open,
Cleave the rocky hills asunder."
　　After this did Ilmarinen
Speak aloud the words which follow:
"How shall I myself, unhappy,
How shall I, the weak, defend me,
And shall armour me, and belt me,
'Gainst the risks of land and water?　　　　　120
Shall I clothe myself in armour,
In a coat of mail the strongest,
Gird a belt of steel around me?
Stronger is a man in armour,
In a coat of mail is better,
With a belt of steel more mighty."
　　Then arrived the time for starting,
And preparing for departure;
First the aged Väinämöinen,
Secondly smith Ilmarinen,　　　　　　　　130
And they went to seek the courser,
And to find the yellow-maned one,
And the one-year old to bridle,
And to see the foal was rough-shod.
Then they went to seek the courser,
Went to seek him in the forest,
And they gazed around them keenly,
And they sought around the blue wood,
Found the horse among the bushes,
Found the yellow-maned in firwood.　　　　140
　　Väinämöinen, old and steadfast,
Secondly smith Ilmarinen,
On his head the bit adjusted,
And the one-year old they bridled,
And they drove upon their journey.
On the shore drove both the heroes,
On the shore they heard lamenting,
From the haven heard complaining.
　　Then the aged Väinämöinen
Spoke aloud the words which follow:　　　　150

"Perhaps it is a girl complaining,
Or perchance a dove lamenting.
Shall we go to look about us,
Shall we nearer go to listen?"
　　Therefore to the spot they sauntered,
Nearer went to gaze around them,
But no maiden there was weeping,
And no dove was there lamenting,
But they found a vessel weeping,
And a boat was there lamenting. 160
　　Said the aged Väinämöinen
As he went towards the vessel,
"Wherefore weep, O wooden vessel,
Boat with rowlocks, why lamentest?
Dost thou weep that thou art clumsy,
And art dreaming at thy moorings?"
　　Then the wooden boat made answer,
Thus replied the boat with rowlocks:
"Know, a vessel longs for water,
And its tarry sides desire it, 170
As a maiden may be longing
For the fine home of a husband.
Therefore weeps the boat unhappy,
And the hapless boat lamenteth,
And I weep to speed through water,
And to float upon the billows.
　　"It was said when I was fashioned,
When my boards were sung together,
That I should become a warship,
And should be employed for warboat, 180
And should bear the plunder homeward,
In my hold should carry treasure,
But I have not been in battle,
Neither have been stored with plunder.
　　"Other boats, and even bad ones,
Always wander forth to battle,
And are led to battle-struggle
Three times in the course of summer,
And return with money loaded,
In their hold they carry treasure, 190

But for me, though well constructed,
Of a hundred boards constructed,
Here upon my rests I'm rotting,
Lying idly at my moorings,
And the worst worms of the country
Underneath my ribs are lurking,
While the birds, of all most horrid,
In my masts their nests are building,
All the toads from out the forest
Over all my deck are leaping.   200
Twice it had been better for me,
Two or three times were it better
Had I been a mountain pine-tree,
Or upon the heath a fir-tree,
With a squirrel in my branches,
Underneath my boughs a puppy."

  Väinämöinen, old and steadfast,
Answered in the words which follow:
"Do not weep, O wooden vessel,
Fret thyself, O boat with rowlocks!   210
Soon shalt thou go forth to battle,
There to mix in furious conflict.
Boat, who wast by builder fashioned,
'Twas this gift the builder gave thee,
That thy prow should reach the water,
And thy sides the billows traverse,
Even though no hand should touch thee,
Neither arm be thrust against thee,
Though no shoulder should direct thee,
And although no arm should guide thee."   220

  Then replied the wooden vessel,
Answered thus the boat with rowlocks:
"None of all my race so mighty,
Neither will the boats, my brothers,
Move unpushed into the water,
Nor unrowed upon the billows,
If no hand is laid upon us,
And no arm should urge us forward."

  Said the aged Väinämöinen,
"If I push you in the water,   230

Will you make, unrowed, your journey,
Unassisted by the oars,
By the rudder undirected,
When the sails no breeze is filling?"
   Answer made the wooden vessel,
Thus replied the boat with rowlocks:
"None of all my race so noble,
Nor the host of other vessels,
Speed along unrowed by fingers,
Unassisted by the oars,   240
By the rudder undirected,
When the sails no breeze is filling."
   Väinämöinen, old and steadfast,
Answered in the words which follow:
"Can you speed if some one rows you,
If assisted by the oars,
By the rudder if directed,
When the sails the breeze is filling?"
   Answered then the wooden vessel,
Thus replied the boat with rowlocks: 250
"Yes, my race would hasten onward,
All the other boats my brothers,
Speed along if rowed by fingers,
If assisted by the oars,
By the rudder if directed,
When the sails the breeze is filling."
   Then the aged Väinämöinen
Left his horse upon the sandhills,
On a tree he fixed the halter,
Tied the reins upon the branches,   260
Pushed the boat into the water,
Sang the vessel in the billows,
And he asked the wooden vessel,
And he spoke the words which follow:
"O thou boat, of shape so curving,
O thou wooden boat with rowlocks,
Art thou just as fit to bear us,
As thyself art fair to gaze on?"
   Answered thus the wooden vessel,
Thus replied the boat with rowlocks: 270

"I am fitted well to bear you,
And my floor is very spacious,
And a hundred men might row me,
And a thousand others stand there."
    So the aged Väinämöinen
Softly then began to carol,
Sang on one side of the vessel
Handsome youths, with hair brushed smoothly,
Hair smoothed down and hands all hardened,
And their feet were finely booted;   280
Sang on other side of vessel
Girls with tin upon their head-dress,
Head-dress tin, and belts of copper,
Golden rings upon their fingers;
And again sang Väinämöinen,
Till the seats were full of people,
Some were very aged people,
Men whose lives were nearly over,
But for these the space was scanty,
For the young folks came before them.   290
    In the stern himself he seated,
Sat behind the birchwood vessel,
And he steered the vessel onward,
And he spoke the words which follow:
"Speed thou on through treeless regions,
O'er the wide expanse of water,
O'er the lake do thou float lightly,
As on waves a water-lily."
    Then he set the youths to rowing,
But he left the maidens resting;   300
Rowed the youths, and bent the oars,
Yet the vessel moved not onward.
    Then he set the girls to rowing,
But he left the youths reposing;
Rowed the girls, and bent their fingers,
Yet the vessel moved not onward.
    Then the old folks set to rowing,
While the young folks gazed upon them;
Rowed they till their heads were shaking,
Still the vessel moved not onward.   310

Thereupon smith Ilmarinen
Sat him down, and set to rowing ;
Now moved on the wooden vessel,
Sped the boat and made good progress,
Far was heard the splash of oars,
Far the splashing of the rudder.

On he rowed, while splashed the water,
Cracked the seats, and shook the planking,
Clashed the mountain-ashwood oars,
Creaked like hazel-grouse the rudders,   320
And their tips like cry of blackcock.
Like a swan the prow clove onward,
Croaked the stern as croaks a raven,
Hissed the rowlocks just as geese hiss.

And the aged Väinämöinen
Steered the vessel quickly onward,
From the stern of the red vessel,
With the aid of the strong rudder,
Till they saw a cliff before them,
And perceived a wretched village.   330

On the cape was Ahti dwelling,
In its bend was Kauko living,
Weeping that the fish had failed him,
Weeping that the bread had failed him ;
For the smallness of his storehouse,
Wept the scamp his wretched fortune.

At a boat's planks he was working,
At a new boat's keel was working,
On this hungry promontory,
And beside the wretched village.   340

Very keen was Ahti's hearing,
But his sight was even keener ;
As he gazed afar to north-west,
And to south his head was turning,
Suddenly he saw a rainbow,
And a single cloud beyond it ;
What he saw was not a rainbow,
Nor a little cloud beyond it ;
But a boat that speeded swiftly,
And a vessel rushing onward   350

O'er the broad lake's shining surface,
Out upon the open water,
In the stern a noble hero,
And a handsome man was rowing.
    Said the lively Lemminkainen,
"What this boat may be I know not,
Whose may be this handsome vessel,
Which is hither rowed from Suomi,
From the east, with strokes of oars,
And its rudder to the north-west."   360
    Then with all his might he shouted,
Shouted, and continued shouting,
From the cape the hero shouted,
Shouted loudly o'er the water,
"Whose the boat that cleaves the water,
Whose the vessel on the billows?"
    From the boat the men made answer,
And the women answered likewise,
"Who art thou, O forest-dweller,
Hero, breaking through the thicket,   370
That thou dost not know this vessel,
Whose from Väinöla this vessel,
Dost not even know the steersman,
Nor the hero at the oars?"
    Said the lively Lemminkainen,
"Now do I perceive the steersman,
And I recognize the oarsman.
Väinämöinen, old and steadfast,
In the vessel's stern is sitting,
Ilmarinen at the oars.   380
Whither then away, O heroes,
Whither do you journey, heroes?"
    Said the aged Väinämöinen,
"To the northward do we journey,
Journey through the foaming billows,
And above the foam-flecked billows.
Forth we go to seize the Sampo,
Gaze upon its pictured cover,
There in Pohjola's stone mountain,
And within the hill of copper."   390

Said the lively Lemminkainen,
"O thou aged Väinämöinen,
Take me with you as your comrade,
As the third among the heroes,
When you go to seize the Sampo,
Bear away the pictured cover.
Perhaps my manly sword may aid you,
In the combat may be useful,
As my hands may bear you witness,
And my shoulders witness to you."　　400

Väinämöinen, old and steadfast,
Took the man upon his journey,
In the boat he took the rascal,
And the lively Lemminkainen
Hurried on to climb upon it,
And he hastened quick to board it,
And his planks he carried with him
To the boat of Väinämöinen.

Said the aged Väinämöinen,
"In my boat is wood in plenty,　　410
Planks sufficient for the vessel,
And besides 'tis heavy laden.
Wherefore do you bring more planking,
Bringing timber to the vessel?"

Said the lively Lemminkainen,
"Foresight will not sink the vessel,
Nor o'erturns a prop the haystack.
Often on the lake of Pohja,
Does the wind destroy the planking,
When the sides are dashed together."　　420

Said the aged Väinämöinen,
"Therefore in a ship for battle,
Are the sides composed of iron,
And the prow of steel constructed,
Lest the wind aside should turn it,
Storms should shatter it to pieces."

Runo XL.—The Pike and the Kantele

Argument

The Sampo-raiders come to a waterfall, beneath which the boat is caught fast on the back of a great pike (1–94). The pike is killed, and the front part is taken into the boat, cooked, and eaten (94–204). Väinämöinen makes the jaws of the pike into a kantele, on which several of the party attempt to play, but without success (205–342).

VÄINÄMÖINEN, old and steadfast,
Steered the vessel swiftly forward,
On beyond the jutting headland,
On beyond the wretched village,
Singing songs upon the water,
Joyous songs upon the billows.
    On the cape were maidens standing,
And they looked around and listened.
" From the lake there comes rejoicing,
And what song from lake re-echoes,   10
Far more joyous than aforetime,
And a finer song than any ? "
    Onward steered old Väinämöinen,
For a day o'er lake was steering,
For the next through marshy waters,
For the third day past a cataract.
    Then the lively Lemminkainen
Thought of spells he heard aforetime,
For the ears of furious cataract,
And the sacred river's whirlpool.   20
And he spoke the words which follow,
And expressed himself in singing :
    " Cease, O Cataract, thy foaming,
Mighty water, cease thy rushing,
Thou, foam-maiden, Cataract's daughter,
On the foam-flecked stones, O seat thee,
On the wet stones do thou seat thee,
In thy lap the waters gather,

And in both thy hands collect them,
With thy hands repress their fury, 30
That upon our breasts they splash not,
Nor upon our heads are falling.
    "Thou, old dame, beneath the billows,
Lady, pillowed on the waters,
Raise thy head above the waters,
Rise from bosom of the waters,
That the foam be heaped together,
And that thou mayst watch the foam-wreaths,
Lest they should o'erwhelm the guiltless,
And should overthrow the faultless. 40
    "Stones that stand amid the river,
Slabs of stone with foam o'ercovered,
Be ye sunk into the water,
And your heads be pressed beneath it,
From the red boat's pathway banished,
From the course the tarred boat follows.
    "If this is not yet sufficient,
Kimmo-stone, O son of Kammo,
Make an opening with thy auger,
Pierce an opening with thy auger, 50
Through the stones in river standing,
And the dangerous slabs that border,
That the boat may pass uninjured,
And the vessel pass undamaged.
    "If this is not yet sufficient,
Water-Father, 'neath the river,
Into moss the rocks transform thou,
Make the boat like pike's light bladder,
As amid the foam it rushes,
As beneath the banks it passes. 60
    "Maiden in the cataract dwelling,
Girl who dwell'st beside the river,
Do thou spin a thread of softness,
In a soft ball do thou wind it,
Drop thy thread into the water,
Through the blue waves do thou guide it,
That the boat its track may follow,
While its tarry breast speeds onward,

So that men the least instructed,
E'en the inexperienced find it. 70
"Melatar, thou gracious matron!
Of thy favour, take the rudder,
That with which thou guid'st the vessel,
Safely through the streams enchanted,
To the house that lies beyond them,
And beneath the sorcerer's windows.
"If this is not yet sufficient,
Ukko, Jumala in heaven,
With thy sword direct the vessel,
With thy naked sword direct it, 80
That the wooden boat speed onward,
Journey on, the pinewood vessel."
Then the aged Väinämöinen,
Steered the vessel swiftly forward,
Through the river-rocks he steered it,
Steered it through the foaming waters,
And the wooden vessel wedged not,
Nor the wise man's boat was grounded.
But as they their voyage continued
Once again in open water, 90
Suddenly the vessel halted,
Stopped the boat upon its journey
In its place remained it fastened,
And the vessel rocked no longer.
Thereupon smith Ilmarinen,
With the lively Lemminkainen,
Pushed into the lake the rudder,
In the waves the spar of pinewood,
And they tried to loose the vessel,
And to free the wooden vessel, 100
But they could not move the vessel,
Nor release the wooden vessel.
Väinämöinen, old and steadfast,
Uttered then the words which follow :
"O thou lively son of Lempi,
Stoop thou down, and look around thee.
Look what stops the boat from moving,
Look what keeps the vessel moveless

Here amid the open water;
What the force beneath that holds it,   110
Whether stopped by rocks or branches,
Or by any other hindrance."
    Then the lively Lemminkainen
Stooped him down to look about him,
And he looked beneath the vessel,
And he spoke the words which follow:
" Not on rock the boat is resting,
Not on boat, and not on branches,
But upon a pike's broad shoulders,
And on water-dog's great backbone."   120
    Väinämöinen, old and steadfast,
Answered in the words which follow:
" All things may be found in rivers,
Whether they are pikes or branches.
If we rest on pike's broad shoulders,
And on water-dog's great backbone,
Plunge your sword into the water,
Thus in twain the fish to sever."
    Then the lively Lemminkainen
Ruddy youth, accomplished rascal,   130
Drew his sword from out his sword-belt,
From his side the bone-destroyer,
In the lake his sword plunged deeply,
Thrust it underneath the vessel,
But he splashed into the water,
Plunged his hands into the billows.
    Thereupon smith Ilmarinen
By the hair seized fast the hero,
Dragged from out the lake the hero,
And he spoke the words which follow: 140
" All pretend to grow to manhood,
And are ready to be bearded,
Such as these we count by hundreds,
And their number mounts to thousands."
    From his belt he drew his sword-blade,
From the sheath the keen-edged weapon,
And he struck the fish with fury,
Striking down beneath the vessel,

But the sword in pieces shivered,
And the pike was injured nothing.   150
     Väinämöinen, old and steadfast,
Uttered then the words which follow:
"Not the half of manhood have you,
Not the third part of a hero,
But a man is now required,
And a man's sense now is needed,
All the sense of the unskilful,
All the efforts of the others."
     Then himself he drew his sword-blade,
Firmly grasped the keen-edged weapon,   160
In the lake his sword then thrust he,
Underneath the boat he struck it,
At the pike's great shoulders striking
At the water-dog's great backbone.
     But the sword was fixed securely,
In the fish's jaws fixed firmly ;
Then the aged Väinämöinen
Presently the fish uplifted,
Dragged it up from out the water,
And the pike in twain he severed.   170
To the bottom sank the fish-tail,
In the boat the head he hoisted.
     Now again moved on the vessel,
And the boat-prow now was loosened.
Väinämöinen, old and steadfast
To the shoals steered on the vessel,
To the shore the boat he guided,
And he turned and looked about him,
And the pike's great head examined,
And he spoke the words which follow :   180
"Let the eldest of the yeomen,
Come and cleave the pike to pieces,
Let him carve it into slices,
Let him hew the head to pieces."
     From the boat the men made answer,
From the boat replied the women,
"But the captor's hands are finer,
And the speaker's fingers better."

Väinämöinen, old and steadfast,
Drew from out the sheath his knife-blade,   190
From his side the cold sharp iron,
That the pike might be divided,
And he cut the fish to pieces,
And he spoke the words which follow:
" Let the youngest of the maidens,
Cook the pike that we have captured,
Let her mince it for our breakfast,
That on fish we make our dinner."

Then the maidens set to cooking,
Ten there were who made the effort,   200
And they cooked the pike for eating,
And they minced it for their breakfast;
On the reefs the bones they scattered,
On the rocks they left the fishbones.

Väinämöinen, old and steadfast,
Saw the bones where they were lying,
And he turned to look upon them,
And he spoke the words which follow:
" What might perhaps be fashioned from them,
From the pike s teeth be constructed,   210
From the fragments of the jawbones,
Were they to the smithy taken,
To the skilful smith entrusted,
To the hands of one most skilful?"

Said the smith, said Ilmarinen,
"Nothing comes from what is useless,
Nothing can be made of fishbones,
By a smith in smithy working,
Though to skilful smith entrusted,
To the hands of one most skilful."   220

Väinämöinen, old and steadfast,
Answered in the words which follow:
" Yet a harp might be constructed
Even of the bones of fishes,
If there were a skilful workman,
Who could from the bones construct it."

As no craftsman there was present,
And there was no skilful workman

Who could make a harp of fishbones,
Väinämöinen, old and steadfast,   230
Then began the harp to fashion,
And himself the work accomplished,
And he made a harp of pikebones,
Fit to give unending pleasure.
Out of what did he construct it?
Chiefly from the great pike's jawbones,
Whence obtained he pegs to suit it?
Of the teeth of pike he made them;
Out of what were harpstrings fashioned?
From the hairs of Hiisi's gelding.   240

Now the instrument was ready,
And the kantele completed,
Fashioned from the pike's great jawbones,
And from fins of fish constructed.

Thereupon the youths came forward,
Forward came the married heroes,
And the half-grown boys came forward,
And the little girls came likewise,
Maidens young, and aged women,
And the women middle-agèd,   250
All advanced the harp to gaze on,
And the instrument examine.

Väinämöinen, old and steadfast,
Bade the young folks and the old ones,
And the people middle-agèd,
With their fingers play upon it,
On the instrument of fishbone,
On the kantele of fishbone.

Played the young and played the aged,
Likewise played the middle-agèd,   260
Played the young, and moved their fingers,
Tried the old, whose heads were shaking,
But they drew no music from it,
Nor composed a tune when playing.

Said the lively Lemminkainen,
" O ye boys half-witted only,
And ye maidens, all so stupid,
And you other wretched people,

'Tis not thus you play upon it,
Neither are you skilled musicians.   270
Give me now the harp of fishbone,
Let me try to play upon it,
On my knees now place it for me,
At the tips of my ten fingers."
   Then the lively Lemminkainen
In his hands the harp uplifted
And he drew it nearer to him,
Held it underneath his fingers,
And he tried to play upon it,
And the kantele he twisted,   280
But could play no tune upon it,
Draw no cheerful music from it.
   Said the aged Väinämöinen,
"There are none among the youthful,
Nor among the growing people,
Nor among the aged people,
Who can play upon these harpstrings,
Drawing cheerful music from them.
Perhaps in Pohjola 'twere better,
Tunes might perhaps be played upon it,   290
Cheerful music played upon it,
If to Pohjola I took it."
   So to Pohjola he took it,
And to Sariola he brought it,
And the boys they played upon it,
Boys and girls both played upon it,
And the married men played on it,
Likewise all the married women,
And the Mistress played upon it,
And they turned the harp and twisted,   300
Held it firmly in their fingers,
At the tips of their ten fingers.
Thus played all the youths of Pohja,
People played of every station,
But no cheerful notes came from it,
And they played no music on it,
For the strings were all entangled,
And the horsehair whined most sadly,

And the notes were all discordant,
And the music all was jarring.　　　　　　310
　　In the corner slept a blind man,
By the stove there lay an old man,
And beside the stove he wakened.
From the stove he raised an outcry,
From his couch he grumbled loudly,
And he grumbled, and he mumbled,
"Leave it off, and stop your playing,
Cut it short and finish quickly,
For the noise my ears is bursting,
Through my head the noise is echoing,　　　320
And through all my hair I feel it,
For a week you've made me sleepless.
　　"And the harp of Suomi's people
Cannot really give us pleasure,
Lulls us not to sleep when weary,
Nor to rest does it incline us.
Cast it forth upon the waters,
Sink it down beneath the billows,
Send it back to where it came from,
And the instrument deliver　　　　　　330
To the hands of those who made it,
To the fingers which constructed."
　　With its tongue the harp made answer,
As the kantele resounded:
"No, I will not sink in water,
Nor will rest beneath the billows,
But will play for a musician,
Play for him who toiled to make me."
　　Carefully the harp they carried,
And with greatest care conveyed it　　　340
Back to him whose hands had made it,
To the knees of its constructor.

RUNO XLI.—VÄINÄMÖINEN'S MUSIC

Argument

Väinämöinen plays on the kantele, and all living things, whether belonging to the air, earth, or water, hasten to the spot to listen (1–168). The hearts of all listeners are so affected by the music that tears fall from their eyes, and Väinämöinen's own eyes shed large drops which fall to the ground and trickle into the water, where they are changed into beautiful blue pearls (169–266).

VÄINÄMÖINEN, old and steadfast,
He the great primeval minstrel,
Presently stretched out his fingers,
Washed his thumbs, the harp for playing,
On the stone of joy he sat him,
On the singer's stone he sat him,
On a hill all silver-shining,
From a golden heath arising.

Then the harp he grasped with fingers,
And upon his knee he propped it,   10
And his hands he placed beneath it,
Then he spoke the words which follow:
"Come ye now to listen to me,
Ye before who never heard me,
Hear with joy my songs primeval,
While the kantele is sounding."

Then the aged Väinämöinen,
Quick commenced his skilful playing
On the instrument of pikebone,
On the kantele of fishbone,   20
And he raised his fingers nimbly,
And his thumb he lifted lightly.

Now came pleasure after pleasure,
As the sweet notes followed others,
As he sat and played the music,
As he sang his songs melodious,
As he played upon the pike-teeth,
And he lifted up the fish-tail,

And the horsehair sounded sweetly,
And the horsehair sounded clearly.   30
    Played the aged Väinämöınen.
Nothing was there in the forest,
Which upon four feet was running,
Or upon their legs were hopping,
And which came not near to listen,
Came not to rejoice and wonder.

    Gathered round him all the squirrels,
As from branch to branch they clambered,
And the ermines flocked around him,
Laid them down against the fences,   40
On the plains the deer were springing,
And the lynxes shared the pleasure.

    In the swamp each wolf awakened,
From the heath the bear aroused him,
From his lair among the fir-trees,
And the thickly growing pine-trees,
And the wolves ran lengthy journeys,
And the bears came through the heather,
Till they sat upon the fences,
Side by side against the gateway.   50
On the rocks the fence fell over,
On the field the gate fell over,
Then they climbed upon the pine-trees,
And they ran around the fir-trees,
Just to listen to the music,
All rejoicing, and in wonder.

    Sage of Tapiola illustrious,
He of Metsola the Master,
And the whole of Tapio's people,
All the boys and all the maidens,   60
Climbed upon a mountain summit,
That they might enjoy the music,
While the Mistress of the Forest,
Keen-eyed matron of Tapiola,
(Fine her stockings, blue in colour,
Firmly tied with crimson ribands,)
Climbed into a crooked birch-tree,
Rested in a curving alder,

To the kantele to listen,
That she might enjoy the music.   70
   And the birds of air assembled,
Those upon two wings that raise them,
Backwards sailing, forwards sailing,
And with all their speed came flying,
Swift to listen to the music,
All in wonder and rejoicing.
   When the eagle in his eyry,
Heard the sweet tones sound from Suomi,
In the nest she left her fledgelings,
And she hovered round to listen   80
To the gallant hero's playing,
And to Väinämöinen's singing.
High in air there soared the eagle,
Through the clouds the hawk was sailing,
Came the ducks from deepest waters,
Came the swans from snow-wreathed marshes,
And the smallest of the finches,
All the twittering birds assembled,
Singing-birds flocked round by hundreds,
And in thousands they assembled   90
In the air, and heard delighted,
And alighted on his shoulders,
All rejoicing in the patriarch,
And in Väinämöinen's playing.
   E'en the Daughters of Creation,
Of the air the charming maidens,
Gathered to rejoice and wonder,
To the kantele to listen.
Some on arch of air were seated,
Seated on the dazzling rainbow,   100
Some on little clouds were seated,
Resting on their crimson borders.
There were Kuutar, slender damsel ;
Päivätär, that maid accomplished ;
Casting with their hands the shuttle,
Drawing threads that they were weaving,
As they wove a golden fabric,
And they wove the threads of silver,

High upon the red cloud-borders,
On the borders of the rainbow.   110
    But when they began to listen
To the notes of charming music,
From their hands they let the comb fall,
Cast from out their hands the shuttle,
And the golden bands were broken,
And the silver shaft was broken.

    There remained no living creature,
None of those who dwell in water,
None who with six fins are moving,
Nor the largest shoals of fishes,   120
Which assembled not to listen,
Came not to rejoice and wonder.
Thither came the pikes all swimming,
And the water-dogs swam forward,
From the rocks swam swift the salmon,
From the deeps there came the powans,
Perch and little roach came also,
Powans white, and other fishes;
Through the reeds they pushed their bodies,
Straightway to the shore they hastened,   130
There to hear the songs of Väinö,
And to listen to his playing.

    Ahto, king of all the billows,
Grass-beard ancient of the waters,
Mounted to the water's surface,
Climbed upon a water-lily,
To the notes with joy he listened,
And he spoke the words which follow:
" Never have I heard such music,
In the course of all my lifetime,   140
As is played by Väinämöinen,
Joyous and primeval minstrel."

    And the sisters, Sotko's daughters,
Cousins of the reeds on lakeshore,
At the time their hair were brushing,
And their locks were deftly combing,
With a comb composed of silver,
And with golden brush they brushed it.

When they heard the strains unwonted,
And they heard the skilful playing,   150
In the waves they dropped the brushes,
Dropped the comb among the lake-waves,
And their hair unsmoothed was hanging,
Nor they smoothed it in the middle.

E'en the Mistress of the Waters,
Water-Mother, towards the rushes,
From the lake herself ascended,
Raised herself from out the billows,
Quickly moved her to the rushes,
Climbed a rock in water standing,   160
And she listened to the music,
And to Väinämöinen playing,
Listened to the wondrous music,
And to the delightful playing,
And she fell in deepest slumber,
Sank upon the ground in slumber,
On the mottled rocky surface,
Underneath a great rock's shelter.

Then the aged Väinämöinen,
Played one day, and played a second.   170
There was none among the heroes,
None among the men so mighty,
None among the men or women,
None of those whose hair is plaited,
Whom he did not move to weeping,
And whose hearts remained unmelted.
Wept the young and wept the aged,
All the married men were weeping,
Likewise all the married women,
And the half-grown boys were weeping,   180
All the boys, and all the maidens,
Likewise all the little children,
When they heard the tones so wondrous,
And the noble sage's music.

He himself, old Väinämöinen,
Felt his own tears rolling downward,
From his eyes the tears dropped downward,
And the water-drops fell downward;

They were tears than cranberries larger,
They were tears than peas much larger,   190
Then the eggs of grouse still rounder,
Larger than the heads of swallows.

    From his eyes there fell the tear-drops,
Others followed after others,
Tears upon his cheeks were falling,
Down upon his cheeks so handsome,
Rolling from his cheeks so handsome,
Down upon his chin's expansion,
Rolling from his chin's expansion,
Down upon his panting bosom,   200
Rolling from his panting bosom,
Down upon his strong knee's surface,
Rolling from his strong knee's surface
Down upon his feet so handsome,
Rolling from his feet so handsome,
Down upon the ground beneath them,
And five woollen cloaks were soaking,
Likewise six of gilded girdles,
Seven blue dresses too were soaking,
And ten overcoats were soaking.   210

    And the tear-drops still were falling,
From the eyes of Väinämöinen,
Till they reached the blue lake's margin,
Overflowed the blue lake's margin,
Down below the sparkling water,
To the black ooze at the bottom.

    Then the aged Väinämöinen
Spoke aloud the words which follow:
"Is there in this youthful party,
'Mid the young and fair here gathered,   220
'Mid these high-descended people,
Any darling child of father,
Who the tears I shed can gather,
From beneath the sparkling water?"

    And the young folks gave him answer,
And the old folks likewise answered:
"There are none among the youthful,
In this young and fair assemblage,

'Mid these high-descended people,
Not a darling child of father,   230
Who the tears you shed can gather,
From beneath the sparkling water."

Then the aged Väinämöinen,
Spoke again in words that follow :
" He who brings my tears unto me,
And the tears again can gather,
From beneath the sparkling waters,
Shall receive a dress of feathers."

Forth there came a raven passing ;
Said the aged Väinämöinen :   240
" Bring me now my tears, O raven,
From beneath the sparkling water,
And receive the dress of feathers."
But the raven could not do it.

And the blue duck heard him likewise,
And the blue duck next came forward.
Said the aged Väinämöinen :
" Often, blue duck, does it happen
That thy beak thou plungest downward,
As thou speedest through the water.   250
Go thou forth my tears to gather,
From beneath the sparkling water,
Bounteous guerdon will I give thee,
And will give a dress of feathers."

Then the duck went forth to seek them,
Seek the tears of Väinämöinen,
Underneath the sparkling water,
On the black ooze of the bottom.
In the lake she found the tear-drops,
And to Väinö's hands she brought them,   260
But they were transformed already,
Suffered beauteous transformation.
Into pearls were they developed,
Like the blue pearls of the mussel,
Fit for every king's adornment,
To the great a lifelong pleasure.

Runo XLII.—The Capture of the Sampo

Argument

The heroes arrive at Pohjola, and Väinämöinen announces that he has come to take possession of the Sampo, either with good-will, or by force (1–58). The Mistress of Pohjola refuses to yield it either by consent or by compulsion, and calls together her people to oppose him (59–64). Väinämöinen takes the kantele, begins to play, and lulls to sleep all the people of Pohjola, and goes with his companions to search for the Sampo ; they take it from the stone mountain and convey it to the boat (65–164). They sail homewards well satisfied, carrying the Sampo with them (165–308). On the third day the Mistress of Pohjola wakes from her sleep, and when she finds that the Sampo has been carried off, she prepares a thick fog, a strong wind, and other impediments, to oppose the robbers of the Sampo, which reach the vessel, and during the tempest Väinämöinen's kantele falls into the water (309–562).

VÄINÄMÖINEN, old and steadfast,
Secondly, smith Ilmarinen,
Third, the lively son of Lempi,
He the handsome Kaukomieli,
Sailed upon the lake's broad surface,
O'er the far-extending billows,
To the cold and dreary village,
To the misty land of Pohja,
To the land where men are eaten,
Where they even drown the heroes.   10
　　Who should row the vessel onward ?
First, the smith named Ilmarinen.
He it was who rowed the vessel,
He was first among the rowers,
And the lively Lemminkainen
Was the last among the rowers.
　　Väinämöinen, old and steadfast,
In the stern himself was seated,
And he steered the vessel onward,
Through the waves he steered it onward,   20
Through the foaming waves he steered it,
Steered it o'er the foam-capped billows,

Unto Pohja's distant haven,
To his well-known destination.
　　When they reached the goal they sought for,
And the voyage at length was ended,
To the land they drew the vessel,
Up they drew the tarry vessel,
Laid it on the steely rollers,
At the quay with copper edging.　　　　　　　30
　　After this the house they entered,
Crowding hastily within it,
Then did Pohjola's old Mistress,
Ask the purport of their coming.
" Men, what tidings do you bring us,
What fresh news, O heroes, bring you ? "
　　Väinämöinen, old and steadfast,
Answered in the words which follow :
" Men are speaking of the Sampo,
Heroes, of its pictured cover.　　　　　　　40
We have come to share the Sampo,
And behold its pictured cover."
　　Then did Pohjola's old Mistress
Answer in the words which follow :
" Two men cannot share a grouseling,
Nor can three divide a squirrel,
And the Sampo loud is whirring,
And the pictured cover grinding,
Here in Pohjola's stone mountain,
And within the hill of copper.　　　　　　　50
I myself rejoice in welfare,
Mistress of the mighty Sampo."
　　Väinämöinen, old and steadfast,
Answered in the words which follow :
" If you will not share the Sampo,
Give us half to carry with us,
Then the Sampo, all entire,
To our vessel will we carry."
　　Louhi, Pohjola's old Mistress,
Heard him with the greatest anger,　　　　　60
Called together all her people,
Summoned all her youthful swordsmen,

Bade them all to aim their weapons
At the head of Väinämöinen.
    Väinämöinen, old and steadfast,
Took the kantele and played it,
Down he sat and played upon it,
And began a tune delightful.
All who listened to his playing
Heard it with delight and wonder,   70
And the men were all delighted,
And the women's mouths were laughing,
Tears from heroes' eyes were falling,
Boys upon the ground were kneeling.
    At the last their strength forsook them,
And the people all were wearied,
All the listeners sank in slumber,
On the ground sank all beholders,
Slept the old and slept the youthful,
All at Väinämöinen's playing.   80
    Then the crafty Väinämöinen,
He the great primeval minstrel,
Put his hand into his pocket,
And he drew his purse from out it,
And sleep-needles took he from it,
And their eyes he plunged in slumber,
And their eyelashes crossed tightly,
Locked their eyelids close together,
Sank the people all in slumber.
Into sleep he plunged the heroes,   90
And they sank in lasting slumber,
And he plunged in lasting slumber
All the host of Pohja's people,
All the people of the village.
    Then he went to fetch the Sampo,
And behold its pictured cover,
There in Pohjola's stone mountain,
And within the hill of copper.
Nine the locks that there secured it,
Bars secured it, ten in number.   100
    Then the aged Väinämöinen
Gently set himself to singing

At the copper mountain's entrance,
There beside the stony fortress,
And the castle doors were shaken,
And the iron hinges trembled.
  Thereupon smith Ilmarinen,
Aided by the other heroes,
Overspread the locks with butter,
And with bacon rubbed the hinges,   110
That the doors should make no jarring,
And the hinges make no creaking.
Then the locks he turned with fingers,
And the bars and bolts he lifted,
And he broke the locks to pieces,
And the mighty doors were opened.
  Then the aged Väinämöinen
Spoke aloud the words which follow:
"O thou lively son of Lempi,
Of my friends the most illustrious,   120
Come thou here to take the Sampo,
And to seize the pictured cover."
  Then the lively Lemminkainen,
He the handsome Kaukomieli,
Always eager, though unbidden,
Ready, though men did not praise him,
Came to carry off the Sampo,
And to seize the pictured cover,
And he said as he was coming,
Boasted as he hastened forward,   130
"O, I am a man of mettle,
And a hero-son of Ukko!
I can surely move the Sampo,
And can seize its pictured cover,
Standing on my right foot only,
If I touch it with my shoe-heel."
  Lemminkainen pushed against it,
Turned himself, and pushed against it,
Pushed his arms and breast against it,
On the ground his knees down-pressing,   140
But he could not move the Sampo,
Could not stir the pictured cover,

For the roots were rooted firmly
In the depths nine fathoms under.
There was then a bull in Pohja,
Which had grown to size enormous,
And his sides were sleek and fattened,
And his sinews of the strongest ;
Horns he had in length a fathom,
One-half more his muzzle's thickness.　　　　150
So they led him from the meadow,
On the borders of the ploughed field,
Up they ploughed the roots of Sampo,
Those which fixed the pictured cover,
Then began to move the Sampo,
And to sway the pictured cover.
Then the aged Väinämöinen,
Secondly, smith Ilmarinen,
Third, the lively Lemminkainen
Carried forth the mighty Sampo,　　　　160
Forth from Pohjola's stone mountain,
From within the hill of copper,
To the boat away they bore it,
And within the ship they stowed it.
In the boat they stowed the Sampo,
In the hold the pictured cover,
Pushed the boat into the water,
In the waves the hundred-boarded ;
Splashed the boat into the water,
In the waves its sides descended.　　　　170
Asked the smith, said Ilmarinen,
And he spoke the words which follow:
" Whither shall we bear the Sampo,
Whither now shall we convey it,
Take it from this evil country,
From the wretched land of Pohja ? "
Väinämöinen, old and steadfast,
Answered in the words which follow:
" Thither will we bear the Sampo,
And will take the pictured cover,　　　　180
To the misty island's headland,
At the end of shady island,

There in safety can we keep it,
There it can remain for ever.
There's a little spot remaining,
Yet a little plot left over,
Where they eat not and they fight not,
Whither swordsmen never wander."

Then the aged Väinämöinen
Steered away from Pohja's borders,   190
Sailed away in great contentment,
Joyous to his native country,
And he spoke the words which follow:
"Speed from Pohjola, O vessel,
Make thy way directly homeward,
Leave behind the foreign country.

"Blow, thou wind, and sway the vessel,
Urge the boat upon the water,
Lend assistance to the rowers,
To the rudder give thou lightness,   200
On the wide expanse of water,
Out upon the open water.

"If the oars should be too little,
And too weak should be the oarsmen,
In the stern too small the steerer,
And the vessel's masters children,
Ahto, give thyself thy oars
To the boat, O Water-Master,
Give the best and newest oars,
Give us, too, a stronger rudder.   210
Do thou seat thee at the oars,
Do thou undertake the rowing,
Speed thou on this wooden vessel,
Urge the iron-rowlocked forward,
Drive it through the foaming billows,
Through the foam-capped billows drive it."

Then the aged Väinämöinen
Steered the vessel swiftly forward,
While the smith named Ilmarinen,
And the lively Lemminkainen,   220
Set themselves to work the oars,
And they rowed, and speeded onward

O'er the sparkling water's surface,
O'er the surface of the billows.
    Said the lively Lemminkainen,
"Formerly when I was rowing,
There was water for the rowers,
There was singing for the minstrels,
But at present time, when rowing,
Nothing do we hear of singing,   230
In the boat we hear no singing,
On the waves we hear no chanting."
    Väinämöinen, old and steadfast,
Answered in the words which follow:
"Do not sing upon the waters,
Do not chant upon the billows;
Singing brings the boat to halting,
Songs would but impede the rowing,
Then would wane the golden daylight,
And the night descend upon us,   240
On the wide expanse of water,
On the surface of the billows."
    Then the lively Lemminkainen
Answered in the words which follow:
"Anyway, the time is passing,
Fades away the lovely daylight,
And the night is swift approaching,
And the twilight comes upon us,
Though no song our life enlivens,
Nor the time is given to chanting."   250
    Steered the aged Väinämöinen
O'er the blue lake's shining water,
And he steered one day, a second,
And at length upon the third day.
Then the lively Lemminkainen
For a second time inquired,
"Wherefore sing not, Väinämöinen?
O thou great one, sing unto us!
We have won the splendid Sampo;
Straight the course that now we follow."   260
    Väinämöinen, old and steadfast,
Gave him a decided answer:

" 'Tis too early yet for singing,
'Tis too early for rejoicing.
Soon a time will come for singing,
Fitting time for our rejoicing,
When we see our doors before us,
And we hear our own doors creaking."

Said the lively Lemminkainen,
" In the stern I'll take position,   270
And with all my might will sing there,
And with all my force will bellow.
Perhaps indeed I cannot do so,
Loud enough I cannot bellow:
If you will not sing unto us,
Then will I commence the singing."

Then the lively Lemminkainen,
He the handsome Kaukomieli,
Quickly pursed his mouth for singing,
And prepared himself to carol,   280
And began to sing his carols,
But his songs were most discordant,
And his voice it sounded hoarsely,
And his tones were most discordant.

Sang the lively Lemminkainen,
Shouted loudly Kaukomieli,
Moved his mouth, his beard was wagging,
And his chin was likewise shaking.
Far away was heard his singing,
Far away across the water,   290
In six villages they heard it,
Over seven the song resounded.

On a stump a crane was sitting,
On a mound from swamp arising,
And his toe-bones he was counting,
And his feet he was uplifting,
And was terrified extremely
At the song of Lemminkainen.

Left the crane his strange employment,
With his harsh voice screamed in terror,   300
From his perch he flew in terror,
Over Pohjola in terror,

And upon his coming thither,
When he reached the swamp of Pohja,
Screaming still, and screaming harshly,
Screaming at his very loudest,
Waked in Pohjola the people,
And aroused that evil nation.

Up rose Pohjola's old Mistress
From her long and heavy slumber,   310
And she hastened to the farmyard,
Ran to where the corn was drying,
And she looked upon the cattle,
And the corn in haste examined.
Nought was missing from the cattle,
And the corn had not been plundered.

To the hill of stone she wandered,
And the copper mountain's entrance,
And she said as she was coming,
"Woe to me, this day unhappy,   320
For a stranger here has entered,
And the locks have all been opened,
And the castle's doors been opened,
And the iron hinges broken.
Has the Sampo perhaps been stolen,
And the whole been taken from us?"

Yes, the Sampo had been taken,
Carried off the pictured cover,
Forth from Pohjola's stone mountain,
From within the hill of copper,   330
Though by ninefold locks protected,
Though ten bars protected likewise.

Louhi, Pohjola's old Mistress,
Fell into the greatest fury,
But she felt her strength was failing,
And her power had all departed,
So she prayed to the Cloud-Maiden.
"Maiden of the Clouds, Mist-Maiden,
Scatter from thy sieve the cloudlets,
And the mists around thee scatter,   340
Send the thick clouds down from heaven,
Sink thou from the air of vapour,

O'er the broad lake's shining surface,
Out upon the open water,
On the head of Väinämöinen,
Falling on Uvantolainen.
    " But if this is not sufficient,
Iku-Turso, son of Äijö,
Lift thy head from out the water,
Raise thy head above the billows,   350
Crush thou Kaleva's vile children,
Sink thou down Uvantolainen,
Sink thou down the wicked heroes
In the depths beneath the billows,
Bring to Pohjola the Sampo,
Let it fall not from the vessel.
    " But if this is not sufficient,
Ukko, thou, of Gods the highest,
Golden king in airy regions,
Mighty one, adorned with silver,   360
Let the air be filled with tempest,
Raise a mighty wind against them,
Raise thou winds and waves against them,
With their boat contending ever,
Falling on the head of Väinö,
Rushing on Uvantolainen."
    Then the Maid of Clouds, Mist-Maiden,
From the lake a cloud breathed upward,
Through the air the cloud she scattered,
And detained old Väinämöinen,   370
And for three whole nights she kept him
Out upon the lake's blue surface,
And he could not move beyond it,
Nor could he escape beyond it.
    When for three nights he had rested
Out upon the lake's blue surface,
Spoke the aged Väinämöinen,
And expressed himself in thiswise :
" There's no man, how weak soever,
Not among the laziest heroes,   380
Who by clouds would thus be hindered,
And by mists would thus be worsted."

With his sword he clove the water,
In the lake his sword plunged deeply,
Mead along his blade was flowing,
Honey from his sword was dropping.
Then the fog to heaven ascended,
And the cloud in air rose upward,
From the lake the mist ascended,
And the vapour from the lake-waves,   390
And the lake extended widely,
Wider spread the whole horizon.

But a little time passed over,
Short the time that then passed over,
When they heard a mighty roaring,
At the red boat's side they heard it,
And the foam flew wildly upwards,
Near the boat of Väinämöinen.

Thereupon smith Ilmarinen,
Felt the very greatest terror.   400
From his cheeks the blood departed,
From his cheeks the ruddy colour;
O'er his head he drew his felt-cap,
And above his ears he drew it,
And his cheeks with care he covered,
And his eyes he covered better.

Then the aged Väinämöinen
Looked into the water round him,
Cast his gaze beside the vessel,
And he saw a little wonder.   410
Iku-Turso, son of Äijö,
By the red boat's side was lifting
High his head from out the water,
Raising it from out the billows.

Väinämöinen, old and steadfast,
Grasped his ears upon the instant,
By his ears he dragged him upward,
And he sang aloud, and questioned,
And he said the words which follow :
"Iku-Turso, son of Äijö,   420
Wherefore from the lake uplift thee,
Wherefore rise above the lake-waves,

Thus thyself to men revealing,
Even Kaleva's own children ? "
   Iku-Turso, son of Äijö,
Was not pleased with this reception,
But he was not very frightened,
And no answer he returned him.
   Väinämöinen, old and steadfast,
Asked again an explanation,   430
And a third time asked him loudly,
" Iku-Turso, son of Äijö,
Wherefore from the lake uplift thee,
Wherefore rise above the billows ? "
   Iku-Turso, son of Äijö,
When for the third time he asked him,
Answered in the words which follow :
" Therefore from the lake I raise me,
Therefore rise above the billows,
For that in my mind I purpose   440
Kaleva's great race to ruin,
Bear to Pohjola the Sampo.
In the waves if you will send me,
And my wretched life concede me,
Not another time ascending,
In the sight of men I'll venture."
   Then the aged Väinämöinen
Cast the wretch into the billows,
And he said the words which follow :
" Iku-Turso, son of Äijö,   450
Nevermore from lake arising,
Or ascending from the lake-waves,
Venture forth where men can see thee,
From this very day henceforward."
   Therefore from that day thenceforward,
Never from the lake rose Turso,
In the sight of men to venture,
Long as sun and moon are shining,
Or the pleasant day is dawning,
And the air is most delightful.   460
   Then the aged Väinämöinen
Once again steered on the vessel.

But a little time passed over,
Short the time that then passed over,
When did Ukko, God the Highest,
Of the air the mighty ruler,
Winds arouse in magic fury,
Made the tempests rage around them.
Then the winds arose in fury,
And the tempests raged around them,   470
And the west wind blew most fiercely,
From the south-west just as fiercely,
And the south wind still more fiercely,
And the east wind whistled loudly,
Roared the south-east wind tremendous,
And the north wind howled in fury.
From the trees the leaves were scattered,
And the pine-trees lost their needles,
And the heather lost its flowerets,
And the grasses lost their tassels,   480
And the black ooze was uplifted
To the sparkling water's surface.
Still the winds were wildly blowing,
And the waves assailed the vessel,
Swept away the harp of pikebone,
And the kantele of fish-fins,
Joy for Vellamo's attendants,
And to Ahtola a pleasure.
Ahto on the waves perceived it,
On the waves his children saw it,   490
And they took the harp so charming,
And unto their home conveyed it.
Then the aged Väinämöinen
From his eyes wept tears of sadness,
And he spoke the words which follow:
"Thus has gone what I constructed,
And my cherished harp has vanished,
And is lost my life-long pleasure.
Never will it happen to me,
In the course of all my lifetime   500
To rejoice again in pike-teeth,
Or to play on bones of fishes."

Thereupon smith Ilmarinen
Felt the very greatest sadness,
And he spoke the words which follow:
"Woe to me, this day unhappy,
That upon the lake I travel,
On this wide expanse of water,
That I tread on wood that's rolling,
And on planks that shake beneath me.   510
Now my hair has seen the tempest,
And my hair begins to shudder,
And my beard ill days has witnessed,
Which it saw upon the water,
Yet have we but seldom witnessed,
Such a storm as rages round us,
Witnessed such tremendous breakers,
Or have seen such foam-capped billows.
Let the wind be now my refuge,
And the waves have mercy on me."   520
    Väinämöinen, old and steadfast,
Heard his words, and thus responded:
"In the boat's no place for weeping,
Room is none for lamentation,
Weeping helps not in misfortune,
Howling, not when days are evil."
    Then he spoke the words which follow,
And he sang and thus expressed him:
"Water, now restrain thy children,
And, O wave, do thou restrain them.   530
Ahto, do thou calm the billows,
Vellamo, o'ercome the waters,
That they splash not on our timbers,
Nor may overwhelm my boat-ribs.
    "Rise, O wind, aloft to heaven,
And among the clouds disport thee,
To thy race, where thou wast nurtured,
To thy family and kindred.
Do not harm this wooden vessel,
Sink thou not this boat of pinewood.   540
Rather fell burnt trees in clearings,
On the slopes o'erthrow the pine-trees."

Then the lively Lemminkainen,
He the handsome Kaukomieli,
Spoke aloud the words which follow:
"Come, O eagle, thou from Turja,
Do thou bring three feathers with thee,
Three, O eagle, two, O raven,
To protect this little vessel,
To protect this bad boat's timbers."   550

He himself enlarged the bulwarks,
Fixed the timbers in their places,
And to these fresh boards he added,
And to fathom-height he raised them,
Higher than the waves were leaping,
Nor upon his beard they splashed him.

All his work was now completed,
And the bulwarks raised protecting,
Though the winds might blow most fiercely,
And the waves might beat in fury,   560
And the foam be wildly seething,
And like hillocks be uprising.

RUNO XLIII.—THE FIGHT FOR THE SAMPO

Argument

The Mistress of Pohjola equips a war-vessel and goes in pursuit of the robbers of the Sampo (1–22). When she overtakes them a fight ensues between the forces of Pohjola and Kalevala in which the latter conquer (23–258). Nevertheless the Mistress of Pohjola succeeds in dragging the Sampo from the boat into the lake, where it breaks to pieces (259–266). The larger portions sink in the lake, and form its riches, while the smaller pieces are thrown on shore by the waves, at which Väinämöinen is much pleased (267–304). The Mistress of Pohjola threatens to send all evil upon Kalevala, to which Väinämöinen pays no attention (305–368). The Mistress of Pohjola returns home in great distress, taking with her only a small fragment of the cover of the Sampo (369–384). Väinämöinen carefully collects the fragments of the Sampo on the shore, and plants them, hoping for continuous good fortune (385–434).

LOUHI, Pohjola's old Mistress,
Called together all her forces,

Bows delivered to her army,
And the men with swords provided,
Fitted out a ship of Pohja,
As a war-ship she prepared it.

In the ship the men she stationed,
And equipped for war the heroes,
As the duck her ducklings musters,
Or the teal her children marshals;   10
There she ranged a hundred swordsmen,
And a thousand men with crossbows.

In the boat the mast she lifted,
Put the yards and spars in order,
On the mast the sails adjusted,
Spread the canvas o'er the sailyards;
Like a hanging cloud it waved there,
Like a cloud in heaven suspended;
Then upon her voyage she started,
Sailed away and speeded onward,   20
Soon to struggle for the Sampo,
With the boat of Väinämöinen.

Väinämöinen, old and steadfast,
O'er the blue lake steered his vessel,
And he spoke the words which follow,
From the stern where he was seated:
"O thou lively son of Lempi,
Of my friends the dearest to me,
Climb thou quickly to the masthead,
And among the canvas hasten.   30
Look thou to the air before thee,
Look thou to the sky behind thee,
Whether clear is the horizon,
Or the sky is somewhat clouded."

Then the lively Lemminkainen,
Ruddy youth, accomplished scoundrel,
Very active, though unbidden,
Very quick, though never boastful,
To the masthead then ascended,
Up aloft among the canvas.   40
East he looked, and looked to westward,
Looked to north-west and to southward,

Looked across to Pohja's coast-line,
And he spoke the words which follow:
"Clear in front is the horizon,
Dark behind is the horizon,
Rises north a cloud, a small one,
Hangs a single cloud to north-west."
    Said the aged Väinämöinen,
"What you say is surely nonsense,   50
For no cloud is there ascending,
Nor a single cloud arising,
But perchance a sailing vessel;
Look again, and look more sharply."
    Then he looked again more sharply,
And he spoke the words which follow:
"Far away I see an island,
Dimly looming in the distance,
Aspens covered o'er with falcons,
Speckled grouse upon the birch-trees."   60
    Said the aged Väinämöinen,
"What you say is surely nonsense,
For no falcons do you see there,
And no speckled grouse you see there,
But perchance the sons of Pohja;
Look more sharply for the third time."
    Then the lively Lemminkainen
For the third time looked around him,
And he spoke the words which follow,
And in words like these expressed him: 70
"'Tis a ship from Pohja sailing,
With a hundred rowlocks fitted,
And I see a hundred oarsmen,
And a thousand men beside them."
    Then the aged Väinämöinen,
All the truth at once perceiving,
Spoke aloud the words which follow:
"Row, thou smith; row, Ilmarinen;
Row, O lively Lemminkainen;
Row ye also, all ye people,   80
That the boat be hurried forward,
And the vessel onward driven."

Rowed the smith, rowed Ilmarinen,
Rowed the lively Lemminkainen,
All the people joined in rowing.
Swayed about the pinewood oars,
Loudly rang the rowan rowlocks,
And the pinewood boat was swaying.
Like a seal the prow dashed onward,
Boiled the waves behind like cataract,   90
Like a bell uprose the water,
And the foam flew up in masses.

As for wager rowed the heroes,
As in race the heroes struggled,
But they rowed, and made no progress,
Nor could urge the wooden vessel
Further from the sailing vessel,
And the ship that came from Pohja.
Then the aged Väinämöinen
Saw misfortune fast approaching.   100
On his head was doomsday falling,
And he pondered and reflected,
How to act and how to save him,
And he spoke the words which follow
"Still I know a plan of safety,
Still I see a little marvel."
Then he took a piece of tinder,
In his tinder-box he found it,
And of pitch he took a little,
And a little piece of tinder,   110
And into the lake he threw it,
O'er his shoulder left he threw it,
And he spoke the words which follow,
And in words like these expressed him ·
"Let a reef of this be fashioned,
And a cliff be fashioned from it,
Where may run the ship of Pohja,
Fitted with a hundred rowlocks,
And may strike in lake tempestuous,
And amid the waves be shattered."   120
Thereupon a reef grew upward,
In the lake a cliff was fashioned,

Half its length to east directed,
And its breadth to north directed.
    Onward sped the ship of Pohja,
Gliding swiftly through the lake-waves,
And upon the reef came rushing,
And upon the rocks wedged firmly.
Broke across the wooden vessel,
And to splinters it was broken;   130
In the lake the masts fell crashing,
And the sails fell drooping downward,
By the wind away were carried,
And the spring wind all dispersed them.
    Louhi, Pohjola's old Mistress,
Plunged her feet into the water,
And she tried to push the vessel,
And she tried to raise the vessel,
But no spear could lift the vessel,
And she could not even move it,   140
For the ribs had all been shattered,
All the rowlocks had been broken.
    And she pondered and reflected,
And she spoke the words which follow:
"Who can aid me now with counsel?
Who can help me in this trouble?"
    Then her form she quickly altered,
To another shape transformed her,
And she took five scythes the sharpest,
And six hoes, worn out completely;   150
These she fashioned into talons,
Into claws did she convert them;
Half the broken vessel's fragments
Did she then arrange beneath her,
And the sides to wings she fashioned,
And to tail she turned the rudder,
'Neath her wings took men a hundred,
On her tail she took a thousand,
And the hundred men were swordsmen,
And the thousand men were archers.   160
Then she flew, her wings extending,
And she soared aloft as eagle,

And she poised herself and hovered,
To attack old Väinämöinen ;
In the clouds one wing was flapping,
In the water splashed the other.
      Then the fairest Water-Mother
Spoke aloud the words which follow :
"O thou aged Väinämöinen,
Turn thy head beneath the sunrise,   170
Do thou turn thine eyes to north-west,
Look a little now behind thee."
      Väinämöinen, old and steadfast,
Turned his head beneath the sunrise,
And he turned his eyes to north-west,
Looked a little just behind him.
Onward came the crone of Pohja,
And the wondrous bird was hovering
Like a hawk about his shoulders,
With the body of an eagle.   180
      Soon she came near Väinämöinen,
And she flew upon the masthead,
Clambered out upon the sailyard,
And upon the pole she sat her,
And the boat was nearly sinking,
And the vessel's side lurched downward.
      Thereupon smith Ilmarinen
Sought from Jumala assistance,
And invoking the Creator,
Then he spoke the words which follow :   190
"Save us, O thou good Creator,
Gracious Jumala, protect us,
That the son may not be hurried,
Nor the mother's child hurled downward,
From among the living creatures,
From the creatures whom thou rulest.
      "Ukko, Jumala the Highest,
Thou our Father in the heavens,
Cast a fiery robe around me,
Over me a shirt of fire,   200
That I thus may fight protected,
And may thus contend protected,

That my head may fear no evil,
Nor my hair may be disordered,
When the shining swords are clashing,
And the steely points are meeting."
 Said the aged Väinämöinen,
And he spoke the words which follow:
"Hail, O Pohjola's great Mistress!
Wilt thou now divide the Sampo,   210
Out upon the jutting headland,
On the misty island's summit?"
 Then said Pohjola's old Mistress,
"No, I'll not divide the Sampo,
Not with thee, thou wretched creature,
Not with thee, O Väinämöinen!"
And she swooped to snatch the Sampo
From the boat of Väinämöinen.
 Then the lively Lemminkainen
Drew his sword from out his swordbelt, 220
Firm he grasped the sharpened iron,
And from his left side he drew it,
Striking at the eagle's talons,
At the claws of eagle striking.
 Struck the lively Lemminkainen,
As he struck, these words he uttered:
"Down ye men, and down ye swordsmen,
Down with all the sleepy heroes!
From her wings, ye men a hundred,
Ten from ends of every feather."   230
 Answered then the crone of Pohja,
And she answered from the masthead:
"O thou lively son of Lempi,
Wretched Kauko, worthless fellow,
For thou hast deceived thy mother,
Lied unto thy aged mother!
Thou wast pledged to seek no battle
In the space of sixty summers,
Whether need of gold should tempt thee,
Or the love of silver urge thee."   240
 Väinämöinen, old and steadfast,
He the great primeval minstrel,

Thought his doom had come upon him,
And he felt his bane approaching;
From the lake he drew the rudder,
Took the oak-spar from the billows,
And with this he struck the monster,
On the claws he struck the eagle,
All the other claws he shattered,
There remained the smallest only.   250

From her wings the youths dropped downward,
In the lake the men splashed downward,
From beneath her wings a hundred,
From her tail a thousand heroes;
Down there dropped the eagle likewise,
Crashing down upon the boat-ribs,
As from tree the capercailzie,
Or from fir-branch drops the squirrel.

Then she tried to seize the Sampo,
Seized it with her nameless finger,   260
From the boat she dragged the Sampo,
Down she pulled the pictured cover,
From the red boat's hold she pulled it,
'Mid the blue lake's waters cast it,
And the Sampo broke to pieces,
And was smashed the pictured cover.

Then the fragments all were scattered,
And the Sampo's larger pieces
Sank beneath the peaceful waters
To the black ooze at the bottom;   270
Thence there springs the water's riches,
And the wealth of Ahto's people.
Nevermore in all his lifetime,
While the golden moon is shining,
Shall the wealth of Ahto fail him,
Neither shall his watery honours.

Other pieces were remaining,
Rather small those other fragments,
On the blue lake's surface floating,
Tossing on the broad lake's billows,   280
And the wind for ever rocked them,
And the billows drove them onward.

And the wind still rocked the fragments,
And the lake-waves ever tossed them,
On the blue lake's surface floating,
Tossing on the broad lake's billows;
To the land the wind impelled them,
To the shore the billows drove them.
    Väinämöinen, old and steadfast,
In the surf beheld them floating,   290
Through the breakers shoreward driving,
Then on shore upcast by billows,
Saw the fragments of the Sampo,
Splinters of the pictured cover.
    Very greatly did it please him,
And he spoke the words which follow:
"From these seeds the plant is sprouting,
Lasting welfare is commencing,
Here is ploughing, here is sowing,
Here is every kind of increase,   300
Thence there comes the shining moonlight,
Thence there comes the lovely sunlight,
O'er the mighty plains of Suomi,
And the lovely land of Suomi."
    Then did Pohjola's old Mistress
Speak aloud the words which follow:
"Still can I devise a method,
Find a method and contrivance,
'Gainst thy ploughing and thy sowing,
'Gainst thy cattle and thine increase,   310
That thy moon shall cease its shining,
And thy sun shall cease its shining.
In the rocks the moon I'll carry,
Hide the sun in rocky mountains,
And will send the Frost to freeze you,
That the frozen air destroyeth
What thou ploughest and thou sowest,
Thy provisions and thy harvests.
I will send a hail of iron,
And a hail of steel o'erwhelming,   320
Over all thy finest clearings,
And the best among the cornfields.

"On the heath the bear I'll waken,
From the pines the wide-toothed monster,
That he may destroy thy geldings,
And that he thy mares may slaughter,
And that he may kill thy cattle,
And that he thy cows may scatter.
I'll with sickness slay thy people,
And thy race will wholly slaughter,   330
That so long as shines the moonlight,
In the world no more 'tis mentioned."
    Then the aged Väinämöinen
Answered in the words that follow :
"Never Lapland spell affects me,
Neither threats from Turjalainen.
Jumala is lord of weather,
Keys of fate are the Creator's,
Not to wicked men entrusted,
Neither to malicious fingers.   340
    "If I turn to my Creator,
To my Jumala upreaching,
From my corn he'll banish maggots,
That they do not spoil my harvests,
That they may not harm my seed-corn,
Nor destroy my corn when growing,
Nor may take my seed-corn from me,
Nor my splendid corn when growing.
    "Go thou, Pohjola's great Mistress,
Drag unto the stones the lost ones,   350
Crush thou in the rocks the wicked,
Evils in thy chosen mountain,
Not the shining of the moonlight,
Nor the shining of the sunlight.
    "Send the Frost to freeze the country,
Send the frozen air destroying,
Send it only on thy seed-corn,
That thy corn when sown be injured.
Send thou forth a hail of iron,
And a hail of steel o'erwhelming,   360
Let it fall on thine own ploughing,
Only on the fields of Pohja.

"On the heath the bear awaken,
And the fierce cat in the bushes,
From the wood the curving-clawed one,
'Neath the pines the wide-toothed monster,
But to range the paths of Pohja,
And to prey on Pohja's cattle."
Then did Pohjola's old Mistress
Answer in the words which follow:⠀⠀⠀⠀370
"Now my might has all departed,
And my strength has greatly weakened.
By the lake my wealth was taken,
By the waves was crushed the Sampo."
Then she hastened homeward weeping,
Back to Pohjola lamenting.
Nothing worthy to be mentioned
Of the Sampo brought she homeward,
Nothing but a little fragment,
By her nameless finger carried,⠀⠀⠀⠀380
But a fragment of the cover,
Which to Sariola she carried:
Hence the poverty of Pohja,
And the starving life of Lapland.
Väinämöinen, old and steadfast,
Went back likewise to his country,
But he took the Sampo's fragments,
And the fragments of the cover,
From the lakeshore where he found them,
From the fine sand of the margin.⠀⠀⠀⠀390
And he sowed the Sampo's fragments,
And the pieces of the cover,
Out upon the jutting headland,
On the misty island's summit,
That they there might grow and flourish,
Might increase and yield their produce,
As the ale obtained from barley,
As the bread that rye is yielding.
Then the aged Väinämöinen
Spoke aloud the words which follow:⠀⠀⠀⠀400
"Grant, O Jumala, Creator,
That we now may live in comfort,

And be joyous all our lifetime,
And thereafter die in honour,
In our pleasant land of Suomi,
And in beautiful Carelia.

" Keep us, O thou great Creator,
Guard us, Jumala most gracious,
From the men to us unfriendly,
And from that old woman's malice.   410
Guard us from terrestrial evils,
And the spells of water-sorcerers.

" O protect thy sons for ever,
May'st thou always aid thy children,
Guard them always in the night-time,
And protect them in the daytime,
Lest the sun should cease from shining,
Lest the moon should cease from beaming,
Lest the winds should cease from blowing,
Lest the rain should cease from falling,   420
Lest the Frost should come and freeze us,
And the evil weather harm us.

" Build thou up a fence of iron,
And of stone a castle build us,
Round the spot where I am dwelling,
And round both sides of my people.
Build it up from earth to heaven,
Build it down to earth from heaven,
As my own, my lifelong dwelling,
As my refuge and protection,   430
That the proud may not devour us,
And they may not spoil our harvests,
In the course of all our lifetime,
When the golden moon is shining."

Runo XLIV.—Väinämöinen's New Kantele

Argument

Väinämöinen goes to seek for his kantele which was lost in the lake, but cannot find it (1–76). He makes himself a new kantele of birchwood, on which he plays, and delights every creature in the neighbourhood (77–334).

VÄINÄMÖINEN, old and steadfast,
In his mind was thus reflecting:
" Now the time has come for music,
Time to give ourselves to pleasure,
In our dwelling newly chosen,
In our homestead now so charming,
But the kantele is sunken,
And my joy has gone for ever
To the dwelling-place of fishes,
To the rock-caves of the salmon,　　　　10
Where it may enchant the lake-pike,
Likewise Vellamo's attendants;
But they never will return it,
Ahto will no more return it.
　　" O thou smith, O Ilmarinen,
Yestreen and before thou workedst,
Work to-day with equal vigour.
Forge me now a rake of iron,
Let the teeth be close together,
Close the teeth, and long the handle　　　　20
That I rake among the billows,
And may rake the waves together,
And may rake among the lake-reeds,
With the rake rake all the margins,
And my instrument recover,
And the kantele recover,
From the devious paths of fishes,
From the rocky caves of salmon."
　　Thereupon smith Ilmarinen,
He the great primeval craftsman,　　　　30

Forged for him a rake of iron,
Furnished with a copper handle,
Teeth in length a hundred fathoms,
And the handle full five hundred.
　　Then the aged Väinämöinen
Took the mighty rake of iron,
And a little way he wandered,
Made a very little journey,
Till he reached the quay, steel-fitted,
And the landing-stage of copper.   40
There he found a boat, found two boats,
Both the boats were waiting ready
On the quay, with steel all fitted,
On the landing-stage of copper,
And the first boat was a new one,
And the second was an old one.
　　Said the aged Väinämöinen,
To the new boat firstly speaking:
"Go, thou boat, into the water,
To the waves, O vessel, rush thou,   50
Even though no arm should turn thee,
Even though no thumbs should touch thee."
　　Sped the boat into the water,
Rushed amid the waves the vessel.
Old and steadfast Väinämöinen,
In the stern made haste to seat him,
And he went to sweep the water,
And to sweep among the billows.
Scattered leaves of water-lilies,
Raked he up among the shore-drift,   60
All the rubbish raked together,
All the rubbish, bits of rushes,
Every scrap he raked together,
All the shoals with care raked over,
But he found not, nor discovered,
Where his pike-bone harp was hidden,
And this joy was gone for ever,
With the kantele was sunken.
　　Väinämöinen, old and steadfast,
Then returned unto his dwelling,   70

Head bowed down, and sadly grieving,
And his cap awry adjusted,
And he said the words which follow:
"Unto me is lost for ever
Pleasure from the harp of pike-teeth,
From the harp I made of fish-bone."

    As he wandered through the country,
On the borders of the woodlands,
There he heard a birch-tree weeping,
And a speckled tree lamenting,   80
And in that direction hastened,
Walking till he reached the birch-tree.

    Thereupon he spoke and asked it,
"Wherefore weep'st thou, beauteous birch-tree,
Shedding tears, O green-leaved birch-tree,
By thy belt of white conspicuous?
To the war thou art not taken,
Longest not for battle-struggle."

    Answer made the leaning birch-tree,
And the green-leaved tree responded: 90
"There is much that I could speak of,
Many things I might reflect on,
How I best might live in pleasure,
And I might rejoice for pleasure.
I am wretched in my sorrow,
And can but rejoice in trouble,
Living with my life o'erclouded,
And lamenting in my sorrow.

    "And I weep my utter weakness,
And my worthlessness lament for,   100
I am poor, and all unaided,
Wholly wretched, void of succour,
Here in such an evil station,
On a plain among the willows.

    "Perfect happiness and pleasure
Others always are expecting,
When arrives the beauteous summer,
In the warm days of the summer.
But my fate is different, wretched,
Nought but wretchedness awaits me;   110

And my bark is peeling from me,
Down are hewed my leafy branches.
  "Often unto me defenceless
Oft to me, unhappy creature,
In the short spring come the children,
Quickly to the spot they hurry,
And with sharpened knives they score me,
Draw my sap from out my body,
And in summer wicked herdsmen,
Strip from me my white bark-girdle,   120
Cups and plates therefrom constructing,
Baskets too, for holding berries.
  "Often unto me defenceless,
Oft to me, unhappy creature,
Come the girls beneath my branches,
Come beneath, and dance around me.
From my crown they cut the branches,
And they bind them into besoms.
  "Often too, am I, defenceless,
Oft am I, unhappy creature,   130
Hewed away to make a clearing,
Cut to pieces into faggots.
Thrice already in this summer,
In the warm days of the summer,
Unto me have come the woodmen,
And have hewed me with their axes,
Hewed the crown from me unhappy,
And my weak life has departed.
  "This has been my joy in summer,
In the warm days of the summer,   140
But no better was the winter,
Nor the time of snow more pleasant.
  "And in former times already,
Has my face been changed by trouble,
And my head has drooped with sadness,
And my cheeks have paled with sorrow,
Thinking o'er the days of evil,
Pondering o'er the times of evil.
  "And the wind brought ills upon me,
And the frost brought bitter sorrows.   150

Tore the wind my green cloak from me,
Frost my pretty dress from off me.
Thus am I of all the poorest,
And a most unhappy birch-tree,
Standing stripped of all my clothing,
As a naked trunk I stand here,
And in cold I shake and tremble,
And in frost I stand lamenting."
　　Said the aged Väinämöinen,
"Weep no more, O verdant birch-tree!　　　　160
Leafy sapling, weep no longer,
Thou, equipped with whitest girdle,
For a pleasant future waits thee,
New and charming joys await thee.
Soon shalt thou with joy be weeping,
Shortly shalt thou sing for pleasure."
　　Then the aged Väinämöinen
Carved into a harp the birch-tree,
On a summer day he carved it,
To a kantele he shaped it,　　　　170
At the end of cloudy headland,
And upon the shady island,
And the harp-frame he constructed,
From the trunk he formed new pleasure,
And the frame of toughest birchwood;
From the mottled trunk he formed it.
　　Said the aged Väinämöinen
In the very words which follow:
"Now the frame I have constructed,
From the trunk for lasting pleasure.　　　　180
Whence shall now the screws be fashioned,
Whence shall come the pegs to suit me?"
　　In the yard there grew an oak-tree,
By the farmyard it was standing,
'Twas an oak with equal branches,
And on every branch an acorn,
In the acorns golden kernels,
On each kernel sat a cuckoo.
　　When the cuckoos all were calling,
In the call five tones were sounding,　　　　190

Gold from out their mouths was flowing,
Silver too they scattered round them,
On a hill the gold was flowing,
On the ground there flowed the silver,
And from this he made the harp-screws,
And the pegs from that provided.
   Said the aged Väinämöinen
In the very words which follow:
" Now the harp-screws are constructed,
And the harp-pegs are provided.   200
Something even now is wanting,
And five strings as yet are needed.
How shall I provide the harp-strings,
Which shall yield the notes in playing?"
   Then he went to seek for harp-strings,
And along the heath he wandered.
On the heath there sat a maiden,
Sat a damsel in the valley,
And the maiden was not weeping,
Neither was she very joyful.   210
To herself she sang full softly,
Sang, that soon might come the evening,
Hoping for her lover's coming,
For the dear one she had chosen.
   Väinämöinen, old and steadfast,
Crept without his shoes towards her,
Sprang to her without his stockings,
And as soon as he approached her,
He besought her hair to give him,
And he spoke the words which follow: 220
" Give thy hair to me, O maiden,
Give me of thy hair, O fair one,
Give me hair to form my harp-strings,
For the tones of lasting pleasure."
   Then her hair the maiden gave him,
From her soft locks hair she gave him,
And she gave him five and six hairs,
Seven the hairs she gave unto him,
That he thus might form his harp-strings,
For the tones of lasting pleasure.   230

Now the harp at last was finished,
And the aged Väinämöinen
On a rock his seat selected,
Near the steps, upon a stone bench.
In his hands the harp then taking,
Very near he felt his pleasure,
And the frame he turned to heaven,
On his knees the knob then propping,
All the strings he put in order,
Fit to make melodious music.   240
When he had the strings adjusted,
Then the instrument was ready ;
Underneath his hands he placed it,
And across his knees he laid it,
With his ten nails did he play it,
And he let five active fingers
Draw the tunes from out the harp-strings,
Making most delightful music.
When the aged Väinämöinen
Thus upon his harp was playing,   250
Fine his hands, his fingers tender,
And his fingers curving outwards,
Then rang out the wood so speckled,
Sang the sapling green full loudly,
Loudly called the golden cuckoo,
And rejoiced the hair of maiden.
Thus played Väinämöinen's fingers,
And the harp-strings loud resounded,
Mountains shook and plains resounded,
All the rocky hills resounded,   260
In the waves the stones were rocking,
In the water moved the gravel,
And the pine-trees were rejoicing,
On the heath the stumps were skipping.
All of Kaleva's step daughters,
All the fair ones flocked together,
And in streams they rushed together,
Like a river in its flowing.
Merry laughed the younger women,
And the mothers all were joyful,   270

As they heard the music playing,
And they wondered at their pleasure.
  Likewise many men were present,
In their hands their caps all holding,
All the old dames in the party
To their sides their hands were holding,
And the maidens' eyes shed tear-drops,
On the ground the boys were kneeling,
To the kantele all listening,
And they wondered at their pleasure.   280
With one voice they all were singing,
With one tongue they all repeated :
" Never have we heard aforetime,
Heard before such charming music,
In the course of all our lifetime,
When the brilliant moon was shining."
  Far was heard the charming music,
In six villages they heard it,
There was not a single creature
But it hurried forth to listen,   290
And to hear the charming music
From the kantele resounding.
  All the wild beasts of the forest
Upright on their claws were resting
To the kantele to listen,
And they wondered at their pleasure.
  All the birds in air then flying,
Perched upon the neighbouring branches,
All the fish that swam the waters,
To the margin hastened quickly,   300
And the worms in earth then creeping,
Up above the ground then hastened,
And they turned themselves and listened,
Listened to the charming music,
In the kantele rejoicing,
And in Väinämöinen's singing.
  Then the aged Väinämöinen
Played in his most charming manner,
Most melodiously resounding ;
And he played one day, a second,   310

Playing on, without cessation,
Every morning after breakfast,
Girded with the selfsame girdle,
And the same shirt always wearing.

When he in his house was playing,
In his house of fir constructed,
All the roofs resounded loudly,
And the boards resounded likewise,
Ceilings sang, the doors were creaking,
All the windows were rejoicing,   320
And the hearthstones all were moving,
Birchwood columns sang in answer.

When he walked among the pinewoods,
And he wandered through the firwoods,
All the pines bowed down before him,
To the very ground the fir-trees ;
On the grass the cones rolled round him,
On the roots the needles scattered.

When he hurried through the greenwood,
Or across the heath was hastening,   330
All the leaves called gaily to him,
And the heath was all rejoicing,
And the flowers breathed fragrance round him,
And the young shoots bowed before him.

RUNO XLV.—THE PESTILENCE IN KALEVALA

Argument

The Mistress of Pohjola sends terrible diseases to Kalevala (1–190).
Väi ämöinen heals the people by powerful incantations and unguents
(191–362).

LOUHI, Pohjola's old Mistress,
In her ears received the tidings
That in Väinölä it prospered,
And that Kalevala had flourished,
Through the fragments of the Sampo,
Fragments of the pictured cover.

Thereupon she grew most envious,
And for evermore reflected
On the death that she might fashion,
How she best might bring destruction   10
On the people in Väinölä,
And on Kalevala's whole people.
　　Then she prayed aloud to Ukko,
And she thus implored the Thunderer
"Ukko, thou of Gods the highest,
Slay thou Kaleva's whole people,
Slay them with thy hail of iron,
With thy steely needles slay them,
Or by sickness let them perish,
Let the evil nation perish,   20
Let the men die in the farmyard,
On the cowshed floor the women."
　　Lived in Tuonela a blind maid,
Loviatar, an aged woman,
She the worst of Tuoni's daughters,
And of Mana's maids most hideous,
She, the source of every evil,
Origin of woes a thousand,
With a face of perfect blackness,
And a skin of hue most hideous.   30
　　Then this daughter black of Tuoni,
Ulappala's blind-eyed damsel,
Made her bed upon the pathway,
On the straw in evil country,
And her back she turned to windward,
Sideways to the bitter weather,
Backwards to the blast so freezing,
And the chilling winds of morning.
　　Then a great wind rose in fury,
From the east a mighty tempest,   40
Blew this wretched creature pregnant,
And she quickened from the tempest,
On a barren waste all treeless,
On the bare and grassless meadows.
　　And she bore a heavy burden,
Bore a heavy painful burden,

Bore it two months, bore it three months,
And for four and five months bore it,
Bore it seven months, bore it eight months,
For the ninth month also bore it,   50
As old wives are wont to reckon,
And for half the tenth month likewise.

When the ninth month had passed over,
And the tenth month was beginning,
Then she writhed about in anguish,
And the greatest pain oppressed her,
But as yet she brought forth nothing,
And no brood as yet resulted.

From her lair at length she moved her,
In another place she laid her,   60
And the wench in childbed laid her,
Sport of winds, in hopes of children.
There betwixt two rocks she laid her,
In the clefts among five mountains,
But as yet she brought forth nothing,
And no brood as yet resulted.

And she sought a place for breeding,
Sought a place for bearing suited,
In the quaking swamps she sought it,
And among the waves she sought it,   70
But she found no place to suit her,
Where she could relieve her burden.

Then she fain would bring forth children,
And relieve her body's burden
In the foam of furious cataract,
'Neath where whirl the furious waters,
Where three waterfalls are falling,
Under nine of precipices,
But as yet she brought forth nothing,
Nor the foul one eased her burden.   80
Then began to weep, the foul one,
And to howl, the wicked monster.
Whither now to go she knew not,
And in what direction wander,
Where she might relieve her burden,
Where to go to cast her offspring.

From the clouds then bespoke her Jumala,
The Creator spoke from heaven:
"Stands in swamp a hut three-cornered,
Just upon a lakelet's margin,   90
In the gloomy land of Pohja,
Near where Sariola's bay stretches.
There thou may'st bring forth thy offspring,
There lay down thy heavy burden,
There it is that people need thee,
There do they expect thy offspring."

Therefore Tuoni's blackest daughter,
Manala's most hideous damsel,
Came unto the house of Pohja,
Came to Sariola's great bathroom,   100
That she there might bear her children,
And she might bring forth her offspring.

Louhi, Pohjola's old Mistress,
Old and gap-toothed dame of Pohja,
Secret led her to the bathroom,
Secretly into the bathroom,
But the village did not know it,
Nought was spoken in the village.

Secretly she warmed the bathroom,
Hastily she made it ready,   110
And with ale the doors smeared over,
And with beer the hinges wetted,
That the doors should make no jarring,
And the hinges make no creaking.

Then she spoke the words which follow,
And expressed herself in thiswise:
"Noble dame, Creation's daughter,
Noble one, as gold all lustrous,
Thou the oldest of all women,
Thou the first of all the mothers,   120
Knee-deep in the lake descend thou,
To thy waist among the billows,
From the perch the slime obtain thou,
And the slime from creeping creatures,
Do thou smear with this the gateway,
And upon the sides anoint it,

Free the damsel from her burden,
And the woman from her sufferings,
Free her from this grievous torment,
And release her from her sufferings.   130
　　" But if this is not sufficient,
Ukko, thou of Gods the highest,
Hither come where thou art needed,
Come thou at our supplication.
Here there is a girl in childbed,
And a woman suffering greatly,
Here amid the bathroom's vapour,
Brought into the village bathroom.
　　" Do thou take thy club all golden,
In thy right hand do thou take it,   140
Each impediment remove thou,
And the door-posts move asunder,
Bend thou the Creator's castles,
Break thou all the bars asunder,
Push the large ones and the small ones,
Even to the very smallest."
　　Then this foul and wicked creature,
She, the daughter blind of Tuoni,
Presently relieved her burden,
And she brought forth evil children,   150
'Neath a rug adorned with copper,
Underneath the softest blankets.
　　Thus became she nine sons' mother,
In a single night of summer,
With the bath prepared once only,
With the bath but once made ready,
With a single effort only,
From the fulness of her body.
　　To the boys their names assigned she,
And she nurtured well the children   160
Just as each one names the children
Whom themselves have brought to being.
One as Pleurisy she destined,
One did she send forth as Colic,
And as Gout she reared another,
One as Scrofula she fashioned,

Boil, another designated,
And as Itch proclaimed another,
Thrust another forth as Cancer,
And as Plague she formed another.   170
    One remained, and he was nameless,
In the straw the lowest lying,
Therefore did she send him onward,
As a sorcerer on the waters,
Also to bewitch the lowlands,
Everywhere to practise malice.
    Louhi, Pohjola's old Mistress,
Sent the others forth to journey
To the cloud-encompassed headland,
And the shady island's summit,   180
Sent in rage these evil monsters,
These diseases all unheard of,
Forth to Väinölä she sent them,
Kaleva's great race to slaughter.
    Sickened Väinölä's own people,
Kaleva's descendants sickened,
With diseases all unheard of,
And whose names were known to no one,
And the floors beneath them rotted,
And the sheet above corrupted.   190
    Then the aged Väinämöinen,
He the great primeval sorcerer,
Went to drive away the evil,
And his people's lives to succour,
Forth he went to war with Tuoni,
And against disease to struggle.
    Thereupon he warmed the bathroom,
And the stones prepared to heat it,
And the finest wood provided,
Faggots, too, he laid in water;   200
Water brought in covered vessels,
Bath-whisks also, well-protected,
Warmed the bath-whisks to perfection,
And the hundred twigs he softened.
    Then he raised a warmth like honey,
Raised a heat as sweet as honey,

From the heated stones he raised it,
From the glowing stones he raised it,
And he spoke the words which follow,
And in words like these expressed him :   210
"Now the bath approach, O Jumala,
To the warmth, O heavenly Father,
Healthfulness again to grant us,
And our peace again secure us.
Drive away these foul diseases,
From these dread diseases save us,
Calm thou down this heat excessive
Drive away this heat so evil,
That it may not burn thy children,
Neither may destroy thy offspring.   220

    "Therefore will I sprinkle water,
On the glowing stones I cast it,
Let it now be changed to honey,
May it trickle down like honey,
Let it flow a stream like honey,
Flowing to a lake of honey,
As it flows along the hearthstones,
Flowing through the mossy bathroom

    "Do not let us guiltless perish,
Nor be overcome by sickness,   230
'Gainst the great Creator's mandate,
When sends Jumala our death not.
He who slaughters us, the sinless,
Let his mouth his own words swallow
On his head cast back the evils,
Evil thoughts recoil upon him.

    "If myself I am not manly,
Nor is Ukko's son a hero,
Nor can drive away these evils,
Nor from off my head can lift them,   240
Ukko is a man and hero,
He it is the clouds who marshals,
And the rainless clouds he governs,
Ruling o'er the clouds so scattered.

    "Ukko, thou of Gods the highest,
Thou above the clouds who dwellest,

Come thou here where thou art needed,
Listen to our supplications,
Do thou look upon our sufferings,
Do thou end our days of anguish,   250
Free us from this evil magic,
Free us now from every evil.

" Bring me now a sword of fire,
Bring me now a flashing sword-blade,
That I may oppose these evils
Quite subdue these frightful evils,
On the wind's path drive our sufferings,
Drive them far amid the deserts.

" Thence I'll drive these sorcerers' torments,
Thence these sufferings will I banish,   260
Far away to rocky caverns,
Rocky caves as hard as iron,
Torments to the stones to carry,
And upon the rocks heap suffering.
Never weeps the stone for anguish,
Nor the rock complains of suffering,
Though it should be greatly beaten,
And though blows be heaped upon it.

" Kiputytto, Tuoni's maiden,
Sitting on the Stone of Sickness,   270
In the rush of three great rivers,
Where three waters are divided,
Turning round the torture-millstone,
And the Mount of Sickness turning!
Go and turn away these sufferings,
To the blue stone gorge direct them,
Or amid the waters send them,
To the deep lake, O condemn them,
Which by wind is never troubled,
Where the sun is never shining.   280

" If this is not yet sufficient,
Kivutar, O noble Mistress,
Vammatar, O noble matron,
Come ye all, and come together,
Once again to work us healing,
And restore our peace unto us!

Take the sufferings from the suffering,
And the ulcers from the ulcered,
That the sick may fall in slumber,
And the weak may rise from weakness,   290
And the sufferer hope recover,
And our mourning have an ending.
  " Put the sufferings in a barrel,
And with copper hasps enclose them,
Carry thou away the sufferings,
And do thou cast down the tortures,
In the midst of Torture-Mountain,
On the peak of Mount of Suffering,
Do thou there boil up the tortures
In the very smallest kettle,   300
Larger not than round a finger,
And no wider than a thumb-breadth.
  "There's a stone in midmost mountain,
'Mid the stone there is an opening,
Which has there been bored by auger,
Where the auger has transpierced it.
Do thou thrust therein the sufferings,
Overcome these painful ulcers,
Crush thou in these raging tortures,
Do thou end our days of suffering,   310
That by night they may be harmless,
And be harmless in the daytime."
  Then the aged Väinämöinen,
He the great primeval sorcerer,
Salved o'er all the ulcered places,
And the open wounds anointed,
With nine various salves anointed,
With eight magic drugs he rubbed them,
And he spoke the words which follow,
And in words like these expressed him :   320
" Ukko, thou of Gods the highest,
O thou aged man in heaven !
Let a cloud appear to eastward,
Let another rise from north-west,
Send thou from the west another,
Grant us honey, grant us water,

That our sores may be anointed,
And our wounds be all salved over.
    "Yet to me no power is given,
Save by my Creator granted.   330
Grant us now thy grace, Creator,
Grant us, Jumala, thy mercy.
With my eyes have I been seeing,
And my hands have been uplifting,
With my mouth have I been speaking,
With my breath have I been sighing.
    "Where my hands avail to reach not,
Let the hands of God be resting;
Where I cannot reach my fingers,
There let God extend his fingers;   40
Far more skilful are his fingers,
The Creator's hands more active.
    "O Creator, work thy magic,
Speak, O Jumala, unto us,
Deign to gaze on us, Almighty!
Let those who at night are healthy,
Likewise in the day be healthy,
Let no suffering fall upon them,
And no sickness come among them,
Nor their hearts be filled with anguish,   350
That they feel no slightest evil,
Feel no more the slightest suffering,
In the course of all their lifetime,
While the golden moon is shining."
    Väinämöinen, old and steadfast,
He the great primeval sorcerer,
Thus at length dispelled the evils,
Raised their burdens from his people,
Drove away the plagues of magic,
Healed the magical diseases,   360
And from death he saved his people,
Thus saved Kaleva's descendants.

Runo XLVI.—Väinämöinen and the Bear

Argument

The Mistress of Pohjola sends a bear to destroy the herds of Kalevala
(1–20).   Väinämöinen kills the bear, and a great feast is held in Kalevala
in honour of the occasion (21–606).   Väinämöinen sings, plays on the
kantele, and hopes that a time of great happiness and prosperity is
coming to Kalevala (607–644).

UNTO Pohjola came tidings,
To the village cold the tidings
That in Väinölä 'twas healthy,
Freed was Kalevala completely
From the evil plagues of magic,
And the scourge of nameless sickness.
  Louhi, Pohjola's old Mistress,
Old and gap-toothed dame of Pohja,
Thereupon again grew furious,
And she spoke the words which follow :   10
" Still I know another method,
And a cunning scheme have thought on.
On the heath the Bear I'll waken,
On the waste the curving-clawed one,
Väinölä's fine flocks to ravage,
Herds of Kalevala to slaughter."
  On the heath the bear she wakened,
From his native land she drove him
To the heathlands of Väinölä,
And to Kalevala's green pastures.   20
  Väinämöinen, old and steadfast,
Uttered then the words which follow :
" Ilmarinen, smith and brother,
Make a new spear quickly for me,
Make it with three cutting edges,
With a copper shaft construct it.
With the bear I now must struggle,
Overthrow the shaggy monster,

That he slay no more my geldings,
Nor shall fall upon my brood-mares,   30
Neither shall destroy my cattle,
Or attempt my cows to injure."
    Then the smith a spear constructed,
Not a long one, not a short one,
But of middle length he forged it.
On the blade a wolf was sitting,
On the edge a bear was standing,
At the joint an elk was trotting,
On the shaft a colt was running,
At the end a reindeer leaping.   40
Then fresh snow was gently falling,
And a little snow had drifted
As it drifts in early autumn,
White as is the hare in winter.
    Said the aged Väinämöinen,
And he spoke the words which follow:
" Now my inclination leads me
Unto Metsola to travel ;
To the forest's daughter's dwelling,
And to the Blue Maiden's homestead.   50
Leaving men, I seek the forest,
Heroes leave, for distant regions.
Take me as thy man, O forest,
Take me, Tapio, for thy hero.
May good fortune now be granted,
And to fell the forest-beauty.
    " Mielikki, the forest's Mistress,
Tellervo, the wife of Tapio,
Do thou bind thy dogs securely,
Do thou keep thy whelps in order,   60
In the paths, 'mid honeysuckle,
And beneath the roof of oakwood.
    " Otso, apple of the forest,
O thou lazy honey-pawed one !
If thou hearest me approaching,
Hearest me, the hero, coming,
In thy hair thy claws conceal thou,
In thy gums thy teeth conceal thou,

That thou never more may'st move them,
That they motionless remain there. 70
 "O my Otso, O my darling,
Fair one with the paws of honey,
Do thou rest in hilly country,
And among the rocks so lovely,
Where the pines above are waving,
And the firs below are rustling.
Turn thyself around, O Otso,
Turn thee round, O honey-pawed one,
As upon her nest the woodgrouse,
Or as turns the goose when brooding." 80
  Then the aged Väinämöinen
Heard his dog was barking loudly,
And the dog was fiercely baying
Just beside the Small-eye's dwelling,
In the pathway of the Broad-nose;
And he spoke the words which follow:
"First I thought it was a cuckoo,
Thought I heard a love-bird singing,
But no cuckoo there is calling,
And no love-bird there is singing, 90
But it is my dog that's baying,
Here my faithful hound awaits me,
At the door of Otso's dwelling,
At the handsome hero's homestead."
  Then the aged Väinämöinen
Struck the bear where he was lying,
Overturned his bed of satin,
Overthrew his lair so golden,
And he spoke the words which follow,
And in words like these expressed him: 100
"Praise, O Jumala, unto thee,
Praise to thee alone, Creator,
Unto me the bear who gavest,
And the forest gold hast granted."
  Gazed he on the golden booty,
And he spoke the words which follow:
"O my Otso, O my darling,
Fair one with the paws of honey,

Be not filled with causeless anger,
I myself have not o'erthrown thee,   110
Thou thyself hast left the forest,
Wandered from thy pine-tree covert,
Thou hast torn away thy clothing,
Ripped thy grey cloak in the thicket.
Slippery is this autumn weather,
Cloudy are the days and misty.
  " Golden cuckoo of the forest,
Shaggy-haired and lovely creature,
Do thou quit thy chilly dwelling,
Do thou quit thy native desert,   120
And thy home of birchen branches,
Wattled wigwam where thou dwellest.
Go to wander in the open,
O thou beauty of the forest,
On thy light shoes wandering onward,
Marching in thy blue-hued stockings,
Leaving now this little dwelling.
Do thou leave this narrow dwelling,
Leave it for the mighty heroes,
To the race of men resign it.   130
There are none will treat thee badly,
And no wretched life awaits thee.
For thy food they'll give thee honey,
And for drink, of mead the freshest,
When thou goest to a distance,
Whither with the staff they guide thee.
  " From this place depart thou quickly,
From thy little nest depart thou,
From beneath these famous rafters,
From beneath this roof so handsome ;   140
Glide along upon thy snowshoes,
As on pond a water-lily,
Then glide on among the fir-trees,
Like a squirrel in the branches."
  Then the aged Väinämöinen,
He the great primeval minstrel,
Walked across the plains, loud-playing,
O'er the heath he wandered singing,

And he brought the noble stranger.
With his shaggy friend he wandered.   150
In the house was heard his playing,
'Neath the roofs they heard his singing.

In the house there cried the people,
And exclaimed the handsome people,
" Listen to the noise resounding,
To the music from the forest,
Like the singing of the crossbill,
Or a maiden's flute in forest."

Väinämöinen, old and steadfast,
Then the house was fast approaching.   160
From the house there called the people,
And the handsome people asked him,
" Have you brought the bright gold with you,
Have you brought the silver hither,
Brought our darling money with you,
Gathered money on your journey?
Gave the wood the honey-eater,
And a lynx to lord of forest,
That you come among us singing,
On your snowshoes come rejoicing?"   170

Väinämöinen, old and steadfast,
Answered in the words which follow :
" Singing would I bring the otter,
Give to Jumala my praises,
So I sing as I am coming,
On my snowshoes come rejoicing.

" What I bring is not an otter,
Not a lynx, and not an otter,
One more famous is approaching,
Comes the pride of all the forest.   180
Comes an old man wandering hither,
With his overcoat he cometh.
If it be a pleasure to you,
Let the doors be widely opened ;
But if you dislike the stranger,
Close the doors against him firmly."

And the people gave him answer,
Shouted all the handsome people,

"Welcome, Otso, be thy coming,
Honey-pawed, who now approachest   190
To our dwelling, freshly scoured,
To our household, now so charming.
  "This I wished for all my lifetime,
All my youth I waited for it,
Tapio's horn to hear resounding,
And to hear the wood-pipe whistling,
Wandering through the golden forest,
Coming through the silver woodland,
And our little house approaching,
And along the narrow pathway.   200
  "I had hoped a year of fortune,
Waiting for the coming summer,
As for new-fallen snow the snowshoe,
Or a path for gliding suited,
As a maiden for her lover,
Or a consort for a red-cheek.
  "In the eve I sat at window,
Morning, at the door of storehouse,
At the gate a week I waited,
And a month at pathway's opening.   210
In the lane I stayed a winter,
Stood in snow while ground was hardened,
Till the hardened land grew softer,
And the soft ground turned to gravel,
And to sand was changed the gravel,
And the sand at length grew verdant,
And I pondered every morning,
In my head reflected daily,
'Wherefore is the Bear delaying?
Why delays the forest's darling?   220
Has he travelled to Esthonia,
Wandered from the land of Suomi?'"
  Then the aged Väinämöinen
Answered in the words that follow:
"Where's my guest to be conducted,
Whither shall I lead my gold one?
To the barn shall I conduct him
On a bed of straw to lay him?"

And the people gave him answer,
Shouted all the handsome people,   230
" Better lead our guest illustrious,
And conduct our golden beauty
Underneath these famous rafters,
Underneath this roof so handsome.
There is food arranged for eating,
There is drink poured out for drinking,
All the floors have there been dusted,
And the floors been swept most cleanly,
All the women finely dressed them,
In their very finest garments,   240
Donned their head-dresses the finest,
In their brightest robes arrayed them."
    Then the aged Väinämöinen
Spoke aloud the words which follow :
"O my Otso, O my birdling,
O my charge, with paws of honey,
Still there's ground for thee to walk on,
And upon the heath to wander.
    "Golden one, go forth to wander,
Dear one, range about the country,   250
Forth to march with sable stockings,
Wander in thy cloth-made trousers,
On the pathway of the titmouse,
And the path where sparrows wander,
Underneath five rafters straying,
Underneath six roof-trees walking.
    "Now be careful, luckless woman,
That the herd may not be frightened,
Terrified the little cattle,
Nor the mistress' calves be frightened,   260
If the bear approach the homestead,
And his shaggy jaws should seize them.
    "Now, ye boys, the porch abandon,
Girls, depart ye from the door-posts,
To the house there comes the hero,
And the pride of men approaches.
    "Otso, apple of the forest,
Fair and bulky forest dweller,

Be not frightened at the maidens,
Fear not the unbraided maidens,   270
Be not fearful of the women,
They the wearers of the stockings.
All the women of the household
Quickly round the stove will gather,
When they see the hero enter,
And behold the youth advancing."
    Said the aged Väinämöinen,
" Jumala be gracious to us,
Underneath these famous rafters,
Underneath this roof so handsome.   280
Whither shall I take my darling,
And shall bring the shaggy creature?"
    And the people spoke in answer,
" Hail, all hail to thee who comest!
Thither shalt thou bring thy birdling,
Thither take thy golden beauty
To the end of pole of pinewood,
To the end of bench of iron,
That his shaggy coat we gaze on,
And his hair may well examine.   290
    " Be not grieved for this, O Otso,
Neither let it make thee angry,
That we take thy hide an hour,
And thy hair to gaze on always.
For thy hide will not be injured,
And thy hair will not be draggled,
Like the rags of evil people,
Or the clothing of the beggars."
    Then the aged Väinämöinen
From the bear stripped off the bearskin,   300
On the storehouse floor he laid it,
Put the flesh into the kettles,
Put it in the gilded kettles,
In the copper caldrons placed it.
    On the fire the pots arranged he,
In the blaze their sides of copper,
Filled them up, and overfilled them,
With the meat he overfilled them,

Salt unto the stew he added,
Brought from very distant regions, 310
From the Saxon land they brought it,
And from distant waters brought it,
Through the Sound of Salt they rowed it,
And they from the ships conveyed it.

When the meat enough was sodden,
From the fire they took the kettles,
And the booty then was carried.
And the crossbill then they carried
Quickly to the long deal table,
In the golden dishes laid it, 320
Where they sat the mead enjoying,
And the beer they were imbibing.

And of firwood was the table,
And the dishes were of copper,
And the spears were all of silver,
And the knives of gold constructed.
All the plates were overloaded,
Brimming o'er were all the dishes,
With the darling of the forest,
Booty of the golden woodland. 330

Then the aged Väinämöinen
Spoke aloud the words that follow:
"Comrade old, with golden bosom,
Master thou of Tapio's household;
Thou of Metsola sweet matron,
Gracious Mistress of the Forest;
Handsome man, the son of Tapio,
Handsome red-capped son of Tapio;
Tellervo, the maid of Tapio;
All the rest of Tapio's people, 340

"Come ye to the feast of cattle,
Where the shaggy beast is eaten;
Here is plenty to be eaten,
Here is food and drink abundant,
Here there is enough for storage,
Plenty too, to give the village."

And the people then responded,
Answered thus the handsome people:

"Where was Otso born and nurtured,
Whence was formed his hide so shaggy, 350
Was he born perchance in straw-bed,
Was he born near stove in bathroom?"
   Then the aged Väinämöinen
Answered in the words which follow:
"Otso was not born in straw-bed.
Nor was born on chaff in malt-house;
There was Otso brought to being,
There was born the honey-pawed one,
Near the moon, in gleams of sunshine,
And upon the Great Bear's shoulders, 360
There beside the Air's fair maiden,
Near the daughter of Creation.
   "On Air's borders walked a maiden,
Through mid heaven there walked a damsel,
Through the rifted clouds she wandered,
On the borders of the heavens,
Clad in stockings, blue in colour,
And with shoes most gaily coloured,
In her hand a wool-filled satchel,
'Neath her arm a hair-filled basket. 370
Wool she cast upon the waters,
Hair she threw among the billows,
And the wind arose and tossed it,
And the air unceasing rocked it,
And the breeze on water rocked it,
To the shore the waves impelled it,
To the edge of honeyed forest,
To the end of honeyed headland.
   "Mielikki, the forest's Mistress,
Tapiola's accomplished matron, 380
Took the wool from out the water,
Took the soft wool from the billows.
Then she wrapped it all together,
With a handsome band she wrapped it,
Put it in her maple basket,
In a beauteous cradle laidi t,
Then she lifted up the bundle,
And the golden chains she carried

Where the branches were the thickest
And the leaves were most abundant.   390
  "Then she rocked the charming object,
And she rocked the lovely creature
Underneath a spreading fir-tree,
Underneath a blooming pine-tree.
Thus it was the bear was nurtured,
And the furry beast was fostered,
There beside a bush of honey,
In a forest dripping honey.
  "Now the bear grew up most handsome,
And attained his perfect stature.   400
Short his legs, his knees were crooked,
Broad his nose, both thick and stumpy,
Broad his head and short his muzzle,
And his handsome hair was shaggy,
But as yet the bear was tailless,
And with claws was unprovided
  "Mielikki, the forest's Mistress,
Uttered then the words which follow:
'Now let claws be granted to him,
And let teeth be also sought for,   410
If he does no mischief with them,
Nor to evil purpose turns them.'
  "Then the bear by oath engaged him,
Kneeling by the forest's Mistress,
And in Jumala's high presence,
'Fore the face of Him Almighty,
Never would he work a mischief,
And would work no evil with them.
  "Mielikki, the forest's Mistress,
Tapiola's accomplished matron,   420
Went to seek the teeth he needed,
And to seek the claws he wanted,
From the wood of mountain ash-tree,
And from juniper the hardest,
From the hardest roots of any,
From the hardest resinous tree-stumps,
But she found no claws among them,
Neither found she teeth among them.

"On the heath there grew a pine-tree,
On the hill there rose a fir-tree,   430
And the pine had silver branches,
And the fir-tree golden branches.
With her hands she plucked the branches,
And from these the claws constructed,
Others fixed in Otso's jawbones,
In his gums securely fixed them.
    "Forth she sent the shaggy creature,
Sent her darling forth to wander,
Let him wander through the marshes,
Let him wander through the forest,   440
Walk along the woodland's borders,
Step along across the heathland,
And she bade him walk discreetly,
And to march along demurely,
And to live a life of pleasure,
And upon fine days to wander,
Through the plains and o'er the marshes,
Past the heaths where men are dancing,
Wandering shoeless in the summer,
Wandering sockless in the autumn,   450
Resting in the worst of weather,
Idling in the cold of winter,
In a hollow stump of cherry,
In the castle of the pine-trees,
At the foot of beauteous fir-trees,
'Mid the junipers close-growing,
Underneath five woollen mantles,
'Neath eight mantles was he hidden,
And from thence I fetched my booty,
There I found it on my journey."   460
    Then the younger people asked him,
And the old folks asked him likewise:
"Wherefore was the wood so gracious,
Gracious wood, and forest lavish,
And the greenwood's lord so joyous,
So propitious friendly Tapio,
That he thus his pet has given,
And resigned the honey-eater?

Did you with the spear attack him,
Was he overcome with arrows ? "   470
    Väinämöinen, old and steadfast,
Answered in the words which follow :
" Very gracious was the forest,
Gracious wood, and forest lavish,
And the greenwood's lord was joyous,
And propitious friendly Tapio.

    " Mielikki, the forest's Mistress,
Tellervo, the maid of Tapio,
Fair-haired damsel of the forest,
Little damsel of the forest,   480
Went along the path to guide me,
And to raise the landmarks for me,
By the roadside posts erected,
And directed all my journey,
And the trees she blazed before me,
Marks she set upon the mountains,
To the door of noble Otso,
To the borders of his dwelling.

    " When I reached the place I sought for,
And arrived upon its borders,   490
With the spear I smote not Otso,
And I shot no arrows at him.
He himself lurched from the archway,
Tumbled from the pine-tree's summit,
And the branches broke his breastbone,
Others ripped his belly open."

    Then he spoke the words which follow,
And in words like these expressed him :
" O my Otso, O my dearest,
O my birdling, O my darling,   500
Now resign to us thy headland,
Lay aside thine eye-teeth likewise,
Cast away the few teeth left thee,
And thy wide jaws give us also,
Yet thou needest not be angry,
That I come to thee in thiswise,
And thy bones and skull have broken,
And have dashed thy teeth together.

"Now I take the nose from Otso,
That my own nose may be lengthened,   510
But I take it not completely,
And I do not take it only.

"Now I take the ears of Otso,
That my own ears I may lengthen,
But I take them not completely,
And I do not take them only.

"Now I take the eyes of Otso,
That my own eyes I may lengthen,
But I take them not completely,
And I do not take them only.   520

"Now will I take Otso's forehead,
That my forehead I may lengthen,
But I take it not completely,
And I do not take it only.

"Now I take the mouth of Otso,
That my own mouth may be lengthened,
But I take it not completely,
And I do not take it only.

"Now I take the tongue of Otso,
That my own tongue may be lengthened,   530
But I take it not completely,
And I do not take it only.

"He shall be a man respected,
And as hero shall be reckoned,
Who the bear's teeth now can number,
And the rows of teeth can loosen
From the jaws of steely hardness,
With his grasp as strong as iron."

As no other man came forward,
And no hero would attempt it,   540
He himself the bear's teeth numbered,
And the rows of teeth he reckoned,
Kneeling down beneath the jawbones,
With his grasp as strong as iron.

From the bear the teeth then taking,
Uttered he the words which follow :
"Otso, apple of the forest,
Fair and bulky forest-dweller,

Thou must go upon thy journey,
Leap along upon the journey,   550
Forth from out this narrow dwelling,
From this low and narrow cottage,
To a lofty house that waits thee,
To a wide and pleasant dwelling.
   "Golden one, go forth to wander,
Dearest treasure, march thou onward,
On the swine's path march thou onward,
Traversing the road of piglings,
To the firwood so luxuriant,
To the needle-covered pine-trees,   560
To the hills all clothed with forest,
To the lofty-rising mountains.
Here for thee to dwell is pleasant,
Charming is it to abide there,
Where the cattle-bells are ringing,
And the little bells are tinking."
   Väinämöinen, old and steadfast,
After this his dwelling entered,
And the younger people asked him,
All the handsome people asked him,   570
"Where have you bestowed your booty,
Whither did you make your journey?
Have you left him in the icefield,
In the snow-slush have you sunk him,
Pushed him down in the morasses,
Buried him upon the heathland?"
   Väinämöinen, old and steadfast,
Answered in the words which follow:
"In the ice I did not leave him,
Sunk him not among the snow-slush,   580
For the dogs from thence would drag him,
Likewise would the birds befoul him.
In the swamp I have not sunk him,
Nor upon the heath have buried,
For the worms would there destroy him
And the black ants would devour him.
   "Thither have I brought my booty,
There bestowed my little captive,

On a golden mountain's summit,
On a copper mountain's summit.   590
In a splendid tree I laid him,
Pine-tree with a hundred needles,
In the very largest branches,
In the broad and leafy summit,
As a joy to men for ever,
And a pleasure to the travellers.
    "Then I turned his gums to eastward,
And his eyes I turned to north-west,
Not too high upon the summit,
Lest if they were in the summit,   600
Then the wind might perhaps destroy them,
And the spring wind treat them badly.
Nor too near the ground I placed them,
Lest if I too low had laid them,
Then the pigs might perhaps disturb them,
And the snouted ones o'erturn them."
    Then the aged Väinämöinen
Once again prepared for singing,
For a splendid evening's pleasure,
And a charm to day departing.   610
    Said the aged Väinämöinen,
And in words like these expressed him:
" Keep thy light, O holder, shining,
So that I can see while singing,
For the time has come for singing,
And my mouth to sing is longing."
    Played and sang old Väinämöinen,
Charming all throughout the evening,
And when he had ceased his singing,
Then a speech he made concluding: 620
    "Grant, O Jumala, in future,
Once again, O good Creator,
That once more we meet rejoicing,
And may once again assemble
Here to feast on bear so fattened,
Feasting on the shaggy creature.
    "Grant, O Jumala, for ever,
Grant again, O good Creator,

That the posts be raised to guide us,
And the trees be blazed before us,   630
For the most heroic people,
For the manly race of heroes.
  " Grant, O Jumala, for ever,
Grant again, O good Creator,
That may sound the horn of Tapio,
And the forest-pipe may whistle
Even in this little courtyard,
Even in this narrow homestead.
  " In the day may we be playing,
And at eventide rejoicing,   640
In this firm and solid country,
In the wide expanse of Suomi,
With the young who now are growing,
With the rising generation."

RUNO XLVII.—THE ROBBERY OF THE SUN AND MOON

Argument

The moon and sun descend to listen to Väinämöinen's playing. The
Mistress of Pohjola succeeds in capturing them, hides them in a mountain, and steals the fire from the homes of Kalevala (1–40). Ukko, the
Supreme God, is surprised at the darkness in the sky, and kindles fire
for a new moon and a new sun (41–82). The fire falls to the ground,
and Väinämöinen and Ilmarinen go to search for it (83–126). The
Virgin of the Air informs them that the fire has fallen into Lake Alue,
and has been swallowed by a fish (127–312). Väinämöinen and
Ilmarinen try to catch the fish with a net of bast, but without success
(313–364).

VÄINÄMÖINEN, old and steadfast,
On his kantele was playing,
Long he played, and long was singing,
And was ever full of gladness.
  In the moon's house heard they playing,
Came delight to the sun's window,
And the moon came from his dwelling,
Standing on a crooked birch-tree,

And the sun came from his castle,
Sitting on a fir-tree's summit,   10
To the kantele to listen,
Filled with wonder and rejoicing.
   Louhi, Pohjola's old Mistress,
Old and gap-toothed dame of Pohja,
Set to work the sun to capture,
In her hands the moon seized likewise.
From the birch the moon she captured,
And the sun from fir-tree's summit;
Straightway to her home she brought them,
To the gloomy land of Pohja.   20
   Then she hid the moon from shining,
In the mottled rocks she hid him,
Sang the sun to shine no longer,
Hidden in a steel-hard mountain;
And she spoke the words which follow:
"Never more again in freedom
Shall the moon arise for shining,
Nor the sun be free for shining,
If I come not to release them,
If I do not go to fetch them,   30
When I bring nine stallions with me,
Which a single mare has littered."
   When the moon away was carried,
And the sun had been imprisoned
Deep in Pohjola's stone mountain,
In the rocks as hard as iron,
Then she stole away the brightness,
And from Väinölä the fires,
And she left the houses fireless,
And the rooms no flame illumined.   40
   Therefore was the night unending,
And for long was utter darkness,
Night in Kalevala for ever,
And in Väinölä's fair dwellings,
Likewise in the heavens was darkness,
Darkness round the seat of Ukko.
   Life without the fire was weary,
And without the light a burden,

Unto all mankind 'twas dismal,
And to Ukko's self 'twas dismal.   50
   Ukko, then, of Gods the highest,
In the air the great Creator,
Now began to feel most strangely,
And he pondered and reflected,
What strange thing the moon had darkened,
How the sun had been obstructed,
That the moon would shine no longer,
And the sun had ceased his shining.
   Then he stepped to cloudland's borders,
On the borders of the heavens,   60
Wearing now his pale blue stockings,
With the heels of varied colour,
And he went the moon to seek for,
And he went to find the sunlight,
Yet he could not find the moonlight,
Nor the sun he could discover.
   In the air a light struck Ukko,
And a flame did Ukko kindle,
From his flaming sword he struck it,
Sparks he struck from off the sword-blade,   70
From his nails he struck the fire,
From his limbs he made it crackle,
High above aloft in heaven,
On the starry plains of heaven.
When the fire had thus been kindled,
Then he took the spark of fire,
In his golden purse he thrust it,
Placed it in his silver casket,
And he bade the maiden rock it,
Told the maid of air to rock it,   80
That a new moon might be fashioned,
And a new sun be constructed.
   On the long cloud's edge she sat her,
On the air-marge sat the maiden,
There it was she rocked the fire,
There she rocked the glowing brightness,
In a golden cradle rocked it,
With a silver cord she rocked it.

Then the silver props were shaken,
Rocked about the golden cradle,   90
Moved the clouds and creaked the heavens,
And the props of heaven were swaying,
With the rocking of the fire,
And the rocking of the brightness.

Thus the maid the fire was rocking,
And she rocked the fire to brightness,
With her fingers moved the fire,
With her hands the fire she tended,
And the stupid maiden dropped it,
Dropped the flame the careless maiden,   100
From her hands the fire dropped downward
From the fingers of its guardian.

Then the sky was cleft asunder,
All the air was filled with windows,
Burst asunder by the fire-sparks,
As the red drop quick descended,
And a gap gleamed forth in heaven,
As it through the clouds dropped downward,
Through nine heavens the drop descended,
Through six spangled vaults of heaven.   110

Said the aged Väinämöinen,
"Smith and brother, Ilmarinen,
Let us go and gaze around us,
And the cause perchance discover,
What the fire that just descended,
What the strange flame that has fallen
From the lofty height of heaven,
And to earth beneath descended.
Of the moon 'tis perhaps a fragment,
Of the sun perchance a segment."   120

Thereupon set forth the heroes,
And they wandered on, reflecting
How they might perchance discover,
How they might succeed in finding,
Where the fire had just descended,
Where the brightness had dropped downward.

And a river flowed before them,
And became a lake extensive,

And the aged Väinämöinen
Straight began a boat to fashion, 130
In the wood he worked upon it,
And beside him Ilmarinen
Made a rudder out of firwood,
Made it from a log of pinewood.

    Thus the boat at length was ready,
Rowlocks, rudder all completed,
And they pushed it in the water,
And they rowed and steered it onward,
All along the river Neva,
Steering round the Cape of Neva. 140

    Ilmatar, the lovely damsel,
Eldest Daughter of Creation,
Then advanced to meet the heroes,
And in words like these addressed them:
"Who among mankind may ye be?
By what names do people call you?"

    Said the aged Väinämöinen,
"You may look on us as sailors.
I am aged Väinämöinen,
Ilmarinen, smith, is with me, 150
But inform us of your kindred;
By what name do people call you?"

    Then the matron made them answer,
"I am oldest of all women,
Of the air the oldest damsel,
And the first of all the mothers.
Five times now have I been married,
Six times as a bride attired.
Whither do you take your journey,
Whither, heroes, are you going?" 160

    Said the aged Väinämöinen,
And he spoke the words which follow:
"All our fires have been extinguished,
And their flames died down in darkness,
Long already were we fireless,
And in darkness were we hidden,
But at length have we determined
That the fire we ought to seek for,

Which has just dropped down from heaven,
From above the clouds has fallen."   170
　　Then the woman gave them answer,
And she spoke the words which follow :
" Hard it is to track the fire,
And the bright flame to discover.
It has evil wrought already,
And the flame has crime committed,
For the red spark has shot downward,
And the red ball has descended
From the realms of the Creator,
Where it was by Ukko kindled,   180
Through the level plains of heaven,
Through the void aërial spaces,
Downwards through the sooty smoke-hole,
Downward through the seasoned roof-tree
Of the new-built house of Tuuri,
Of a wretched roofless dwelling.
　　" When the fire at length came thither,
In the new-built house of Tuuri,
Evil deeds he then accomplished,
Shocking deeds he then accomplished,   190
Burning up the maidens' bosoms,
Tearing at the breasts of maidens,
And the knees of boys destroying,
And the master's beard consuming.
　　" And her child the mother suckled,
In a cradle of misfortune.
Thither, too, the fire rushed onward,
And its evil work accomplished,
In the cradle burned the baby,
Burning, too, the mother's bosom,   200
And the child went off to Mana,
And the boy went straight to Tuoni.
Thus it was the infant perished,
And was cast into destruction,
In the red flame's fiery torture,
In the anguish of its glowing.
　　" Great the knowledge of the mother,
And to Manala she went not.

Means she knew to ban the fire,
And to drive away its glowing,   210
Through the little eye of needle,
And across the back of axe-blade,
Through the sheath of glowing sword-blade,
Past the ploughed land did she drive it."
    Väinämöinen, old and steadfast,
Heard her words, and then made answer:
" Whither has the fire retreated,
Whither did the pest take refuge,
Was it in the field of Tuuri,
In a lake, or in a forest ? "   220
    Then the matron made him answer,
And she spoke the words which follow:
" When from thence the fire departed,
And the flame went wandering onward,
First it burned o'er many districts,
Many districts, many marshes,
Rushed at last into the water,
In the billows of Lake Alue,
And the fire rose up all flaming,
And the sparks arose all crackling.   230
    " Three times in the nights of summer,
Nine times in the nights of autumn,
Rose the lake the height of fir-trees,
Roaring rose above the lake-banks,
With the strength of furious fire,
With the strength of heat all flaming.
    " On the bank were thrown the fishes,
On the rocks the perch were stranded,
And the fishes looked around them,
And the perch were all reflecting   240
How they could continue living.
Perch were weeping for their dwellings,
Fish were weeping for their homesteads,
Perches for their rocky castles.
    " And the perch with back all crooked,
Tried to seize the streak of fire,
But the perch was not successful;
Seized upon it the blue powan.,

Down he gulped the streak of fire,
And extinguished thus its brightness.   250
    "Then retired the Lake of Alue,
And fell back from all its margins,
Sinking to its former level
In a single night of summer.
    "When a little time passed over,
Fire-pain seized on the devourer,
Anguish came upon the swallower,
Grievous suffering on the eater.
    "Up and down the fish swam turning,
Swam for one day and a second,   260
All along the powan's island,
Clefts in rocks where flock the salmon,
To the points of capes a thousand,
Bays among a hundred islands.
Every cape made declaration,
Every island spoke in thiswise :
    "'Nowhere in these sluggish waters,
In the narrow Lake of Alue,
Can the wretched fish be swallowed,
Or the hapless one may perish   270
In the torture of the fire,
In the anguish of its glowing.'
    "But a salmon-trout o'erheard it,
And the powan blue he swallowed.
When a little time passed over,
Fire-pain seized on the devourer,
Anguish came upon the swallower,
Grievous suffering on the eater.
    "Up and down the fish swam turning,
Swam for one day and a second,   280
Through the clefts where flock the salmon,
And the depths where sport the fishes,
To the points of capes a thousand,
Bays among a hundred islands.
Every cape made declaration,
Every island spoke in thiswise :
    "'Nowhere in these sluggish waters,
In the narrow Lake of Alue,

Can the wretched fish be swallowed,
Or the hapless one may perish   290
In the pain of burning fire,
In the anguish of its glowing.'
    " But a grey pike hurried forward,
And the salmon-trout he swallowed.
When a little time passed over,
Fire-pain seized on the devourer,
Anguish came upon the swallower,
Grievous suffering on the eater.
    " Up and down the fish swam turning,
Swam for one day and a second,   300
Past the cliffs where flock the seagulls,
And the rocks where sport the seamews,
To the points of capes a thousand,
Bays among a hundred islands.
Every cape made declaration,
Every island spoke in thiswise :
    " ' Nowhere in these sluggish waters,
In the narrow Lake of Alue,
Can the wretched fish be swallowed,
Or the hapless one may perish   310
In the pain of burning fire,
In the anguish of its glowing.' "
    Then the aged Väinämöinen,
Secondly, smith Ilmarinen,
Wove a net of bast constructed,
Which from juniper they gathered,
Steeped it in the juice of willow,
And of sallow-bark they made it.
    Väinämöinen, old and steadfast
Sent the women to the drag-net ;   320
To the net there went the women,
Sisters came to draw the drag-net ;
And he steered, and glided onward
Past the capes and round the islands,
To the clefts where flock the salmon,
And along the powan's island,
Where the red-brown reeds are waving,
And among the beauteous rushes.

Eager now to make a capture,
Then he cast the net and sunk it,   330
But he cast the net out twisted,
And in wrong direction drew it,
And the fish they could not capture,
Though with eagerness they laboured.

In the water went the brothers,
To the net the men proceeded,
And they swung it and they pushed it,
And they pulled it and they dragged it
Through the deeps, and rocky places,
Drew it o'er Kalevala's shingle ;   340
But the fish they could not capture ;
Not the fish so greatly needed.
Came the grey pike never near them,
Neither on the placid water,
Nor upon its ample surface ;
Fish are small, and nets not many.

Now the fish were all complaining ;
Said one pike unto another,
And the powan asked the ide-fish,
And one salmon asked another :   350
" Can the famous men have perished,
Perished Kaleva's great children,
They who drag the net of linen,
And of yarn have made the fish-net,
With long poles who beat the water,
With long sticks who move the waters ? "

Old and famous Väinämöinen
Answered in the words which follow :
" No, the heroes have not perished,
Kaleva's great race has died not,   360
When one dies, is born another,
And the best of staves they carry,
Longer sticks to sound the water,
And their nets are twice as fearful."

RUNO XLVIII.—THE CAPTURE OF THE FIRE

Argument

The heroes prepare a linen net, and at length capture the fish which has swallowed the fire (1–192). The fire is found in the fish's belly, but flashes up suddenly, and burns Ilmarinen's cheeks and hands severely (193–248). The fire rushes into the forest, burns over many countries, and spreads further and further, till at length it is captured and carried to the dark dwellings of Kalevala (249–290). Ilmarinen recovers from his burns (291–372).

VÄINÄMÖINEN, old and steadfast,
He the great primeval minstrel,
Thereupon began to ponder,
And reflected on the method
How to make a net of linen,
How to make the hundred meshes.
    Then he spoke the words which follow,
And expressed himself in thiswise :
" Is there one who flax can sow me,
Who can sow the flax and card it,   10
And of this a net can make me,
Weave for me its hundred meshes,
Thus this wretched fish to slaughter,
And destroy the fish unhappy ? "
    So a little spot they found him,
Found a place not yet burned over,
In the wide extent of marshes,
There between two stumps they found it.
    Thereupon they dug the roots out,
And 'twas there they found the flaxseed,   20
Guarded by the worm of Tuoni,
There protected by the earthworm.
    There they found a heap of ashes ;
Dry the ashes that they found there,
Of a wooden burned-up vessel,
Of a boat that once had burned there.

There it was they sowed the flaxseed,
In the loose ash did they sow it,
On the shore of Lake of Alue,
There they sowed it in the clayfield.   30
    Presently the shoot rose upward,
And the flax grew thick and strongly,
Grew beyond their expectations,
In a single night of summer.
Then they steeped it in the night-time,
And they carded it by moonlight,
And they cleansed it and they stripped it,
And they beat it and they rubbed it,
With their tools of steel they scraped it,
And with all their strength they stripped it.   40
Then they took the flax to steeping,
And it soon began to soften,
And they hastened then to pound it,
Afterwards in haste they dried it.
    Then into the house they brought it,
And they hastened then to strip it,
And they hastened next to beat it,
And they hastened then to break it.
    Then with diligence they cleansed it.
In the twilight did they comb it,   50
And upon the loom arranged it,
Quicker brought it to the spindle,
In a single night of summer;
Thus between two days they worked it.
    After this the sisters spun it,
And their brothers' wives were netting,
And the brothers worked the meshes,
And the fathers also aided.
    Quickly did they turn the netter,
And the mesh with speed they twisted,   60
Till the net was quite completed,
And the cords were fixed upon it,
In a single night of summer,
Half another in addition.
    Thus the net was quite completed,
And the cords were fixed upon it.

And its length was hundred fathoms,
And its breadth was hundreds seven;
Stones for weights were fastened to it,
Likewise proper floats provided.　　　　　　70

  With the net the youths were walking,
And at home the old men pondered,
Whether they would make a capture,
And secure the fish they wished for.

  Then they drew the net and dragged it,
Much they toiled, and threshed the water,
Drew it lengthwise through the water,
Dragged it crosswise through the water,
Captured many little fishes,
Many luckless perch they captured,　　　　80
Many bony perch they captured,
And a large-galled Redeye likewise,
But the fish they could not capture
That for which the net was fashioned.

  Said the aged Väinämöinen,
"O thou smith, O Ilmarinen,
Let us now go forth together
Where the net is in the water."

  Thereupon went both the heroes,
And they drew it through the water,　　　90
And upon one side they spread it
Round the islands in the water,
And the other side directed,
Round about the promontories,
And the balance-pole was guided
Just as aged Väinö pushed it.

  Thus they cast the net and pushed it,
And they drew the net and dragged it,
Captured fishes in abundance,
And they captured perch in plenty,　　　100
Salmon-trout in great abundance,
Bream and salmon too they captured,
All the fishes of the water,
Only not the fish they sought for,
That for which the net was woven,
And the ropes were fastened to it.

Then the aged Väinämöinen
Worked to make the net yet longer,
Wider yet the sides expanded,
Perhaps five hundred fathoms broader,   110
Netted full seven hundred fathoms,
And he spoke the words which follow:
"To the depths the nets we'll carry,
And will now extend them further,
Once again will drag the water,
Thus another cast attempting."

To the depths the nets they carried
Further did they then convey them,
And again they dragged the water,
Thus another cast attempting.   120

Then the aged Väinämöinen
Spoke aloud the words which follow:
"Vellamo, O Water-Mother,
Old one with the lavish bosom,
Do thou change the shift upon thee,
Do thou change thy dress completely,
For thou hast a shift of rushes,
On thy head a cap of lake-foam,
Fashioned by the Wind's fair daughter,
Which the billows' daughter gave thee.   130
Now assume a shift of linen,
Of the finest flax that's woven,
Which by Kuutar has been woven,
Päivätär has wrought when spinning.

"Ahto, master of the billows,
Ruler thou of caves a hundred,
Take thy pole in length five fathoms,
Take thy stake, in length full seven,
Thresh with this the open water,
And do thou stir up the lake-bed,   140
Stir thou all the heaps of refuse,
Drive thou on the shoals of fishes,
Where the net is spread to catch them,
And its hundred floats are swimming,
From the bays by fish frequented,
From the caves where hide the salmon,

From the wide lake's seething whirlpool,
And from the profound abysses,
Where the sun was never shining,
Undisturbed the sand for ever."   150
    From the lake a dwarf ascended,
From the waves arose a hero,
Stood upon the lake's broad surface,
And he spoke the words which follow:
"Is there need to thresh the water,
With a long pole to disturb it?"
    Väinämöinen, old and steadfast,
Answered in the words that follow:
"There is need to thresh the water,
With a long pole to disturb it."   160
Then the dwarf, the little hero,
Lifted from the bank a pine-tree,
Took a tall tree from the pinewood,
And prepared to thresh the water,
And he asked, and spoke as follows:
"Shall I thresh with strength sufficient,
Putting forth my utmost efforts,
Or as hard as may be needful?"
    Old and prudent Väinämöinen
Answered in the words which follow: 170
"If you thresh as hard as needful,
You will have to do much threshing."
    Then the man, the little hero,
Set to work to thresh the water,
And he threshed as much as needful,
And he drove the shoals of fishes,
And into the net he drove them,
In the net with floats a hundred.
    Rested now the smith his oars;
Väinämöinen, old and steadfast,   180
Now the net himself drew upward,
At the rope as he was pulling.
    Said the aged Väinämöinen,
"We have caught a shoal of fishes,
In the net that I am lifting,
With a hundred floats provided."

Then the net was soon drawn upward,
And they drew it up and shook it
In the boat of Väinämöinen,
Finding mid the shoal of fishes,   190
That for which the net was fashioned,
And the hundred floats provided.

Väinämöinen, old and steadfast,
To the land then urged the vessel,
To the blue bridge-side he brought it,
To the red bridge-end he brought it,
There the shoal of fishes sorted,
Turned the heap of bony fishes,
And the grey pike found among them,
Which he long had sought to capture.   200

Then the aged Väinämöinen
Thus unto himself reflected:
"Is it wise with hands to seize it,
Save with gauntlets made of iron,
Save with gloves of stone constructed,
Save with mittens made of copper?"

And the Sun's son heard him speaking,
And replied in words that follow:
"I myself would rip the pike up,
Venture in my hand to take him,   210
If I had my large knife only,
Which my noble father gave me."

Then from heaven the knife descended,
From the clouds the knife fell downward,
Golden-hafted, silver-bladed,
To the Sun's son's belt dropped downward.

Thereupon the Sun's son seized it,
Firmly in his hand he grasped it,
And with this the pike ripped open,
Cleft the body of the Broad-snout,   220
And within the grey pike's belly
There the grey trout he discovered,
And within the grey trout's belly
There he found the smooth-skinned powan.

Then he split the smooth-skinned powan,
And a blue clew he discovered,

In the powan's entrails hidden,
In the third fold of the entrails.
    Then the blue clew he unwinded;
From the inside of the blue clew   230
Fell a red clew from within it,
And when he unwound the red clew,
In the middle of the red clew,
There he found a spark of fire
Which had once from heaven descended,
Through the clouds had fallen downward,
From above eight heavens descending,
From the ninth aërial region.
    Väinämöinen then considered
How the spark might best be carried,   240
To the cold and fireless dwellings,
To the rooms so dark and gloomy.
But the fire flashed up most fiercely,
From the Sun's son's hands who held it,
Singed the beard of Väinämöinen,
Burned the smith much more severely,
For upon his cheeks it burned him,
And upon his hands it scorched him.
    And it hastened quickly onward
O'er the waves of Lake of Alue,   250
Through the junipers fled onward,
Burnt its way through all the thicket,
Then rushed upward through the fir-trees,
Burning up the stately fir-trees,
Rushing ever further onward,
Burned up half the land of Pohja,
And the furthest bounds of Savo,
Over both halves of Carelia.
    Väinämöinen, old and steadfast,
Followed hard upon its traces,   260
And he hastened through the forest,
Close behind the furious fire,
And at length he overtook it,
'Neath the roots of two great tree-stumps,
In the stumps of alders hidden,
In the rotten stumps he found it.

Then the aged Väinämöinen
Spoke aloud the words which follow:
"Fire, whom Jumala created,
Creature of the bright Creator,   270
Idly to the depths thou goest,
Aimlessly to distant regions.
It were better far to hide thee
In the hearth of stone constructed,
There thy sparks to bind together,
And within the coals enclose them,
That by day thou may'st be flickering
In the kitchen birchen faggots,
And at night thou may'st be hidden
Close within the golden fire-box."   280

Then he thrust the spark of fire
In a little piece of tinder,
In the fungus hard of birch-tree,
And among the copper kettles.
Fire he carried to the kettles,
Took it in the bark of birch-tree,
To the end of misty headland,
And the shady island's summit.
Now was fire within the dwellings,
In the rooms again 'twas shining.   290

But the smith named Ilmarinen
Quickly hastened to the lakeshore,
Where the rocks the water washes,
And upon the rocks he sat him,
In the pain of burning fire,
In the anguish of its glowing.

There it was he quenched the fire,
There it was he dimmed its lustre,
And he spoke the words which follow,
And in words like these expressed him: 300
"Fire whom Jumala created
And O thou, the Sun's son, Panu!
Who has made ye thus so angry,
As to scorch my cheeks in thiswise,
And to burn my hips so badly,
And my sides so much to injure?

" How shall I the fire extinguish,
How shall I reduce its glowing,
Make the fire for evil powerless,
And its lustre render harmless,   310
That no longer it may pain me,
And may cause me pain no longer ?

"Come, thou girl, from land of Turja,
Come, thou maiden, forth from Lapland,
Frosty-stockinged, icy-booted,
And thy skirts all frosted over,
In thy hand the icy kettle,
And the ice-spoon in the kettle.
Sprinkle me with freezing water,
Sprinkle me with icy water,   320
On the places scorched so badly,
And the burns the fire has caused me.

" But if this is not sufficient,
Come, thou youth, come forth from Pohja,
Come, thou child, from midst of Lapland,
From Pimentola, O tall one,
Tall as is a forest fir-tree,
Tall as pine-tree in the marshes,
On thy hands the gloves of hoarfrost,
On thy feet the boots of hoarfrost,   330
On thy head the cap of hoarfrost,
Round thy waist the belt of hoarfrost.

" Bring from Pohjola the hoarfrost,
Ice from out the frozen village.
Hoarfrost's plentiful in Pohja,
Ice enough in frozen village.
Lakes of ice, and frozen rivers,
All the air with ice is laden.
O'er the hoarfrost hares are skipping,
On the ice the bears are sporting,   340
In the middle of the snow-heaps,
On the edge of the snow mountains,
On the rims the swans are walking,
On the ice the ducks are waddling,
In the midst of snow-filled rivers,
Cornices of icy cataracts.

" On thy sledge bring thou the hoarfrost,
On thy sledge the ice convey thou,
From the slopes of rugged mountains,
From the lofty mountains' borders.   350
Make them hoary with the hoarfrost,
With the ice, O make them icy,
All the hurts by fire occasioned,
All the burns the fire has caused me.

" But if this is not sufficient,
Ukko, thou of Gods the highest,
Ukko, thou the clouds who leadest,
Thou the scattered clouds who herdest,
Send a cloud from out the eastward,
And a thick cloud from the westward,   360
Link the edges close together,
Close thou up the gaps between them,
Send thou ice, and send thou hoarfrost,
Send thou, too, the best of ointment,
For the places scorched so badly,
And the hurts by fire occasioned."

Thus it was smith Ilmarinen
Found a means to quench the fire,
And to dim the brilliant fire.
Thus the smith was healed completely,   370
And regained his former vigour,
Healed from wounds the fire occasioned.

Runo XLIX.—False and True Moons and Suns

Argument

Ilmarinen forges a new moon and sun but cannot make them shine (1–74). Väinämöinen discovers by divination that the moon and sun are hidden in the mountain of Pohjola, goes to Pohjola and conquers the whole nation (75–230). He sees the moon and sun in the mountain, but cannot enter (231–278). He returns home to procure tools with which to break open the mountain. While Ilmarinen is forging them, the Mistress of Pohjola, fearing that it may go ill with her, releases the moon and sun (279–362). When Väinämöinen sees the moon and sun reappear in the sky, he salutes them, hoping that they will always go brightly on their course, and bring happiness to the country (363–422).

Still the sun was never shining,
Neither gleamed the golden moonlight,
Not in Väinölä's dark dwellings,
Not on Kalevala's broad heathlands.
Frost upon the crops descended,
And the cattle suffered greatly,
And the birds of air felt strangely,
All mankind felt ever mournful,
For the sunlight shone no longer,
Neither did there shine the moonlight.

Though the pike knew well the pike-deeps,
And the bird-paths knew the eagle,
And the wind the vessel's journey,
Yet mankind were all unknowing
If the time was really morning,
Or if perhaps it still was night-time,
Out upon the cloudy headland,
And upon the shady island.
And the young men then took counsel,
And the older men considered   20
How to live without the moonlight,
And exist without the sunlight,
In that miserable country,
In the wretched land of Pohja.

And the girls took likewise counsel,
And their cousins too considered;
And they hastened to the smithy,
And they spoke the words which follow:
"Smith, from 'neath the wall arise thou,
From the hearthstone rise, O craftsman,   30
That a new moon thou may'st forge us,
And a new sun thou may'st make us.
Ill it is without the moonlight,
Strange it is without the sunlight."

From the hearth arose the craftsman,
From beneath the wall the craftsman,
That a new moon he might forge them,
And a new sun he might make them,
And a moon of gold constructed,
And a sun he made of silver.   40

Came the aged Väinämöinen,
And beside the door he sat him,
And he spoke the words which follow:
"O thou smith, my dearest brother,
What art thou in smithy forging,
Hammering thus without cessation?"

Thereupon smith Ilmarinen
Answered in the words that follow:
"Out of gold a moon I'm shaping,
And a sun of silver making,   50
In the sky I then will place them,
Over six of starry heavens."

Then the aged Väinämöinen
Answered in the words that follow:
"O thou smith, O Ilmarinen,
What you make is wholly useless.
Gold will never shine like moonlight,
Silver will not shine like sunlight."

Thus the smith a moon constructed,
And a sun completely finished,   60
Eagerly he raised them upward,
Raised them to the best position,
Raised the moon to fir-tree's summit,
Set the sun upon a pine-tree.

From his head the sweat was streaming,
From his forehead sweat was falling,
With the greatness of his efforts,
And the weight that he was lifting.
    Thus the moon was now uplifted,
In his place the sun was stationed,   70
Moon amid the crown of fir-tree,
Sun upon a pine-tree's summit,
But the moon shed forth no lustre,
And the sun was likewise rayless.
    Then the aged Väinämöinen
Spoke aloud the words which follow :
"Time it is the lots to shuffle,
And the signs with care to question
Where the sun is hidden from us,
And the moon has vanished from us."   80
    Then the aged Väinämöinen,
He the great primeval sorcerer,
Hastened alder-sticks to cut him,
And arranged the sticks in order,
And began the lots to shuffle,
With his fingers to arrange them,
And he spoke the words which follow,
And in words like these expressed him :
" Leave I ask of the Creator,
Seek an answer that misleads not.   90
Tell me, signs of the Creator,
Lots of Jumala, instruct me,
Where the sun is hidden from us,
And the moon has vanished from us,
Since no more as time elapses,
In the sky do we behold them ?
    " Speak, O lot, and tell me truly
With man's reason speak unto me,
Speak thou faithful words unto us,
Make thou faithful compacts with us !   100
If the lot should lie unto me,
Then its worth I hold as nothing,
And upon the fire will cast it,
And will burn the signs upon it.

And the lot spoke words most faithful,
And the signs made answer truly,
For they said the sun was hidden,
And the moon was also sunken,
Deep in Pohjola's stone mountain,
And within the hill of copper.   110

Väinämöinen, old and steadfast,
Uttered then the words which follow:
"I to Pohjola must journey,
On the path of Pohja's children,
And will bring the moon to shining,
And the golden sun to shining."

Forth he journeyed, and he hastened
Unto Pohjola's dark regions,
And he walked one day, a second,
And at length upon the third day   120
Came in view the gate of Pohja,
And appeared the rocky mountains.

Then with all his strength he shouted,
As he came to Pohja's river,
"Bring me here a boat directly
Which shall take me o'er the river."

As his shouting was not heeded,
And no boat for him provided,
Wood into a heap he gathered,
And the dead twigs of a fir-tree.   130
On the shore he made a fire,
And thick clouds of smoke rose upward;
To the sky the flame rose upward,
In the air the smoke ascended.

Louhi, Pohjola's old Mistress
Came herself unto the window,
And, at the sound's opening gazing,
Then she spoke the words which follow:
"What's the flame that's burning yonder,
Where the Sound of Saari opens?   140
For a camp too small I think it,
But 'tis larger than a fisher's."

Then the son of Pohja's country
Hurried out into the open,

And he looked about and listened,
Seeking thus for information.
"On the river's other margin,
Is a stately hero marching."
　　Then the aged Väinämöinen
Once again commenced his shouting.   150
"Bring a boat, O son of Pohja,
Bring a boat for Väinämöinen."
　　Answer made the son of Pohja,
And in words like these responded:
"Here the boats are never ready;
You to row must use your fingers,
And must use your hands for rudder,
Crossing Pohjola's deep river."
　　Then the aged Väinämöinen
Pondered deeply and reflected,   160
"Not as man should he be reckoned
Who retreats upon his pathway."
　　Like a pike in lake then plunging,
Powan-like in sluggish river,
Through the sound he swam right quickly,
Speedily the strait he traversed,
And he moved one foot, a second,
And he reached the shore of Pohja.
　　Then spoke out the sons of Pohja,
And the evil army shouted: 170
"Go into the yard of Pohja,"
And on this the yard he entered.
　　Then exclaimed the sons of Pohja,
And the evil army shouted:
"Enter now the house of Pohja."
And on this the house he entered,
On the floor his foot he planted,
Grasped he the door-handle firmly,
Forced his way into the dwelling,
And beneath the roof he entered.   180
There the men the mead were drinking,
And the honey-drink imbibing.
All the men with swords were girded,
And the heroes aimed their weapons

At the head of Väinämöinen,
Thus to slay Suvantolainen.
Then they questioned the intruder
In the very words that follow:
"What's your news, you wretched fellow,
What's your need, O swimming hero?"　　　190
　　Väinämöinen, old and steadfast,
Answered in the words which follow:
"Of the moon are curious tidings,
Of the sun are wondrous tidings.
Where is now the sun imprisoned,
Whither has the moon been taken?"
　　Answered then the sons of Pohja,
And the evil army answered:
"Thus it is the sun is hidden,
Sun is hidden, moon imprisoned,　　　200
In the stones of many colours,
In the rocks as hard as iron,
And from this, escape they cannot,
And release shall never reach them."
　　Then the aged Väinämöinen
Answered in the words that follow:
"If the sun from rock ascends not,
Nor the moon from rocky mountain,
Let us join in closest conflict,
Let us grasp our trusty sword-blades."　　　210
　　Sword they drew, and tried their sword-blades,
Drew from out the sheaths their weapons;
At the point the moon was shining,
On the hilt the sun was shining,
On the back a horse was standing,
At the knob a cat was mewing.
　　After this the swords they measured,
And they thus compared their weapons,
And the sword of aged Väinö
Was a little trifle longer,　　　220
Longer, as a grain of barley,
As the width of straw-stalk longer.
　　Out into the yard they hastened,
On the grass to meet in conflict,

And the aged Väinämöinen
Struck a blow with lightning swiftness,
Struck a blow, and struck a second,
And he sheared, like roots of turnips,
Off he shore, like heads of flax-plant,
Heads of all the sons of Pohja.   230
   Then the aged Väinämöinen
Sought for where the moon was hidden,
Likewise would release the sunlight
From the rocks of varied colour,
From the depths of steely mountain,
From the rocks as hard as iron.
   Then he walked a little distance,
But a very little distance,
When he saw a copse all verdant,
In the copse a lovely birch-tree,   240
And a large stone block beneath it,
And a rock beneath the stone block,
And there were nine doors before it,
In the doors were bolts a hundred.
   In the stone a crack perceiving,
In the rock some lines engraven,
Then he drew his sword from scabbard,
On the coloured stone he scraped it,
With the sharp point of his sword-blade,
With his gleaming blade he scraped it,   250
Till the stone in two divided,
And in three he quickly split it.
   Väinämöinen, old and steadfast,
Looked into the stone all pictured;
Many serpents ale were drinking,
In the wort the snakes were writhing,
In the coloured stone were hiding,
In the cracks of liver-colour.
   Väinämöinen, old and steadfast,
Uttered then the words that follow: 260
"Thus it is the hapless Mistress
Has so little ale acquired,
For the snakes the ale are drinking,
In the wort the snakes are writhing."

Off he cut the heads of serpents,
Broke the necks of all the serpents,
And he spoke the words which follow,
And in words like these expressed him:
"Never while the world existeth,
From this very day henceforward,   270
Let our ale by snakes be drunken,
And our malt-drink by the serpents."
    Then the aged Väinämöinen,
He the great primeval sorcerer,
Sought with hands the doors to open,
And the bolts by spells to loosen,
But to hands the doors would yield not,
By his spells the bolts were moved not.
    Then the aged Väinämöinen
Spoke his thoughts in words that follow: 280
"Man unarmed is weak as woman;
Weak as frog, without a hatchet."
And at once he wended homeward,
Head bowed down, in great vexation,
For the moon was not recovered,
Neither had the sun been captured.
    Said the lively Lemminkainen,
"O thou aged Väinämöinen,
Wherefore didst forget to take me,
As your very trusty comrade?   290
I had brought the locks to creaking,
And the bars asunder broken,
And released the moon for shining,
And had raised the sun for shining."
    Väinämöinen, old and steadfast,
Answered in the words that follow:
"Unto spells the bolts will yield not,
And the locks my magic breaks not;
Strength of hands will never move them,
And no strength of arm will force them."   300
    To the smith's forge then he wandered,
And he spoke the words which follow:
"O thou smith, O Ilmarinen,
Forge me now a mighty trident,

And a dozen hatchets forge me,
And a bunch of keys enormous,
From the stone the moon to rescue,
From the rock the sun deliver."
    Thereupon smith Ilmarinen,
He the great primeval craftsman,   310
Forged the hero what he needed,
And a dozen hatchets forged him,
Forged a bunch of keys enormous,
And of spears a mighty bundle,
Not too large and not too little,
But of middle size he forged them.
    Louhi, Pohjola's old Mistress,
Old and gap-toothed dame of Pohja,
Then with wings herself provided,
And extended them for flying,   320
Near the house at first was flying,
Then her flight extended further,
Straight across the lake of Pohja
Unto Ilmarinen's smithy.
    Then the smith his window opened,
Looking if the wind was blowing;
'Twas no wind that there was blowing,
But a hawk, and grey in colour.
    Thereupon smith Ilmarinen
Spoke aloud the words that follow: 330
"Bird of prey, what brings thee hither,
Sitting underneath my window?"
    Hereupon the bird spoke language,
And the hawk at once made answer:
"O thou smith, O Ilmarinen,
Thou the most industrious craftsman,
Truly art thou very skilful,
And a most accomplished craftsman."
    Thereupon smith Ilmarinen
Answered in the words that follow: 340
"But indeed 'tis not a wonder
If I am a skilful craftsman,
For 'twas I who forged the heavens,
And the arch of air who welded."

Hereupon the bird spoke language,
And the hawk at once responded:
"What is this, O smith, thou makest,
What, O blacksmith, art thou forging?"
    Thereupon smith Ilmarinen
Answered in the words that follow: 350
"'Tis a neck-ring I am forging,
For the aged crone of Pohja,
That she may be firmly fettered
To the side of a great mountain."
    Louhi, Pohjola's old Mistress,
Old and gap-toothed dame of Pohja,
Felt on this her doom was coming,
On her head the days of evil,
And at once to flight betook her,
Swift to Pohjola escaping.   360
    From the stone the moon released she,
From the rock the sun released she,
Then again her form she altered,
And to dove herself converted,
And her flight again directed
Unto Ilmarinen's smithy,
To the door in bird-form flying,
Lit as dove upon the threshold.
    Thereupon smith Ilmarinen
Asked her in the words which follow: 370
"Why, O bird, hast thou flown hither?
Dove, why sit'st thou on the threshold?"
    From the door the wild bird answered,
And the dove spoke from the threshold:
"Here I sit upon the threshold,
That the news I now may bring thee
From the stone the moon has risen,
From the rock the sun is loosened."
    Thereupon smith Ilmarinen
Hastened forth to gaze around him,   380
And he stood at door of smithy,
Gazing anxiously to heaven,
And he saw the moon was gleaming,
And he saw the sun was shining.

Then he went to Väinämöinen,
And he spoke the words which follow:
"O thou aged Väinämöinen,
Thou the great primeval minstrel,
Come to gaze upon the moonlight,
Come to gaze upon the sunlight.   390
Now they stand in midst of heaven,
In their old accustomed places."

Väinämöinen, old and steadfast,
Hurried out into the open,
And at once his head uplifted,
And he gazed aloft to heaven.
Moon was risen, sun was loosened,
In the sky the sun was beaming.

Then the aged Väinämöinen
Made a speech without delaying,   400
And he spoke the words which follow,
And in words like these expressed him:
"Hail, O Moon, who beamest yonder,
Thus thy fair cheeks well displaying,
Golden sun who risest yonder,
Sun who once again arisest!

"Golden Moon from stone delivered,
Fairest Sun from rock arisen,
Like the golden cuckoo rise you,
Like the silver dove arise you,   410
Lead the life ye led aforetime,
And resume your former journeys.

"Rise for ever in the morning,
From this present day hereafter.
Bring us always happy greetings,
That our wealth increases ever,
Game for ever in our fingers,
Fortune at the points of fish-hooks.

"Go ye on your path with blessings,
Go ye on your charming journey,   420
Let your crescent now be beauteous,
Rest ye joyful in the evening."

Runo L.—Marjatta

Argument

The virgin Marjatta swallows a cranberry and brings forth a boy
(1–346).   The child disappears and is found after a long search in a
swamp (347–430).   He is taken to an old man to be baptized, but the
latter will not baptize the fatherless child until after due considera-
tion (431–440).   Väinämöinen comes to inquire into the matter, and
advises that the ill-omened boy should be put to death, but the child
reproaches him for his unjust sentence (441–474).   The old man
baptizes the boy as King of Carelia, at which Väinämöinen is griev-
ously offended and leaves the country, but first declares that he
will again make a new Sampo and kantele, and light for the people.
He sails away in a copper boat to a land between earth and heaven,
but he leaves behind his kantele and his great songs as a parting gift to
his people (475–512).   Concluding verses (513–620).

MARJATTA the petted damsel
In her home long time was growing,
In the home of her great father,
In her tender mother's dwelling,
And five chains wore out completely,
And six rings she wore out likewise ;
For her father's keys she used them,
Which around her waist were hanging.
    And she wore out half the threshold,
With her skirts as she was passing,   10
And she half destroyed the rafters
Where she hung her silken ribands,
And she half destroyed the door-posts
As her fine sleeves rubbed against them,
And the planking of the flooring
Wore away beneath her slippers.
    Marjatta the petted damsel
Was a very little damsel,
And was always pure and holy,
And was ever very modest,   20
And she fed on fish the finest,
And the soft bark of the fir-tree,

But the eggs of hens ate never,
Over which the cocks were crowing,
And the flesh of ewe she ate not,
Had the ewe with ram been running.
  If her mother sent her milking,
Yet she did not go to milking,
And she spoke the words which follow:
" Never such a maid as I am   30
Udders of the cows should handle,
Which with bulls have been disporting,
If no milk from calf is flowing,
Or from calf it is not running."
  If her father sent her sledging,
In a stallion's sledge she went not,
If a mare her brother brought her,
Then these words the maiden uttered:
" Never will I sit in mares' sledge,
Which with stallion has been running,   40
If no foals the sledge are drawing,
Which have numbered six months only."
  Marjatta the petted damsel,
She who always lived a virgin,
Always greeted as a maiden,
Modest maid with locks unbraided,
Went to lead the herds to pasture,
And beside the sheep was walking.
  On the hill the sheep were straying,
To the top the lambs were climbing,   50
On the plain the maiden wandered,
Tripping through the alder bushes,
While there called the golden cuckoo,
And the silvery birds were singing.
  Marjatta the petted damsel,
Looked around her and she listened,
Sitting on the hill of berries,
Resting on the sloping hillside,
And she spoke the words which follow,
And in words like these expressed her: 60
" Call thou on, O golden cuckoo,
Sing thou still, O bird of silver,

Sing thou from thy breast of silver !
Tell me true, O Saxon strawberry,
Shall I long remain unhooded,
Long among the flocks as herd-girl,
On the wide-extending heathlands,
And the far-extending woodlands,
For one summer, for two summers,
Or for five or six of summers,   70
Or perchance for ten long summers,
Or the time fulfilled already ? "

    Marjatta the petted damsel,
For a while lived on as herd-girl.
Evil is the life of shepherd,
Far too heavy for a maiden ;
In the grass a snake is creeping,
In the grass the lizards wriggling.

    But not there a snake was writhing,
Nor in grass the lizards wriggling.   80
From the hill there cried a berry,
From the heath there cried a cranberry,
" O thou maiden, come and pluck me,
Rosy-cheeked one, come and gather,
Come with breast of tin to pluck me,
With thy copper belt to choose me,
Ere the slug should come to eat me,
Or the black worm should disturb me.

    " There are hundreds who have seen me,
Thousands more have sat beside me,   90
Girls by hundreds, wives by thousands,
Children, too, that none can number ;
None among them yet has touched me,
None has gathered me, the wretched."

    Marjatta the petted damsel,
Went a very little distance,
Went to look upon the berry,
And the cranberry to gather,
With her skilful hands to pluck it,
With her beauteous hands to pluck it.   100

    On the hill she found the berry,
On the heath she found the cranberry ;

Twas a berry in appearance,
And it seemed to be a cranberry,
But from ground too high for eating,
On a tree too weak for climbing.

From the heath a stick she lifted,
That she might pull down the berry;
Then from ground the berry mounted
Upward to her shoes so pretty,   110
From her pretty shoes arose it,
Upward to her knees of whiteness,
Rising from her knees of whiteness
Upward to her skirts that rustled.

To her buckled belt arose it,
To her breast from buckled girdle,
From her breast to chin arose it,
To her lips from chin arose it,
Then into her mouth it glided,
And along her tongue it hastened,   120
From her tongue to throat it glided,
And it dropped into her stomach.

Marjatta the petted damsel,
After this had chanced grew pregnant,
And it soon increased upon her,
And her burden soon was heavy.

Then she cast aside her girdle,
Loosely dressed, without a girdle,
Secretly she sought the bathroom,
And she hid her in the darkness.   130

Always was her mother thinking,
And her mother pondered ever:
"What has chanced to our Marjatta,
What has happened to our house-dove,
That she casts aside her girdle,
Always dresses loosely, beltless,
Goes in secret to the bathroom,
And she hides her in the darkness?"

And a baby gave her answer,
And the little child made answer: 140
"This has chanced to our Marjatta,
This befel the wretched creature,

She has been too long a herd-girl,
With the flocks too far has wandered."
  And she bore her heavy burden,
And the pain it brought upon her,
Bore it seven months, bore it eight months,
Bore it through the ninth month also,
By the reckoning of old women,
And for half the tenth month also.   150
  While the tenth month thus was passing,
Then the girl was filled with anguish,
Grievous sufferings came upon her,
And the weight oppressed her sorely.
  For a bath she asked her mother,
"O my very dearest mother,
Make a warm place ready for me,
And a warm room ready for me,
Where the girl awhile may rest her
In the house of suffering women."   160
  But her mother gave her answer,
Answered thus, the aged woman:
"Woe to thee, O whore of Hiisi,
Tell me now with whom thou restedst,
With a man as yet unmarried,
Or beside a married hero?"
  Marjatta the petted damsel,
Then replied to her in thiswise:
"Neither with a man unmarried,
Nor with any married hero,   170
But I sought the hill of berries,
And I went to pluck the cranberries,
And I took what seemed a berry,
And upon my tongue I laid it,
Quickly in my throat it glided,
And it dropped into my stomach.
Thus it is that I am pregnant,
Thus it comes that I am pregnant."
  For a bath she asked her father,
"O my very dearest father,   180
Give me now a well-warmed refuge,
Make a warm room ready for me,

Where the suffering one may rest her,
And the girl endure her suffering."
    But her father gave her answer,
Gave her back a shameful answer:
"Go thou forth from here, O strumpet,
Wander forth, O wench for burning,
To the bears' own rocky caverns,
To the caves where bears are lurking,   190
Thither forth to bear, O strumpet,
Bear thy children, wench of fire."
    Marjatta the petted damsel,
Then returned submissive answer:
"Not at all am I a strumpet,
Neither am a wench for burning;
I shall bear a mighty hero,
And shall bear a noble offspring,
He shall be a mighty conqueror,
Strong as even Väinämöinen."   200
    Then the maid was greatly troubled
Where to go, and how to journey,
Where a bath she might provide her,
And she spoke the words which follow:
"O my little damsel Piltti,
Thou the best of all my handmaids,
Find me now a bath in village,
Find a bath near reed-fringed brooklet,
Where the suffering one may rest her,
And the girl endure her suffering.   210
Go at once, and hasten quickly,
For my need is of the greatest."
    Then the little damsel Piltti,
Answered in the words that follow:
"Where am I to ask a bathroom,
Who will help me to obtain it?"
    Thereupon did our Marjatta
Answer in the words which follow:
"Go and ask a bath from Ruotus,
Near where issues forth the Reed-brook."   220
    Then the little maiden Piltti
Listened to her words obedient,

Always ready, heedless never,
Always quick, avoiding gossip,
Like a mist, away she hurried,
To the yard like snake she hastened,
With her hands her skirts she lifted,
In her hands her dress she twisted,
And upon her course she hastened
Straight unto the house of Ruotus.   230
Hills re-echoed to her footsteps,
Shook the mountains as she climbed them,
On the heath the cones were dancing,
Gravel scattered o'er the marshes ;
Thus she came to Ruotus' dwelling,
And the house she quickly entered.

In his shirt sat wicked Ruotus,
Eating, drinking like the great ones,
In his shirt at end of table,
In a shirt of finest linen,   240
And he asked as he was eating,
Grunted, leaning o'er the table,
"What have you to say, you beggar,
Wretch, why come you running hither ?"

Then the little damsel Piltti
Answered in the words that follow :
"Here I seek a village bathroom,
Seek a bath near reed-fringed brooklet,
That relief may reach the suffering,
For the need is very pressing."   250

Then the wicked wife of Ruotus
Presently with arms a-kimbo,
Slouched along upon the flooring,
Swept to middle of the flooring,
And she asked upon her coming,
Speaking in the words which follow :
"Who is seeking for a bathroom,
Who is seeking for assistance ?"

Said the little damsel Piltti,
"Needed 'tis for our Marjatta."   260

Then the wicked wife of Ruotus
Answered in the words that follow :

"Vacant baths are rare in village,
None at mouth of reed-fringed streamlet.
There's a bath upon the clearing,
And a stable in the pinewood,
Where the whore may bear her children,
And the vile one cast her offspring,
While the horses there are breathing,
Let her take a bath and welcome."   270
    Then the little maiden Piltti,
Hurried back with rapid footsteps,
And upon her course she hastened,
And she said on her arrival :
"In the village is no bathroom,
None beside the rush-fringed streamlet,
And the wicked wife of Ruotus,
Only spoke the words which follow :
'Vacant baths are none in village,
None at mouth of reed-fringed streamlet.   280
There's a bath upon the clearing,
And a stable in the pinewood,
Where the whore may bear her children,
And the vile one cast her offspring,
While the horses there are breathing,
Let her take a bath and welcome.'
This was all she said unto me,
This is truly what she answered."
    Marjatta the hapless maiden
When she heard, burst forth in weeping,   290
And she spoke the words that follow :
"Thither must I then betake me,
Even like an outcast labourer,
Even like a hired servant,
I must go upon the clearing,
And must wander to the pinewood."
    In her hands her skirt she lifted,
With her hands her skirt she twisted,
And she took the bath-whisks with her,
Of the softest leaves and branches,   300
And with hasty steps went onward,
In the greatest pain of body,

To the stable in the pinewood,
And the stall on hill of Tapio.
　　And she spoke the words which follow,
And in words like these expressed her :
"Come thou to my aid, Creator,
To my aid, O thou most gracious,
In this anxious time of labour,
In this time of hardest labour.　　　　　　　310
Free the damsel from her burden,
From her pains release the woman,
That she perish not in torment,
May not perish in her anguish."
　　When at length her journey ended,
Then she spoke the words which follow:
"O thou good horse, breathe upon me,
O thou draught-foal, snort upon me,
Breathe a vapour-bath around me,
Send thou warmth throughout the bathroom,　320
That relief may reach the sufferer,
For the need is very pressing."
　　Then the good horse breathed upon her,
And the draught-foal snorted on her,
Over all her suffering body.
When the horse desisted breathing,
Steam was spread throughout the stable,
Like the steam of boiling water.
　　Marjatta the hapless maiden,
She, the holy little maiden,　　　　　　　330
Bathed her in a bath sufficient,
Till she had relieved her suffering,
And a little boy was born her,
And a sinless child was given,
On the hay in horses' stable,
On the hay in horses' manger.
　　Then she washed the little infant,
And in swaddling-clothes she wrapped him,
On her knees she took the infant,
And she wrapped her garments round him.　　340
There she reared the little infant,
Thus she reared the beauteous infant,

Reared her little golden apple,
And her little staff of silver,
And upon her lap she nursed it,
With her hands did she caress it.
    On her knees she laid the infant,
On her lap she laid the infant,
And began to brush his hair straight,
And began to smooth his hair down,   350
When from off her knees he vanished,
From her lap the infant vanished.
    Marjatta the hapless maiden
Fell into the greatest trouble,
And she hurried off to seek him,
Seek her little boy, the infant,
And she sought her golden apple,
Sought her little staff of silver,
Sought him underneath the millstones,
Underneath the sledge while running,   360
Underneath the sieve while sifting,
Underneath the lidless basket ;
Trees she moved, and grass divided,
Spreading out the tender herbage.
    Long the little boy she sought for,
Sought her son, the little infant,
Sought him through the hills and pinewoods,
On the heath among the heather,
Searched through every tuft of heather,
And in every bush she sought him,   370
Roots of juniper updigging,
And of trees the branches straightening
    Then she thought to wander further,
And she went upon her wanderings,
And there came a star to meet her,
And before the star she bowed her.
"Star, whom Jumala created,
Know you nothing of my infant,
Where my little son is hidden,
Where is hid my golden apple?"   380
    And the star made answer to her:
"If I knew I would not tell it.

He it was who me created,
Made me, through these days of evil
In the cold to shine for ever,
And to glimmer through the darkness."
 Then she thought to wander further,
And she went upon her wanderings,
And the moon came next to meet her,
And she bowed herself before him.   390
"Moon, whom Jumala created,
Know you nothing of my infant,
Where my little son is hidden,
Where is hid my golden apple?"
 And the moon made answer to her:
"If I knew I would not tell it.
He it was who me created,
Always in these days of evil
Through the night to watch all lonely,
And to sleep throughout the daytime."   400
 Then she thought to wander further,
And she went upon her wanderings,
And there came the sun to meet her,
And she bowed herself before him.
"Sun, whom Jumala created,
Know you nothing of my infant,
Where my little son is hidden,
Where is hid my golden apple?"
 And the sun made answer wisely:
"Well indeed I know your infant.   410
He it was who me created,
In these days of finest weather,
Golden rays to shed about me,
Silver rays to scatter round me.
 "Well indeed I know your infant,
Know your son, unhappy mother!
There thy little son is hidden,
There is hid thy golden apple,
In the swamps to waistband sunken,
To his arm-pits in the marshlands."   420
 Marjatta the hapless maiden
Sought her infant in the marshes,

In the swamps her son discovered,
And she brought him home in triumph.
Then the son of our Marjatta
Grew into a youth most beauteous,
But they knew not what to call him,
Did not know what name to give him,
But his mother called him Floweret,
And the strangers called him Sluggard.   430

    And they sought a man to cross him,
And to sprinkle him with water;
And an old man came to cross him,
Virokannas to baptize him.

    Then these words the old man uttered,
And in words like these expressed him:
"With the cross I will not sign him,
Nor will I baptize the infant,
Not till he has been examined,
And a judgment passed upon him."   440

    Who shall dare to come to try him,
Test him, and pass sentence on him?
Väinämöinen, old and steadfast,
He the great primeval sorcerer,
He alone came forth to try him,
And to test him and pass sentence.

    Väinämöinen, old and steadfast,
Sentence gave in words that follow:
"As the boy from marsh has risen,
From the ground, and from a berry,   450
On the ground they now shall lay him,
Where the hills are thick with berries,
Or shall to the swamps conduct him,
On the trees his head to shatter."

    Then the half-month old spoke loudly,
And the fortnight-old cried loudly:
"O thou old and wretched creature,
Wretched old man, void of insight,
O how stupid is your judgment,
How contemptible thy sentence!   460
Thou hast grievous crimes committed,
Likewise deeds of greatest folly,

Yet to swamps they did not lead thee,
Shattered not thy head on tree-trunks,
When thyself, in youthful folly,
Gave the child of thine own mother,
That thou thus mightst 'scape destruction,
And release thyself in thiswise.

"And again thou wast not carried,
And abandoned in the marshes, 470
When thyself in youthful folly,
Caused the young maids to be sunken,
In the depths beneath the billows,
To the black ooze at the bottom."

Then the old man quickly crossed him,
Quick baptized the child with water,
As the king of all Carelia,
And the lord of all the mighty.

Then was Väinämöinen angry,
Greatly shamed and greatly angry, 480
And prepared himself to journey
From the lake's extended margin,
And began his songs of magic,
For the last time sang them loudly,
Sang himself a boat of copper,
With a copper deck provided.

In the stern himself he seated,
Sailing o'er the sparkling billows,
Still he sang on his departure,
And he sang as he was sailing: 490
"May the time pass quickly o'er us,
One day passes, comes another,
And again shall I be needed.
Men will look for me, and miss me,
To construct another Sampo,
And another harp to make me,
Make another moon for gleaming,
And another sun for shining.
When the sun and moon are absent
In the air no joy remaineth." 500

Then the aged Väinämöinen
Went upon his journey singing,

Sailing in his boat of copper,
In his vessel made of copper,
Sailed away to loftier regions,
To the land beneath the heavens.

There he rested with his vessel,
Rested weary, with his vessel,
But his kantele he left us,
Left his charming harp in Suomi,   510
For his people's lasting pleasure,
Mighty songs for Suomi's children.

*   *   *   *   *

Now my mouth must cease from speaking,
And my tongue be bound securely,
Cease the chanting of my verses,
And my lively songs abandon.
Even thus must horses rest them,
When a long course is completed,
Even iron must be wearied
When the grass is mown in summer,   520
And the water-drops be weary,
As they trace the river's windings,
And the fire must be extinguished
When throughout the night 'tis burning.
Wherefore should our songs not falter,
As our sweet songs we are singing,
For the lengthy evenings' pleasure,
Singing later than the sunset?

Thus I heard the people talking,
And again it was repeated: 530
" E'en the waterfall when flowing
Yields no endless stream of water,
Nor does an accomplished singer,
Sing till all his knowledge fail him.
Better 'tis to sit in silence
Than to break off in the middle."

Now my song remains completed,
'Tis completed and abandoned.
In a ball I wind my lays up,
As a ball I cast them from me,   540
On the storehouse floor I lay them,

With a lock of bone secure them,
That from thence escape they never,
Nor in time may be untwisted,
Not unless the lock be opened,
And its jaws should be extended.
Not unless the teeth be opened,
And the tongue again is moving.
     What would now avail my singing,
If the songs I sang were bad ones,   550
If I sang in every valley,
And I sang in every firwood?
For my mother lives no longer,
Wakes no more my own old mother,
Nor my golden one can hear me,
Nought can learn my dear old mother,
None would hear me but the fir-trees,
Learn, save branches of the pine-trees,
Or the tender leaves of birch-trees,
Or the charming mountain ash-tree.   560
     I was small when died my mother,
Weak was I without my mother ;
On the stones like lark she left me,
On the rocks like thrush she left me,
Left me like a lark to sing there,
Or to sing as sings the throstle,
In the wardship of a stranger,
At the will of a step-mother,
And she drove me forth, unhappy,
Forth she drove the unloved infant,   570
To a wind-swept home she drove me,
To the north-wind's home she drove me,
That against the wind defenceless,
Winds might sweep away the orphan,
     Like a lark away I wandered,
Like a hapless bird I wandered
Shelterless about the country ;
Wearily I wandered onward,
Till with every wind acquainted,
I their roaring comprehended ;   580
In the frost I learned to shudder,

And I learned to cry with freezing.
Even now do many people,
Many people I encounter,
Speak to me in angry accents,
Rudest speeches hurl against me,
Curses on my tongue they shower,
And about my voice cry loudly,
Likewise they abuse my grumbling
And they call my songs too lengthy,   590
And they say I sing too badly,
And my song's accented wrongly.

May you not, O friendly people,
As a wondrous thing regard it
That I sang so much in childhood,
And when small, I sang so badly.
I received no store of learning,
Never travelled to the learned.
Foreign words were never taught me,
Neither songs from distant countries.   600
Others have had all instruction,
From my home I journeyed never,
Always did I help my mother,
And I dwelt for ever near her,
In the house received instruction,
'Neath the rafters of my storehouse,
By the spindle of my mother,
By my brother's heap of shavings,
In my very earliest childhood,
In a shirt that hung in tatters.   610

But let this be as it may be,
I have shown the way to singers,
Showed the way, and broke the tree-tops,
Cut the branches, shown the pathways.
This way therefore leads the pathway,
Here the path lies newly opened,
Widely open for the singers,
And for greater ballad singers,
For the young, who now are growing,
For the rising generation.   620

NOTES TO RUNOS XXVI—L

(These are by the translator, when not otherwise stated. K. K. indicates Prof. Kaarle Krohn, and A. M. Madame Aino Malmberg. For proper names, refer to the Glossary at page 281.)

RUNO XXVI

129. Literally, "his teeth."

230. In the *Völuspá*, we read of a Hall of Serpents in Naströnd, one of the Icelandic hells, composed of serpents wattled together, with their heads turned inwards, vomiting floods of venom in which wade murderers, perjurers, and adulterers.

271. Literally, "the toads."

> "Seven monarchs' wealth in that castle lies stowed ;
> The foul fiends brood o'er them like raven and toad." (Scott.)

A diabolical creature, half dragon and half frog, is described in a well-known Esthonian story.

427. *Tetrao tetrix*, known as the Black-cock and Grey-hen.

555. Virsta, a Russian word naturalized in Finnish.

617. This description recalls the serpents of Indian mythology, such as those described in the first book of the *Mahabharata*.

619. Such a passage might have suggested to Longfellow the following :

> "Bigger than the Big-Sea-Water,
> Broader than the Gitche Gumee."
> *Hiawatha*, xxi.

RUNO XXVII

208. Here commences a magical contest somewhat resembling the transformation scenes in the stories of the Second Calendar, and of Nooreddin and Bedreddin, in the *1001 Nights*.

326. "I don't want to have a mess made upon my floor here, or any noise or shooting." (Tanta Coetzee, in Rider Haggard's *Jess*.)

RUNO XXVIII.

15, 16. His horse and sledge seem to have been transformed, like those of Joukahainen in Runo III.

195. In Finnish and Esthonian tales we often find persons transformed into trees and flowers ; sometimes for purposes of concealment.

RUNO XXIX

242. " Grass-widows " are probably intended.

253-268. Even this old woman did not appeal to him in vain. We might compare with this passage Byron's *Don Juan*, VIII., cxxxi., cxxxii.

RUNO XXX

175, 187. Literally, " nails."

185. Pakkanen, Puhurin poika. Frost, the son of the North Wind.

389. The unmanly lamentations of the heroes over a fate that has not befallen them may remind us of Grimm's story of " Die kluge Else." It will also be noticed that the heroes are only concerned about their mothers ; and Tiera has as little thought for his virgin bride as Lemminkainen has for Kyllikki.

RUNO XXXI

1. The tragedy of Kullervo is the favourite episode of the *Kalevala* in Finland, next to that of Aino. The preamble (lines 1–10) is the same as the opening of the Esthonian *Kalevipoeg*. The story of the Esthonian hero, though he was a king and not a slave, resembles that of Kullervo in so many respects that he must have been the same character originally.

19. I think the change of style, indicative of different authorship, in this episode is sufficiently obvious even in a translation. Many words used here do not occur earlier in the poem.

91–96. The same story is told of the infant Kalevipoeg.

107. Esthonians call dwarfs " Ox-knee people " ; *i. e.* people as high as an ox's knee.

137. Like Simple Simon.

337. It is obvious that some of the youthful exploits of Kwasind (slightly varied, after Longfellow's manner) are imitated from those of Kullervo. (Compare also Runo XXXV., 11–68.)

RUNO XXXII

24. The rye-bread, on which the Finnish peasants largely subsist, is described as baked in very hard round loaves, like quoits, which are strung on a pole. But Kullervo's cake seems to have been prepared to look nice on the outside.

156–162. Does this refer to stories of witches milking cattle?

206. Of juniper wood.

498. Literally, an apple-berry. Probably a small crab-apple is intended.

513. I think wolves are here intended, not dogs.

533. In the Esthonian story of the Northern Frog, the monster is secured by an iron stake driven through the jaws. (Kirby's *Hero of Esthonia*, II., 253, 256.)

542. These elaborate and ineffectual prayers and incantations may be compared with the prayers of Achilles for the safety of Patroclus, in *Iliad*, XVI.

RUNO XXXIII

40. Wheat is used in the folk-songs as a term of endearment. (K. K.)

61, 62. The Esthonian Kalevipoeg was constantly instructed by the voice of birds.

285–290. In Esthonia this episode occurs in the story of the Royal Herdboy. (*Hero of Esthonia*, I., pp. 279–305.)

RUNO XXXV

2. Are blue stockings supposed to be an emblem of strength? Ukko is also represented as wearing them.

29.   "All with incredible stupendous force,
            None daring to appear antagonist." (Milton.)

65. As Kalervo appears to have been a chief in his own right, it is not very clear why, or to whom, he had to pay taxes.

107, 108. The lake of course was frozen.

153. As in several other instances in the *Kalevala*, this does not appear to be abduction in the modern sense, but merely marriage by capture.

214. There is another celebrated poem written by a Finn, but in Swedish, Runeberg's *Kong* (King) *Fjalar*, in which a similar chance meeting between a brother and sister forms the principal subject.

343. Sea-beasts are very rarely mentioned in the *Kalevala*, for nearly all aquatic animals referred to are lake- or river-fish. Here the allusion is probably to the story of Jonah.

RUNO XXXVI

80. Literally "the rest of his flesh." Having regard to the supposed powers of Finnish magicians, this passage is not to be taken merely as an impudent rejoinder, but as asserting powers which Kullervo actually claimed to be able to exert.

307. In an old English romance we read concerning the suicide of a sorcerer, "The ground whereon he died was ever afterwards unfortunate, and to this present time it is called in that country, 'a vale of walking spirits.'" (*Seven Champions of Christendom*, Part I., chap. xix.)

327. This reminds us of Sir Peter's "Sword of Vengeance." (Prior's *Danish Ballads*, I., pp. 269–275.)

341. The Esthonian Kalevipoeg was also slain, like Kullervo, by his own sword. (*Hero of Esthonia*, I., pp. 140, 141.)

RUNO XXXVII

56. Literally, their hatless shoulders.
61. Compare the account of the forging of the Sampo in Runo X.

RUNO XXXVIII

94. This might allude to the Viking practice of carving the Blood-Eagle on the backs of enemies ; but Prof. Krohn remarks that this was unknown in Finland.
255. Here it seems that the mere fact of Ilmarinen having carried off the girl, even against her will, was enough to constitute her his lawful wife.
273. Ilmarinen's sword was less bloodthirsty than that of Kullervo ; but it will be noticed that there is as little real chivalry in the *Kalevala* generally as in old Scandinavian literature.

RUNO XL

274. Literally, "at the tips of my ten nails."

RUNO XLI

238. Similar incidents are common in folktales. The reader will recollect the decoration of Mama, the Woodpecker. (*Hiawatha*, IX.)

RUNO XLII

1–3. Here again we notice a difference of expression, indicating a different authorship.
52. "Mistress of the mighty spell." (Southey.)
146. Compare Runo XX., lines 17–118.
295. Literally, his finger-bones.
403. Perhaps the cap had ear-flaps to be worn in bad weather.

RUNO XLIII

37, 38. This seems to be meant ironically.
115–120. This, or something similar, is a common device for impeding a pursuer in European fairy tales.
177. Pohjan eukko. Another epithet for Louhi.
383, 384. The Sampo being not only an unfailing corn, salt, and money-mill, but a palladium of general prosperity, Pohjola would naturally fall into famine and misery when nothing remained but an almost worthless fragment of the cover. It is possible that the story may refer to some great and permanent change for the worse of the climate of the North ; either during the storms and earthquakes of the fourteenth century, which would connect it with the plague described in Runo XLV. ; or perhaps to a much earlier period, when, as old Persian books tell us, the climate of some part of Asia (?) was changed from nine months summer and three months winter, to nine months winter and three months summer.

RUNO XLV

41. Loviatar represents the evil and destructive powers of Nature, as opposed to the beneficent powers, represented in the *Kalevala* under the twin aspects of Ilmatar and Marjatta.

117. This speech or invocation is not addressed to Loviatar, but apparently to some goddess similar to the Roman Lucina.

168. Dr. Russell says that the itch was more dreaded than the plague in Aleppo in the eighteenth century.

181. Pestilence has often been attributed to the anger of gods or demons ; and Finland suffered severely from plague till well into the eighteenth century. But I am inclined to regard the plague described here as the Black Death, which must have ravaged Finland about 1350.

269, 282, 283. All these names have nearly the same significance, and might be rendered by " Dolores, our Lady of Pain."

RUNO XLVI

13, 14. The pestilence having abated at the approach of winter, the wild beasts naturally overran the devastated country. So I would interpret this passage.

25. Literally, three feathers, but the commentary gives the meaning adopted above.

81. For an account of bear-hunting in Finland, compare Acerbi's *Voyage to the North Cape*, I., pp. 288, 289.

168. Tapio is the lord of the forest here alluded to, according to the commentary.

246. The word here rendered "charge" literally means "bundle" or "package."

313. Probably the Danish Sound.

377. A honeyed forest perhaps means a forest abounding in honey-dew.

565, 566 These lines are rather musical :

> Kuuluvilla karjan kellon,
> Luona tiukujen tirinän.

RUNO XLVII

15, 16. There is a Finnish ballad relating how the sun and moon were stolen by German and Esthonian sorcerers, and recovered by the son of Jumala. (*Kanteletar*, III., 2 ; translated by Mr. C. J. Billson, *Folklore*, VI., 343, 344.)

37. Compare the story of Maui stealing the fire in New Zealand legends.

128. Lake Ladoga seems to be intended.

233. Does this refer to tides? Tides can hardly be known in Finland, except by hearsay ; the Baltic itself is almost tideless.

RUNO XLVIII

137, 138. Neptune's trident?

169. Here a different epithet is applied to Väinämöinen.

283. Probably *Polyporus igniarius* or *P. fomentarius*, both of which are much used for tinder.

302. He appears to have thought that Panu was in league with the Fire.

RUNO XLIX

83. This is Rhabdomancy, or divination by twigs. Tacitus describes the priests of the Ancient Germans doing this, and the Druids had a similar practice.

417. Literally, at the end of our thumbs.

RUNO L

1. Marjatta korea kuopus.
Literally, Marjatta the elegant darling; an expression occurring nowhere else in the *Kalevala*. The story in the present Runo seems to exhibit a veneer of Christianity over Shaman legends. Even the name Marjatta, notwithstanding its resemblance to Maria, seems to be really derived from the word marja, a berry. An old writer says that the favourite deities of the Finns in his time were Väinämöinen and the Virgin Mary.

188. That is, a criminal who deserves to be burnt at the stake.

199, 200. She already recognizes her unborn son as an Avatar.

289. The word here rendered "hapless" properly means "little."

465. This is the only passage in the *Kalevala* in which Väinämöinen is spoken of as ever having been young; though he is occasionally called young in variants.

465–468. This passage apparently alludes to Väinämöinen having sent Ilmarinen to Pohjola by a trick.

471–474. This must allude either to the fate of Aino, or to some story not included in the *Kalevala*.

501. In Esthonian legends, Vanemuine is not an Avatar and culture-hero, but the God of Music, who withdrew from men on account of the ribaldry with which some of his hearers received his divine songs. (*Hero of Esthonia*, II., pp. 80–85.) Longfellow also makes Hiawatha depart in a boat after the conclusion of his mission. So also King Arthur.

613, 614. These expressions remind us of the Buddha "breaking down the rafters and the roof-tree" preparatory to reaching Nirvana.

GLOSSARY OF FINNISH NAMES

(The dotted vowels are included with the others.)

AHAVA, *the cold spring East Wind.*

AHTI, *a name of Lemminkainen.*

AHTO, *the God of the Sea and of the Waters.*

AHTOLA, *the dominions of Ahto.*

ÄIJÖ, *the father of Iku-Turso.*

AINIKKI, *Lemminkainen's sister.*

AINO, *a Lapp maiden, Joukahainen's sister.*

ALUE, *name of a lake.*

ANNIKKI, *Ilmarinen's sister.*

ANTERO VIPUNEN, *a primeval giant or Titan, whom some commentators suppose to be the same as Kaleva.*

ETELÄTÄR, *the goddess of the South Wind.*

HÄLLÄPJÖRÄ, *name of a waterfall.*

HÄME, *Tavastland.*

HERMIKKI (SINEWY), *name of a cow.*

HIISI, *the same as Lempo, the Evil Power, somewhat resembling the Scandinavian Loki in character. His name is often used as a term of reprobation.*

HIITOLA, *the dominions of Hiisi.*

HONGATAR, *the goddess of the Fir-trees.*

HORNA (HELL), *name of a mountain.*

IKU-TURSO, *a water-giant; the name is doubtless connected with the Icelandic word Thurs, which means a giant, and which is also the name of the letter* þ, *called* þa *in Old English.*

ILMA (AIR), *name of Ilmarinen's homestead.*

ILMARI, ILMARINEN, *the primeval smith; still used as a proper name in Finland.*

ILMATAR, *the Daughter of the Air; the Creatrix of the world, and the mother of Väinämöinen.*

ILPOTAR, *a name of Louhi.*

IMATRA, *the great falls or rapids in the river Vuoksi.*

INGERLAND, *usually known as Ingermanland.*

JOUKAHAINEN,⎫ *a young*
JOUKO,   ⎭ *Laplander.*
JOUKOLA, *the land of Joukahainen.*
JUMALA, OR UKKO, *God.*
JUOTIKKI (DRINKER), *name of a cow.*
JUUTAS, *a name probably derived from Judas. It is used as a name for Hiisi, and also as a term of reprobation.*

KAATRAKOSKI, *name of a waterfall.*
KALERVO, *a chieftain, the brother of Untamo, and the father of Kullervo.*
KALERVOINEN, *epithet of Kullervo.*
KALEVA, *the ancestor of the heroes, who does not appear in person in the Kalevala.*
KALEVALA, *the land of Kaleva.*
KALEVALAINEN, *a descendant of Kaleva.*
KALEVATAR, OR OSMOTAR, *the daughter of Kaleva.*
KALMA, *Death personified; he is more often called Tuoni or Mana.*
KAMMO, *a rock, the father of Kimmo.*
KANKAHATAR, *the goddess of Weaving.*

KANTELE, *the Finnish harp or zither.*
KANTELETAR, *the Daughter of the Harp; name given by Lönnrot to his published collection of Finnish ballads.*
KARJALA, *Carelia.*
KATAJATAR, *the nymph of the Juniper.*
KAUKO,   ⎫ *Names of*
KAUKOLAINEN, ⎬ *Lemminkainen.*
KAUKOMIELI, ⎭ *kainen.*
KAUPPI, *a Laplander, skilled in making snowshoes.*
KEITOLAINEN, *the Contemptible One, one of the names of the Evil Power.*
KEMI, *name of a river.*
KIMMO, (1) *a stone;* (2) *name of a cow.*
KIPUTYTTÖ, *Maiden of Pain.*
KIRJO (*variegated, or dappled*), *name of a cow.*
KIVUTAR, *Daughter of Pain.*
KUIPPANA, *a name of Tapio.*
KULLERVO,   ⎫ *a hero, the*
KULLERVOINEN, ⎬ *son of Kalervo.*
             ⎭ *lervo.*
KUURA, *a name of Tiera.*
KUUTAR, *the Daughter of the Moon.*
           ⎫ *a maiden of*
KYLLI,   ⎪ *Saari, whom*
KYLLIKKI, ⎬ *Lemminkainen carries off and marries.*
LEMMINKAINEN, *a reckless adventurer.*

LEMPI (LOVE), *the father of Lemminkainen.*

LEMPO, or HIISI, *the Evil Power.*

LOKKA, *the mother of Ilmarinen.*

LOUHI, *the Mistress of Pohjola.*

LOVIATAR, *one of the daughters of Tuoni, and the mother of the Plagues.*

LUONNOTAR, *Daughter of Creation, a name applied to Ilmatar, and other celestial goddesses.*

LUOTOLA, *name of a bay.*

LYYLIKKI, *a name of Kauppi.*

MAIRIKKI, *name of a cow.*

MANA, or TUONI, *the God of Hades.*

MANALA, or TUONELA, *Hades.*

MANALAINEN = *Mana.*

MANALATAR, *Daughter of Mana.*

MANSIKKA (STRAWBERRY) *name of a cow.*

MARJATTA, *the mother of Väinämöinen's supplanter. She is usually identified with the Virgin Mary.*

MÄRKÄHATTU (WET-HAT), *name or epithet of a cowherd who has been exposed to the rain.*

MELATAR, *the goddess of the Rudder.*

METSOLA, *the Woodlands, from metsa, a forest.*

MIELIKKI, *the Mistress of the Forests, the spouse of Tapio.*

MIMERKKI, *a name of Mielikki.*

MUSTI (BLACKIE), *a dog's name.*

MUURIKKI (BLACKIE), *name of a cow.*

NYYRIKKI, *the son of Tapio.*

OSMO, *a name of Kaleva.*

OSMOLA = *Kalevala.*

OSMOINEN, *an epithet of Väinämöinen.*

OSMOTAR, *the daughter of Osmo.*

OTAVA, *the constellation of the Great Bear.*

OTSO, *pet name for the bear.*

PAHALAINEN (THE WICKED ONE), *a name of the Evil Power.*

PÄIVÄTÄR, *the Daughter of the Sun.*

PAKKANEN, *the personified Frost.*

PALVONEN, *apparently the same as Tuuri.*

PANU, *the son of the Sun.*

PELLERVOINEN, *vide Sampsa.*

PIHLAJATAR, *the nymph of the Mountain-Ash tree.*

PILTTI, *the handmaid of Marjatta.*

PIMENTOLA, *a name of Pohjola.*

Pisa, *name of a mountain.*

Pohja, *the North.*

Pohjola, *the North Country, (a) A dark and dismal country to the north of Lapland, but sometimes identified with Lapland itself; (b) The castle or homestead of Louhi, to which the name of the country itself was applied.*

Puhuri, *the North Wind.*

Puolukka (Cranberry), *name of a cow.*

Ruotus, *the headman of a village. (Herod, according to the commentators.)*

Rutja, *a cataract, said to be the same as Turja.*

Saarelainen (The Islander), *an epithet of Lemminkainen.*

Saari, *an island, especially the island now called Kronstadt.*

Sampo, *a magic corn, salt and coin-mill.*

Sampsa Pellervoinen, *the genius of agriculture (from pellon or pelto, a field), the servant or agent of Väinämöinen.*

Sara
Sariola } *names of Pohjola.*

Savo (Savolaks) *a province of Finland.*

Sima, *a Sound in Pohjola.*

Sinetar, *a nymph who colours flowers blue.*

"Sotko's Daughters"; *the protecting nymphs of ducks.*

Suomi, *Finland.*

Suonetar, *the nymph of the veins.*

Surma, *Death, or the God of Death.*

Suovakko, *name of an old woman.*

Suvantola (*the land of still waters*), *a name of Väinölä.*

Suvantolainen, *an epithet of Väinämöinen.*

Suvetar, *the goddess of Summer.*

Syöjätär, *an ogress, the mother of the serpents.*

Syötikki (Eater), *name of a cow.*

Tammatar, *the goddess of the oak tree.*

Tanika, *name of the builder of a castle.*

Tapio, *the God of the Forests.*

Tapiola, *the dominions of Tapio.*

Tellervo, *the daughter of Tapio, but in some passages apparently identified with Mielikki.*

Terhenetär, *the goddess of the Clouds.*

Tiera, *Lemminkainen's comrade in arms.*

Tuometar, *the goddess of the Bird Cherry.*

Tuomikki, *name of a cow.*

TUONELA, or MANALA, *Hades.*

TUONETAR, *the daughter of Tuoni.*

TUONI, or MANA, *the God of Hades.*

TUORIKKI, *name of a cow.*

TURJA, *Lapland; also name of a cataract.*

TURJALAINEN, *a Laplander.*

TURSAS, *vide Iki-Turso.*

TUULIKKI, *a daughter of Tapio.*

TUURI, *the builder of a house where honey is stored.*

UKKO (OLD MAN), *usually identified with Jumala, the God of Heaven, with special authority over the clouds.*

ULAPPALA (*the country of the open sea*), *apparently the same as Tuonela.*

UNTAMO ⎰ (*a*) *the god*
UNTAMOINEN ⎱ *of Sleep and Dreams;* (*b*) *a turbulent chieftain, the brother of Kalervo.*

UNTAMOLA, *the dominions of Untamo; sometimes used for Untamo himself.*

UNTO, *short for Untamo.*

UNTOLA, *the dominions of Unto.*

UVANTO ⎰ *names of*
UVANTOLAINEN ⎱ *Väinämöinen.*

VÄINÄMÖINEN, *the primeval minstrel and culture-hero, the son of Ilmatar (the name, as pronounced, sounds like Vannamœnen).*

VÄINÖ, *short for Väinämöinen.*

VÄINÖLÄ, *the dominions of Väinämöinen* (= *Kalevala.*)

VAMMATAR, *the Daughter of Evil.*

VELLAMO, *the goddess of the Sea and of the Waters, the spouse of Ahto.*

VIPUNEN, *vide Antero Vipunen.*

VIRO, *Esthonia.*

VIROKANNAS, *used as a proper name; apparently meaning the Wise Esthonian.*

VUOJALAINEN, *a name of Lyylikki.*

VUOKSI, *an important river which flows into Lake Ladoga.*

THE END

EVERYMAN'S LIBRARY: A Selected List

This List covers a selection of volumes available in Everyman's Library. Those volumes marked with a * indicate that a paperback edition of this title is also available. Numbers only of hardback editions are given.

BIOGRAPHY

ESSAYS AND CRITICISM

FICTION

HISTORY

LEGENDS AND SAGAS

POETRY AND DRAMA

REFERENCE

RELIGION AND PHILOSOPHY

SCIENCE

TRAVEL AND TOPOGRAPHY